Suppose that one is presented with a report of a miracle as an exception to nature's usual course. Should one believe the report and so come to favour the idea that a god has acted miraculously? Hume argued that no reasonable person should do anything of the kind. Many religiously sceptical philosophers agree with him, and have both defended and developed his reasoning. Some theologians concur or offer other reasons why those who are believers in God should also refuse to accept accounts of miracles as accurate reportage. This book argues to the contrary. For Houston, miracle stories may contribute towards the reasonableness of belief in God, and, appropriately attested, may be accepted by believers in God. To bolster his case he examines historically and intellectually significant writings about the miraculous. And having argued for the rejection of Hume, he explores the implications of this rejection for science, history, and theology.

REPORTED MIRACLES

REPORTED MIRACLES

A critique of Hume

J. HOUSTON

Senior Lecturer, Faculty of Divinity,
University of Glasgow

CAMBRIDGE
UNIVERSITY PRESS

Published by the Press Syndicate of the University of Cambridge
The Pitt Building, Trumpington Street, Cambridge CB2 1RP
40 West 20th Street, New York, NY 10011-4211, USA
10 Stamford Road, Oakleigh, Melbourne 3166, Australia

First published 1994

Printed in Great Britain at the University Press, Cambridge

A catalogue record for this book is available from the British Library

Library of Congress cataloguing in publication data

Houston, J. (Joseph)
Reported miracles: A critique of Hume/J. Houston.
p. cm.
Includes bibliographical references and index.
ISBN 0 521 41549 7 (hardback)
1. Miracles – History of doctrines. 2. Hume, David, 1711–1776 –
Religion. 3. God – Proof. I. Title.
BT97.2.H68 1994
212–dc20 93–29658 CIP

ISBN 0 521 41549 7 (hardback)

To
M. M. H.

Contents

Acknowledgements

I have been advancing (that is, both proposing and developing) some of the main ideas in this book on and off for about twenty-five years, and I am grateful to philosophical colleagues for encouraging me, whether they were inclined to agree with me or not, to think that there might be something in what I was saying; in particular Pat Shaw and Alexander Broadie, at different times, boosted my enthusiasm for the cause by the way in which they responded to the reading of papers on the subject. I am grateful to departmental colleagues for enabling me to have study leave at a time when the book needed sustained, momentum-building effort.

Cambridge University Press have been patient, tactful and unfailingly helpful. I am glad, and it is fitting, that they have wished to publish this book because it was a request from *Religious Studies* (published by Cambridge University Press) to review Mackie's book *The Miracle of Theism* which led me to try to put together the whole case against Hume which is this book's main point. I did not see how I could explain this case, in a way which would convince anyone, in the space of a review. Yet I could not produce a review which left this part of Mackie's discussion unscathed; so no review was ever forthcoming, and I can only offer the editors of *Religious Studies* my apologies. If Cambridge University Press feel that their earlier loss is now their gain, I shall be pleased to have made some amends there.

Many people have given secretarial assistance, and I thank them all. They include Jan Crawford, Jean Johnston, Marion Paton, Margaret Smith and Catherine Vost. Their helpfulness has been exemplary, frequently better than I deserved, and is much appreciated.

At a needy time for us and a formative time for the book, the Buchans let us use a house of theirs. May their roses bloom.

My family has often put up with the distractedness and un-buoyant spirits of one who has something on his mind. My thanks and love to them, and especially to my wife to whom the book is dedicated.

Introduction

An impressive cloud of modern witnesses can be called to support the case that the making, and reading, of this book is vanity.

The first to be cited is Bernard Williams, now a philosophy professor in Oxford; in 1983 when he was (at least) one of Cambridge's leading philosophers he reviewed J. L. Mackie's lucid book *The Miracle of Theism* (Oxford) in which, and prominently among the sequence of confident attacks on standard types of apologetic, Hume's dispatch of apologists' appeals to miracle reports is succinctly re-presented, endorsed and sharpened. Williams writes, 'For a detailed and perspicuous account of how it now stands [that is, with the traditional reasonings in support of theism] I know of no book that does it better than this'.[1] Williams goes on, however, to qualify his praise of the book: 'It concedes too much to these arguments in pretending that it is an open question whether they could deliver their conclusion . . . Hume and Kant . . . broke up most of this furniture a long time ago'. A book attacking Hume's views about the actual or possible significance of miracle-stories, such as this book is, is presumably no less otiose than a book advocating those views, if the matter was long ago settled.

The second witness is Maurice Wiles, Regius Professor of Theology, now Emeritus, at Oxford, who has recently written dismissively about the view that 'The absolute reliability of Scripture can be convincingly proved by the testimony of

---

[1] B. Williams, review of J. L. Mackie's *The Miracle of Theism*, Oxford, 1982, in *The Times Literary Supplement* (11 March 1983), p. 231.

miracle and fulfilled prophecy.'[2] He says, 'Claims of the latter kind [that is the kind just characterised in the previous quotation] have proved quite unable to stand up to the challenges that philosophical critics [he is not now thinking of biblical critics] have levelled against them. I shall not waste time by going over the arguments once again.' Both the passages quoted and their wider context make plain that Wiles regards it as time ill spent to defend or try to reinstate any such claims against the standard objections. Yet this book aims to show that reports or miracles may contribute to the apologists' case for theism.

John Hick is a notable and respected philosopher – theologian who, like very many others (such as Mackie, or T. Penelhum) has argued for the following,[3] as setting out the available acceptable alternatives in relation to alleged miracles: either you are a religious sceptic in which case you discount miracle-stories because of your premises, or else, because you have faith in the supernatural, you have different premises, and so you may accept at least some miracle-stories. However, miracle-stories cannot on this account of the matter, lead you, in reason, from scepticism to belief, nor can belief rest on attestations by miracles. In the following pages it will be argued *inter alia* that the wide consensus on this issue is quite mistaken.

These three witnesses are in no way eccentric in their estimates; and in the body of this book there appear other luminaries who concur with the expert testimony already called, in holding in effect that this book's task is hopeless. Yet expert witnesses in philosophy and theology cannot claim a court's firm confidence in quite the way that an expert metallurgist or pathologist might. Indeed it is surprising to see any professional philosopher appealing, as Williams does, to assured results, those of Hume and Kant, in philosophy; it is the more surprising when much of their Enlightenment anti-theology has come to be challenged in recent years.

---

[2] M. Wiles, in an essay entitled 'The Reasonableness of Christianity', in *The Rationality of Religious Belief*, edited by W. J. Abraham and S. W. Holtzer, Oxford, 1987, pp. 40–1.

[3] See J. Hick, *Philosophy of Religion*, Englewood Cliffs, NJ, 1963, pp. 39f.; also T. Penelhum, *Religion and Rationality*, New York, 1971, pp. 276f.

Although he will have specialist expertise in one or two areas, a systematic theologian cannot engage in detailed careful scrutiny of all the current views of all the specialists whom he must consult: biblical scholars, historians of doctrine and of philosophy, experts in other religions than his own, and philosophers. So Wiles has a better excuse than Williams for receiving rather than assessing the consensual philosophical wisdom. In fact he recognises the contemporary existence of sophisticated challenges to Enlightened philosophical ortho-doxy, but his rejection is summary[4] because he thinks he can rely on merely indicating rather than rehearsing or developing a standard, widely accepted line of criticism.

Some contemporary challengers have accepted that En-lightenment anti-theology is sound enough as far as it sees but have claimed that it failed to notice other perspectives, or features of life in the world, which have been more recently recognised, such as those towards which existentialist or per-sonalist philosophers direct us. However, other challengers have attacked specific Enlightenment arguments which were di-rected against specific theological claims, and these challenges have been much more by way of the sorts of argument whose point or force Enlightenment philosophers would immediately recognise or reckon with. (These challengers include Robert Adams, William Alston, Alvin Plantinga, William Rowe, Richard Swinburne and others from highly reputable centres of learning. It was presumably the work of these writers which led J. L. Mackie to think that his book was called for.) The present book aspires to contribute to this kind of rebuttal of Enlighten-ment anti-theology.

The Enlightenment arguments specifically against the apolo-gists' use of miracle reports are due mainly to Hume. Schleier-macher, it is true, does offer a distinctive, theological and non-Humean argument against believing miracle stories; but although it seems to have been hugely influential, it is a weak argument, whose weakness will be clearly brought out in the context of debate about Hume's line of reasoning. Hume's

---

[4] Wiles, in Abraham and Holtzer, *The Rationality of Religious Belief*, p. 48

arguments have of course been employed by philosophical critics of religious apologetics. Essentially these same arguments have also been appropriated, sometimes transposed, in the kind of idealist standpoint which has been greatly influential on theology. This book aims to reveal specifically the error and weakness of this Humean constellation of arguments. If they are, as will shortly be claimed, erroneous, and fail to justify the significant conclusions which they pretend to support, it is important that they should be assessed and their false pretensions exposed. The fact that large numbers of generally informed people see Hume on miracles as substantially unassailable, and so regard a book like this as a pointless waste of effort, actually makes it the more desirable to examine Hume's reasoning, and if necessary to reveal to those who rely on it the error of their way.

Of course the view which you take about the proper evaluation of miracle-stories will have implications for science, historiography and theological studies, as well as philosophy. The relevances of miracle reports to natural science are to be seen by engaging in some epistemology. Much that is written about miracle-stories in relation to science or history is Humean[5] and can be dealt with by exploring the epistemological implications of adopting or rejecting a Humean attitude. Other recent writers have more extensively discussed changes in modern science itself as these may be thought to impinge on the assessment of miracle reports. However, it is clear that neither the 'new physics' nor chaos theory, for instance, eliminates the usable distinction between what accords with nature's usual course and what runs counter to it, what is law-conforming and what is law-violating. So while some questions of interest are raised by these developments in science, the Humean problematic remains, to be reckoned with. Exploring the epistemological themes begins to open up a world view, alternative to that of the so-called Enlightenment, in which science and history are neither at odds with theistic belief nor unrelated to it.

---

[5] For example, the crudely Humean James Hansen, 'Can Science Allow Miracles?', *New Scientist*, vol. 94, no. 1300, (8 April 1982), pp. 73–6 (main cover story), and the much subtler F. H. Bradley's *Collected Essays*, Oxford 1935, pp. 1–70, discussed at length in Chapter 5, below.

Moreover, scripture scholars may hope for some valuable guidance from this enquiry, in view of the prevalence of miracle narratives in the scriptures. There are ways, certainly, of being a scripture scholar and avoiding the issue. You can simply dismiss or ignore the Humean constraints of historical critical method, as it is commonly understood, and defiantly present all or most miracle-stories as true. A bold but baseless approach. Or you can treat the stories which, just as stories, have many interesting things to be said about them without questions of the stories' truth ever being addressed. For scholars who find these approaches inadequate, but who also, by reason of their specialist study, find unsatisfactorily implausible the Humean claim that all these stories which describe what really would count as miracles (as distinct from events which have a natural explanation, like psychosomatic healings) must be regarded as erroneous, a discussion of the credentials of miracle-stories will be helpful.

In the last part of the book, therefore, significant relationships will be traced and discussed, between what has been said about the Humean case and the assumptions and methods of scientists, historians and, finally, theologians.

The study begins however, with the exposition of the ideas about reported miracles, of Augustine, Aquinas, Locke, Hume, Bradley and Troeltsch. These five chapters (Bradley and Troeltsch being taken together) are offered partly because accurate accounts, which give adequate detail to enable the thinkers' viewpoints about miracles to be properly grasped, are non-existent for all but Hume; not because they serve as a case study which counts (insofar as any case study can) against theses maintaining radical cultural and conceptual discontinuity over the centuries, though, incidentally, they do serve that end; but mainly because these prominent figures between them made points, brought out conceptual connections and engaged in argumentative manoeuvres in relation to reported miracles, knowledge of which is invaluable, perhaps obligatory, for anyone who wishes to reflect responsibly about the topic now. The scholarly description is offered, then, as having a value in its own right, but principally as providing an important resource for the evaluative enterprise which is this book's main point.

The line between description and evaluation cannot admittedly be drawn precisely, and undue concern to avoid the evaluative, for example by refusing to consider how an author could or would deal with a problem, may prevent the emergence of the author's meaning. So although the treatments do go beyond mere reportage, the aim in these first five chapters is fair and full exposition. The six authors chosen are arguably the six most influential writers on the subject. Yet even if that claim can be defeated, the more important point is that the historically occurring, pre-First World War ways of thinking about the miraculous, which are likely to be of interest or value to anyone now seeking the truth, are to be found in the authors who have been selected.

The survey of the older authors reveals more than one conception of miracle, and the twentieth century has generated more. Theologians have particularly wished to reject Hume's conception and have proposed alternatives. The next two chapters explore their contentions and attempt a sufficiently full understanding of the implications, largely desirable, of employing Hume's conception.

Hume's own theories are then criticised, largely adversely. In the course of that critique, accusations of question-begging abound, and some important ones are well justified. Higher critics may infer from the fact that 'begging a question' is never, in this book, employed to mean raising a question, or leaving unanswered some question that has arisen, that these chapters were drafted some time ago, or by a decently educated person. Certainly, here, begging the question is the fallacy *petitio principii*.

One principal outcome is in effect a defence of Locke and of Pannenberg. However, the book is not otiose because it endorses the conclusions of these two distinguished thinkers. Their conclusions, as they appear before us in their own writings and those of their commentators are undermined by the Humean attack. So long as it remains unanswered, the standpoints of Locke and Pannenberg conspicuously lack visible means of support. This book aspires to make good the large deficiency, so as to set the views of Locke and Pannenberg up, well-founded.

The concern here is not historical assessment for its own sake; whatever Locke or Pannenberg or anyone else may have said, the points of greatest import are that miracle stories are not as such incredible, and that they may, properly interpreted as truth-claiming, make a contribution to the advocacy of religious belief.

CHAPTER I

Augustine on the miraculous

St Augustine thought that, to the discerning, anything in the world of time and space could (for example, by its goodness) tell of God. As for Plato, an inevitably imperfect, geometrical figure such as a triangle could prompt an intellectual awareness of the ideal perfect triangle, and an imperfect human being or a somewhat beautiful scene could lead us up to contemplation of perfect humanity or beauty, so, for many Christians who were influenced by him, everything which is in the spatio-temporal world and accessible to our senses can draw the minds of the wise up to knowledge and love of God, whose thoughts the created world (albeit imperfectly) represents. Accordingly, for those such as Augustine who think in this way, no class of things, or events in which things participate, is marked off from others simply as opening up knowledge of, and love for, God. However, not everybody is wise or discerning.

Augustine distinguishes between the 'proper' or 'usual' order whereby events occur 'naturally', and occurrences which are otherwise and 'miraculously' done. While the wise would recognise the call to seek and know and love God by the ordinary usual course of events, the foolish, who ignore or fail to notice the significance of such events as 'constantly meet our senses', 'may be lifted up to God' by the authority which he openly exerts in miracles. Hence by such unusual events, especially those which meet our needs, people whose souls are clouded in folly by misplaced love are moved by God to

8

recognise and love him.[1] None of this would be necessary for the wise man.[2] Augustine says 'Whatever appears that is difficult or unusual, that I call a miracle.'[3] Further, 'When . . . things happen in a continuous kind of river of ever-flowing succession, passing by a regular and beaten track, then they are called natural; when, for the admonition of men they are thrust in by an unusual changeableness, then they are called miracles.'[4] Being didactic, drawing the mind of the onlooker to the mind of God is not a sufficient condition for being miraculous. So Augustine refers, as an example of something which is not a miracle, to the action of the prophet Ahijah who tore his new garment into twelve pieces and gave ten of them to Jeroboam as a sign that God would take the nation from the offending Solomon and give ten of its twelve tribes to Jeroboam (1 Kings, Chapter 11, verses 30 and 31). Such actions 'cannot cause wonder as being miracles'. To do that they must be 'more difficult and more unknown'.[5]

Many more pages of Augustine's writings[6] describe, and argue for the occurrence of, particular miracles, than are devoted to the theory of the miraculous. It is a matter of importance to him, in particular in his later writing, that specified miracles actually took place. There is no question of its being enough for us to come to see the truth and goodness of what God would be setting before us were he to work such and such miracles, which the perceptive reception of an edifying miracle-story simply as a story might be thought to accomplish. Apparently he thought that, following our false loves,[7] our heart may well not rise to know God by the hearing of a pointful miracle-story, which (like one of Aesop's fables) might have

[1] For example, Augustine, *De Cura pro Mortuis Gerenda*, xvi,20; All references in this chapter are to the text of Augustine in *Patrologiae Latinae*, ed. J. P. Migne, Paris, 1861–1900; the reference system is that used by Migne whereby the Book number is given first as a Roman capital (where there is more than one Book in the work), the chapter number is given as a lower-case Roman numeral, and the paragraph number as an Arabic numeral.   [2] Augustine, *De Utilitate Credendi*, xvi, 34.
[3] Ibid.   [4] Augustine, *De Trinitate*, iii, vi, 11.   [5] Ibid. iii, x, 20.
[6] Notably Augustine, *De Civitate Dei*, xxii, viii–ix.
[7] Augustine, *Epistle* cxvii, iii, 10.

point rather than be a true report. Instead, God must compel us towards himself by the actual working of miracles of which we can come to hear. So Augustine gives many examples of actual miracles of which he claims knowledge.

If we ask further whether awareness of the miraculous is essential for salvation, in Augustine's view, the answer must be in the affirmative in that the Incarnation, by which alone we are saved, is, with Creation, a primary miracle. If we ask whether our personally witnessing a miracle is necessary for our salvation, however, the answer is 'no'; and warnings are issued against our coveting the sensational for ourselves,[8] and exhortations given to find and know God rather by the sacraments.

A third question suggests itself: do miracles, or reports of miracles, provide unbelievers with a reason for them to come to faith? Althought the answer here is 'yes', it can hardly be thought that all the miracles of which Augustine speaks can have this kind of apologetic or compulsive force. When Augustine is talking about the wonders done by Christ and in his name it is often upon the conversion of rebellious wills, forgiveness, the birth of true belief, the overthrow of false devotion that he dwells.[9] All this belongs rather to the content of faith, to what the newly convinced Christian believer has come to believe, than to his reasons for the new belief. If the enquirer has been lacking reasons for Christian commitment, at least some of *these* miracles are more likely to be part of what it is he needs to be persuaded about than they are to be persuasive reasons in themselves.

Some of these miracles, such as changes of heart, may seem of doubtful argumentative force, because, if they are free choices, it will not be clear either that there can be a usual order of nature for them to differ from, or what the usual order of nature can be. Since, however, Augustine maintains that there is a usual order of nature in which human wills do not of themselves or within that order turn away from lower, corrupting loves, to love of God and good, and that it is not natural for us to repent, repentance and conversion do count as miraculous on Augustine's account. The fact remains that this belief, that such

---

[8] Augustine, *De Peccatorum Meritis*, II, xxxii, 52.
[9] For example, Augustine, *De Civitate Dei*, x, xxxii.

changes of heart are not natural but from above, may well itself be part of what requires argumentative support from the enquirer's standpoint; so the interpretation of conversions as miraculous, and any appeal to such miracles as arguments for faith, would be doubted.

However, there are other sorts of miracle about which Augustine speaks,[10] for example those which confirm the great miracle of Christ's ascension. The most glorious of these miracles are celebrated in scripture, while others are still being wrought in Christ's name up to Augustine's own day. He clearly thinks that, for at least some people, knowledge of the occurrence of a miracle not part of the faith which is to be confirmed, can give the needed reasons for accepting that faith. So he thinks it important to argue for the genuine occurrence of miracles known to him. He says that the divinity of Christ was corroborated by miraculous signs, and that such miraculous confirmation was necessary for the world to believe.[11] The gift of faith, imparted by God's grace, can, therefore, come by God's exerting his authority in miraculous events.

So far, miracles are contrasted with natural occurrences by being unusual as compared with the ordinary run of events, and by their resultant power to direct the mind and allegiance of otherwise indifferent or unconvinced people to God. Augustine consistently says that the usual order of nature is due to the Creator's implanting causal principles (*causales rationes*) in the Creation at the first.[12] However, we cannot come to any clear, definite or full understanding of these primordial principles; so, about the obvious ordinary order of nature, such as the successions of night and day, and of the seasons, the powers of seeds to grow and so forth, he says 'What more obscure than the causes of these?'[13] The harbouring of such misgivings about our grasp of the causal powers in nature may raise the question of how we can confidently *identify* miracles, if we do not really know what can and should ordinarily be expected of nature. Talk of 'implanted causal principles' as determining nature's ordinary

[10] Ibid. xxii, vii and viii.   [11] Ibid.
[12] For example, Augustine, *De Genesi ad Litteram*, vi, xiv, 18.
[13] Augustine, *De Utilitate Credendi*, xvi, 34.

course may raise the question of how we are to *conceive* of miracles
in relation to the causal powers within nature: for example, are
miracles brought about by causal powers which are implanted
in nature but distinct from the *causales rationes* already spoken of,
or are they brought about by powers from outside nature? We
look first at the identification, the epistemological, question.

   Although Augustine did think that human understanding of
the causal connexions in nature is indefinite and incomplete, he
was not altogether a sceptic in matters of science.[14] He claims
some, limited, capacity to grasp by experience what is in the
nature of things which emerge in (created) time: 'Conformably
with the constraint of human weakness we can know what is in
the nature of each of those things which have emerged in time
because we have perceived in experience . . .'[15] (Our powers of
prediction, are, however, very restricted. Augustine continues,
'but we are ignorant as to what may be. So some youth is in his
nature such as to grow old but we do not know whether even this
is to be, in the will of God.'[16]) Observable phenomena do,
therefore, give us some cognitive access to the causal powers,
which are latent in things, as these things possess particular
natures;[17] but if Augustine is consistent, he does not mean that
we can acquire an accurate, determinate and complete grasp of
the causal factors which are implanted and at work in nature.
What we can do is to discover some powers which the natures of
things appear to exhibit in the ordinary course of events, and
provisionally, standing to be corrected, we may distinguish
miracles as those events which deviate from nature's usual
course and which cannot be accounted for in terms of (*prima
facie*) normal causal powers, events which are for someone's
good and which evoke first wonder and, thereby, belief in and
love for God.

   Turning next to the conceptual question, we can usefully
distinguish three ways in which Augustine conceives of the
miraculous. We can see that there are three conceptions

[14] Cf. Robert M. Grant, *Miracle and Natural Law in Graeco-Roman and Early Christian
   Thought*, Amsterdam, 1952, p. 219.
[15] Augustine, *De Genesi ad Litteram*, VI, xvi, 27; see also ibid. IX, xvi, 29.
[16] Ibid. VI, xvi, 27.   [17] Ibid. IX, xvii, 32 makes this clear.

involved when we ask whether miracles have a natural cause: on the first of his conceptions Augustine would answer 'yes', on the second 'no', and on the third the proper answer is not so straightforward.

On all three conceptions, divinely implanted primordial causal principles control the ordinary course of events. In expounding the first conception, Augustine speaks of hidden seeds 'concealed in the corporeal elements of this world'.[18] Ordinary seeds, which we know in experience, prompt the growth of their organisms both according to God's will and in a familiar sequence of developments; but these hidden seeds, seeds of seeds (*semina seminum*), when they are activated, alter the usual developmental sequence so as, for example, to accelerate it. Augustine represents at least some miracles as bringing about what the ordinary run of nature brings about, but in an exceptionally speedy way.[19] The known seed either is itself a primordial causal principle, or is to be thought of as acting in accordance with more or less understood causal principles, according to whether we take '*rationes*' to mean actual causes (causal reasons for what happens) or the general principles according to which causes operate. The hidden seeds, correspondingly, either are latent causes, or they act in accordance with unknown principles. According to this conception, miracles have causes which are in nature, hidden from our comprehension, exceptionally activated to bring about exceptional results. The role of the hidden seed is, it should be noted, set forth in a discussion which is primarily, though not exclusively, about wonders done by angels and by Pharaoh's magicians; it is therefore a real (but by some writers insufficiently addressed) question whether Augustine intends this account to apply to all instances of the miraculous.

Angels have been given power to work magic, so Augustine also says in *De Trinitate* without explicitly relating this to Pharaoh's magicians and their efforts. Yet, in another place, when discussing these miracles of the Egyptian magicians, Augustine suggests that in order to work their wonders the

---

[18] Augustine, *De Trinitate*, III, viii, 13. [19] For example, ibid. III, v, 11.

magicians entered agreements, in private, presumably with angels or demons (see *Liber de Diversis Quaestionibus* LXXXIII, lxxix). This further factor in his account makes it even harder to be certain what his complete view was of the Egyptians' magic. Did he think that angels or demons could exploit an understanding which they particularly had of the workings of hidden seeds? Or was Augustine, when he discussed this issue in one place, simply forgetfully careless of what he had written about it in another? The former view would maintain consistency and help to explain *how* demons or angels could work wonders. Accordingly, the former view perhaps has some claim on us. The compact-with-demons approach is present in Augustine himself, but it is given greater prominence later by Aquinas, when the undesirable nature of magic is being brought out.

The sorts of wonders which he is talking about here may well raise distinctive, peculiar problems, because the wonders done by magicians cannot generally be accounted for as being brought about by any immediate exercise of God's power in order to corroborate divine truth or to lift people's hearts and minds up to God himself. It may be that the reference to seeds, causal powers which are hidden in nature, is made to explain just this sub-class of magical wonders, a sub-class of which instances are claimed in the Bible and by Augustine's contemporaries. Since this species of wonder does not in any case fall under the central Augustinian characterisation of miracle (since it does not lift up the impious to know God), it is at least possible that Augustine did not propose this view as applying generally, to the properly miraculous. Nevertheless, some writers have seen this as the leading element of Augustine's conception of the miraculous,[20] and have thought the matter confirmed by another Augustinian remark: comparing things which are naturally done with things which are miraculously done, Augustine says, 'God is present to nature that it may exist, and nature is not lacking to miracles.'[21] The context of this, in itself cryptic, remark is not so clear as to rule out the interpretation

---

[20] For example, Grant, *Miracle and Natural Law*, pp. 215–20, and B. Ward, *Miracles and the Mediaeval Mind* London, 1982, pp. 1–4.
[21] Augustine, *De Cura pro Mortuis Gerenda*, xvi, 19.

simply that miracles occur to created things which belong to the natural world. Certainly, we are not compelled to read it as representing the hidden seeds theory, or even as saying that miracles have natural causes.

The principal source of Augustine's second conception of the miraculous is *De Genesi ad Litteram*. There, in his discussion of the creation of woman, Augustine speaks about ordinary natural causation, remarks on the difficulty of establishing what is natural, and spends some paragraphs reflecting on natural and miraculous causality. He holds, in this account of the issue, that miracles do not involve causal principles inherent or latent in nature, but that God brings about miracles according to his sovereign will in a way which is distinct from nature's way, and is not causally dependent on nature. He speaks of causes hidden in God himself and (explicitly) not placed within created things,[22] not belonging to nature and God's providential order, but in God's will by which he rules the natures which he has created, belonging to that order of grace by which sinners are saved. Those events which point to God's grace are accordingly done 'not by the natural movement of things, but miraculously (*mirabiliter*)'.[23] Earlier in the same substantial commentary, Augustine has said, 'In the first created order God did not pre-establish every cause, but retained some in his own will, and those which he has kept in his own will assuredly do not depend on the necessity of created causes'.[24]

It might be wondered whether this conception of the miraculous is, as it has been set out here, perhaps found in a piece of writing considerably earlier than *De Trinitate* which advances the hidden seed conception, and whether we should take the latest thought to be the maturest, constituting Augustine's most considered view. However, there is no good reason to place the composition of *De Genesi ad Litteram* earlier than that of *De Trinitate*[25]; moreover the *De Genesi ad Litteram* conception is unmistakably echoed in the late *De Civitate Dei*, in a passage which we have noticed already, where repentance, conversion,

---

[22] Augustine, *De Genesi ad Litteram*, IX, xviii, 33. [23] Ibid. IX, xviii, 34.
[24] Ibid. VI, xviii, 29.
[25] See B. Altaner and A. Stuiber, *Patrologie*, Freiburg, 1978, p. 426 and p. 430.

forgiveness and true devotion are spoken of as the central miracles.[26] It can be added that Augustine's works were not so much each composed in a period during which he concentrated on that work, as accumulated out of material which he had had occasion to set down over several years, during which other material, now consolidated in other books, was also coming into being. This makes any argument based on the order of composition somewhat complex and tentative. There is no good reason to doubt that this second conception of the miraculous *was* significantly present in Augustine's thinking. Further, this conception is not somehow, awkwardly, to be subsumed under, or accommodated to the hidden seeds conception; this second conception is distinct,[27] and since it relates to (as Augustine sees them) the most significant examples of the miraculous rather than to a peculiar sub-class, this conception has a good claim to be Augustine's central conception of miracle.

The third conception of the miraculous involves God's changing the natures of things, God having first created these natures as he pleased.[28] Such changing of natures gives rise to monsters and portents. In *De Genesi ad Litteram*, Augustine also talks of God's ruling as he wills those natures which he has created, in a way which is to be understood as changing them, and this (quite explicitly) by-passing the providential order of nature.[29] Since natures have a degree of permanence, to be natures, the language of changing natures suggests that new causal factors, newly introduced by God, are now continuingly present within nature itself. This conception fits ill with the hidden seeds view because the causal principles thus newly and strikingly operative in nature were not implanted at the first, but have been newly introduced by the will of God. On the other hand, it may seem to go beyond the second conception because it does involve the implantation in nature of somewhat permanent causal powers by which miracles happen. Accordingly, when we ask whether, on this conception, miracles have a natural cause, the answer cannot be a clear 'yes' or 'no'. Perhaps

---

[26] Augustine, *De Civitate Dei*, x, xxxii.
[27] Cf. R. M. Grant, and B. Ward, as cited in note 20 above.
[28] Augustine, *De Civitate Dei*, xxi, viii.   [29] See note 22 above.

if we desire to reduce the number of Augustinian conceptions of miracle, we can best regard this last concept as a sub-class of the second. Then the alteration of natures is one way by which God acts from outside the natural order of providence to effect the purposes of grace, and he is to be thought of as acting in this way when he wishes to introduce innovations which have some permanence, such as monsters which have a period of time in which to act in the ways which are true to their monstrous natures. Moreover, as we saw in the reference to *De Genesi ad Litteram*[30], Augustine does speak in terms of God's rule over natures precisely in the context in which the second conception is explicit, so that it looks as though he may have regarded what has been called the third conception as a variant on, or elaboration of, the second.

On any of these conceptions, Augustine takes God to bring miracles about in a way which does not go back upon the primordial system which he instituted and the will expressed therein. The hidden seeds were part of that order, implanted to be activated in due time; so that the first conception of miracles is not seen as raising any issue about God's or nature's self-consistency. It is in the context of the presentation of the second conception that Augustine insists[31] on God's not contravening the primitive ordering of nature when miracles happen; in Augustine's view, God acts beyond rather than against the usual course of nature.[32] In relation both to the creation of Adam and to the extension by fifteen years of the life of Hezekiah (in response to prayer), Augustine stresses that 'God does not act [or 'has not acted'] against a cause which he surely instituted purposely in advance, a cause against which he does not act'. He goes on,

In the first created order, God did not pre-establish every cause, but retained some in his own will, and those which he has kept in his own will assuredly do not depend on the necessity of created causes; nevertheless those causes which he has retained in his own will cannot be contrary to those which he laid down by his will, because the will of God cannot be contrary to itself.[33]

[30] See note 22 above.   [31] Augustine, *De Genesi ad Litteram*, ix, xviii, 34.
[32] Ibid. ix, xviii, 31.   [33] Ibid. vi, xviii, 29.

However surprising and wonder-provoking miracles may be to us, they have their place in the consistent divine purpose.

When Augustine speaks, as he does, of natural laws (*naturales leges*)[34] which relate to the ordinary course of nature, and determine what the elements which constitute things in the material world can or cannot become, he seems, if we are to take him literally, to have in mind laws which constrain, limit and control. In one widespread modern usage, by contrast, a law of nature is a descriptive generalisation setting forth what happens in specific sorts of circumstances. Standardly, the distinction is expressed by saying that, on a view like Augustine's, natural laws are normative or prescriptive, whereas on the common modern view they are descriptive. (For some purposes this distinction may not matter much: after all if nature obeys some prescriptive law, say, 'Iron will sink in water', what actually occurs may well (if the law is appropriately expressed) be described by use of the same form of words, 'Iron will sink in water'.)

Now if we ask whether Augustine thought of miracles as events which are contrary to natural laws, we may have in mind Augustine's own conception of natural laws, in which case the answer is 'no'. Natural laws will be seen, here, as (or as implemented by) those causal principles which, having been laid down by the will of God, determine the ordinary course of nature. Natural laws therefore express the will of God which is seen in the order of providence. Miracles happen due to causes which are wholly hidden from us, but also by the will of God; and God's will does not change or become contrary to itself. Hence miracles, so understood, are not contrary to natural laws, so understood.

However, if by 'natural laws' *we* mean summary descriptions of what does happen, with no connotation that it is required, obliged or compelled to happen, Augustine might well have given the answer 'yes' to our question. His frequent assertion that there is a usual course of nature, an assertion which is accompanied by an express disavowal of any confident grasp of

[34] Ibid. IX, xvii, 32.

underlying necessary causes, has a force very like that of the characteristic common modern claim that there are laws of nature, of a descriptive sort. For Augustine a miracle is, specifically, contrary to the observed usual course of nature, which according to the common modern usage is to say that a miracle is contrary to natural law.

Even if this represents Augustine correctly it remains true that he would not take the further step of distinguishing miracles as those events which cannot be given a natural explanation, and cannot be understood scientifically, from events which can be naturally explained and understood. For Augustine, to understand an event is to know by what causal powers or principles it happens; even if we can (as he thinks we can) grasp something of the pattern of nature's ordinary course, this will not in itself yield genuine understanding of events which conform to the pattern.

By contrast, many a modern writer who takes the descriptive view of natural law, would say that to understand an event is just to recognise that its occurrence is covered by a known and specified natural law. Augustine requires more if there is to be genuine explanation, and the scepticism about science which has been attributed to him is, in part, a reflection of the high demand he makes: real scientific knowledge will go behind the apparent regularities of nature's course and will reveal underlying causes. The modern who looks only for observable regularities in nature may seem less sceptical only because he is less demanding; this modern and Augustine agree that miracles are distinguishable from other events as exceptions to nature's apparent normal course, but only the modern can take that to mean that miracles are distinguishable as unexplained, as compared to nature's explained and understood normal course. For Augustine, as we saw, nature's normal course is not fully, properly understood, and so miracles cannot be marked off from ordinary events on the basis that miracles lack explanation, are not well understood.

It is a truism that Augustine's influence on Western Church and society was and is formative and great, and that the Middle Ages drew hugely on the theological legacy left by him. On miracles, the descriptive treatment given of miraculous events,

especially in *De Civitate Dei*, is a forerunner of mediaeval writings
galore. B. Ward's book[35] splendidly surveys this world, and its
world-view. However, she suggests (pp. 4–5) that Anselm and
Abelard, in their conceptions of the miraculous, shift the
emphasis, as compared with Augustine's emphasis, towards the
miraculous as 'caused by the direct intervention of God in
affairs' and away from the wonder which miracles cause in man;
she is rather surprised by this shift, and she points out that
Anselm and Abelard (and others) discuss the matter in relation
to the narratives in Genesis about the creation of man and
woman. It is true that there is then, as one might expect in the
context of the discussion of the Genesis narrative, less interest in
miracles as wonders; when Augustine himself discusses miracles
in the context of the Genesis narratives he also places less stress
than he does elsewhere on the wonder-provoking power of
miracles. Furthermore, the passage from Anselm which Ward
quotes as evidence of the shift of emphasis,[36] and the paragraphs
around it in Anselm's discussion, otherwise faithfully echo the
Augustinian 'second conception' of miracles which has been set
out here. Ward has given insufficient stress to Augustine's own
discussion of the creation narratives in *De Genesi ad Litteram*, and
has therefore failed to recognise, or failed to recognise as distinct,
the important 'second conception' of the miraculous expounded
above. Consequently she has sketched a more substantial shift
than there really was. What Anselm and Abelard say about
miracles is wholly derived, undistorted, from Augustine, and
there is a general continuity from Augustine to the mediaeval
theologians.

---

[35] See note 20 above.
[36] Anselm, *De Conceptu Virginali*, Chapter 11, in *Anselm of Canterbury*, edited and
   translated by J. Hopkins and H. Richardson, Toronto and New York, 1976, vol. III,
   pp. 157–9.

CHAPTER 2

Aquinas on the miraculous

Augustine doubts our human capacity to fully understand nature. He treats nature's usual, observed course as the surface outcome of the operation of somewhat hidden causal powers in things; a consistent, uniform surface is no more than a *prima facie* indication of consistent underlying causal powers, and does not reliably reveal these powers, in the grasping of which a proper understanding of nature consists. Events which cause surprise and wonder in us by their apparent extraordinariness by comparison with nature's normal course, may yet, for all we can say, occur by the normal causal powers of the things involved; still these are the events which, particularly when they compel our minds upwards to God, we call miracles. Of course, some events are apparently so beyond the powers of nature that there will be no room for serious doubt that they exceed the casual powers implanted in things.

Aquinas follows Augustine on the miraculous in many ways, but while he retains being wonderful as part of his conception, he distinguishes between the wonder which derives from ignorance of the causes at work in nature and what is wondrous in an unqualified way because it truly has no natural cause.[1] An example of the former sort of wonder will be the person who is amazed by an eclipse of the sun whereas the astronomer, who knows its cause, is not. The name 'miracle' suggests 'what is of itself filled with admirable wonder, not simply in relation to one

[1] Aquinas, *Summa Contra Gentiles*, translated by Anton C. Pegis, New York, 1955, Book III, Ch. 101, 1: also Aquinas, *Summa Theologiae*, Blackfriars editions and translations, London and New York, from 1964, 1a, 105, 7, Responsio. All references in the notes for this chapter are to these works.

person or another'. When there are miracles the hidden cause is God. 'Therefore, those things must properly be called miraculous which are done by divine power apart from the order generally followed in things.' This Thomist shift in the conception of the miraculous will, to the extent that it is accompanied by Augustinian misgivings about the soundness of human understanding of causality in nature, lead to increased doubts about what is and what is not truly miraculous.

In several other ways, Aquinas recognisably takes up the Augustinian 'second conception'. So, to Aquinas, miraculous occurrences are beyond nature's powers to bring about at all, or to bring about in the way in which they actually happen.[2] Such miracles are not done contrary to nature, Aquinas insists, even though they are done 'apart from the order implanted in things'.[3] Even when what happens seems 'to be opposed to the proper order of a particular nature',[4] this may be because it is acted upon by God. God may act upon what is in nature rather as a force or energy, or by using natural things as his instruments, and in such cases what happens accords with and employs the usual powers in nature.[5]

The woodcarver's knife cannot of itself, unused by the craftsman, carve a figure, but when the carver uses it, he makes use of the knife's natural powers as he carves; the sea, of itself, has no tidal motion, but acted upon by the moon, its tidal motion accords with its natural powers.[6] However, there are other sorts of cases. For example, and carrying the artwork analogy forward, Aquinas points out that an artist 'may work in a different way on his product, even after he has given it its first form', and suggests that 'the whole of nature is like an artifact of the divine artistic mind'. Does it then follow, as Aquinas claims, that it is not 'against nature if God does something to natural things in a different way from that to which the course of nature is accustomed?'[7] Certainly a woodcarver may begin his shaping of the wood by establishing it in the rough shape of, say, a tree,

[2] Aquinas, *Summa Contra Gentiles*, III, 101, 2–4.   [3] Ibid. III, 100, 1.
[4] Ibid. III, 100, 2.   [5] Ibid. III, 100, 2–4. See also *Summa Theologiae*, Ia, 105, 6.
[6] Aquinas, *Summa Theologiae*, Ia, 105, 6.
[7] Aquinas, *Summa Contra Gentiles*, III, 100, 6.

but his final carving may turn out to be a human figure; and in none of this does there seem to be anything against nature, so far as 'against nature' has any meaning. Nor are the craftsman's earlier and later actions inconsistent. However, is this analogy, so employed, relevant to a discussion of the being, or not being, contrary to nature of particular events which occur in a way different from the usual course of nature? Perhaps the composition of a piece of music, in which there is an unexpected passage in a different key or a different tempo from the rest, provides a better analogy; the notes in the new and (as it were) anomalous key will correspond to miraculous events. Human composers who act in this way do not cause there to be anything occurring against nature, in any obvious sense, but if God is thought of as the cosmic composer ordering all events in their particular patterns of succession, as the composer orders the notes of his composition, and if God orders some events so that they occur in ways contrary to an order which he has already established, what *would* be contrary to nature if this is not? Once again, the composer's unity of conception may be perfectly consistently worked out in and through the passage of the (to that point) unexpected sort, so that there is no question of the composer's being self-inconsistent in his purposes. Yet the order of nature, or nature's own causal powers, would seem to be that order or those powers which God has established generally; what then might it *be* for events to be contrary to nature other than that these events occur contrary to the established order or contrary to the established causal powers? If there is no other interpretation of 'being contrary to nature' the God-as-composer analogy will indicate that miracles *are* contrary to nature. Aquinas's point, which he wants to stress, seems to be that nature has of itself no order, no powers, other than those given by God, and as God re-orders, or alters powers, these new orders or powers are now those of nature. Augustine's concern in insisting that God does not act against nature was to affirm God's unchanging steadfast purposes. Nature has no inherent order or powers of its own, apart from what God devises by his wisdom.

Augustine and Aquinas both held (1) that God's purposes in his rule over nature are consistent and (2) that nature has no

order except that which God gives. In their respective developments of the thesis that miracles do not go against nature,
Augustine conspicuously emphasises the first principle, Aquinas
the second.

In discussing the miraculous, Aquinas talks much more than
Augustine in terms of the causal powers in things, perhaps
because he has a greater interest in the way the natural world
works, and because he was more confident about our discove-
ring and reliably identifying such causal powers and, relatedly,
because the concept of causal power has more widely useful
explanatory work to do in Aquinas's philosophising. With a
consequently deeper sense of what is at stake, he distinguishes
the more insistently between the observed usual course of nature
and the underlying powers which cause nature to run as it does.
Since some apparent irregularity in the observed usual course of
nature may be explained in terms of the ordinary causal powers
in things, perhaps interacting in a way that had not been
realised, irregularities in nature's normal course are no more
than *prima facie* indications of powers other than nature's usual
powers. So, when there seems some irregularity compared to the
order generally followed in things, Aquinas has two reasons for
denying that this event is 'contrary to nature': (1) It may turn
out to be explicable by reference to nature's causal powers and if
it is not, we should not conclude that nature has by itself gone
against its own underivative intrinsic causal powers. Rather, (2)
God's powers will be the explanation, acting beyond rather than
against nature. There is the possibility that God might act
beyond nature in such a way that no irregularity is noticed by us
on the surface of nature's course of events. Perhaps (we may
speculate) God might do this to avert dangers which are
unknown to us; if he is supposed to act in the hidden way (we
may further speculate) there may be less incentive for us to
discover how the world works in order to use its powers, with a
consequent reduction of the scope of our responsible action, as
compared with a world in which God is not supposed to act
behind the appearances. Aquinas does not, however, discuss this
possibility, and of course we have *ex hypothesi* no way of knowing
whether God does act beyond nature in this covert way. The

sovereignty of God over natural processes is not only insisted on in Aquinas's discussion of the concept of the miraculous; the divine sovereignty is confirmed by the actual occurrence of miraculous events. When a miracle occurs it is plain that the miraculous event itself is an exercise of divine power over nature, and it is thereby also made plain that the ordinary regular course of nature is not possessed by nature of itself. Rather, nature is *given* its normal ordered character, and retains it as it does because it is ruled by the power of God. Aquinas writes

it is . . . certain that divine power can sometimes produce an effect, without prejudice to its providence, apart from the order implanted in natural things by God. In fact, he does this at times to manifest power. For it can be manifested in no better way, that the whole of nature is subject to the divine will, than by the fact that sometimes He does something outside the order of nature. Indeed, this makes it evident that the order of things has proceeded from Him, not by natural necessity, but by free will.[8]

Some events may look to us like miracles, but are not miracles. One reason already noted may be that we are simply ignorant of the powers of nature by which an event which surprises us has come to pass. Another reason may be that an angel has acted. Aquinas explains why this will not be miraculous, in a passage which helps to make clearer why only God can bring miracles about:

Strictly speaking, a miracle is defined as an event that occurs outside the natural run of things. However, if some event should occur outside the ordinary course of things with respect to any particular thing in nature, this would not be enough to make it a miracle – otherwise, someone throwing a stone up in the air would be working a miracle, since this is outside the ordinary course of the stone's nature. God, however, is the only one who can do this, since whatever an angel or any other created thing does by its own power takes place in accordance with the ordinary processes of nature and so is not miraculous. Thus God alone can work miracles.[9]

Demons, like angels, can so act as to amaze us, but, once again their actions will not be, properly speaking, miraculous because they will not happen 'outside the whole realm of created nature,

[8] Ibid. III, 99, 9.   [9] Aquinas, *Summa Theologiae*, Ia, 110, 4.

in which realm every created power is contained'.[10] Only in a wide sense can these events be called miraculous, because they go beyond the human power to grasp.[11]

So, whereas 'God alone works miracles',[12] magic is otherwise to be accounted for; the distinction between miracles and magic is so insisted upon and developed by Aquinas that nobody could confuse his views about the one with his views about the other in anything like the way Augustine's respective views on these two topics can be confused and are only distinguished (to the extent that they are distinct) by analysis.[13] If, for example, a magician were to exploit any hidden powers in nature, such as those of the hidden seeds, the seeds of seeds, of which Augustine spoke, Aquinas is quite clear that the unexpected, exceptional, marvellous events which were brought about would not be miracles. Such wonders would be surprising to the onlooker only because, and to the extent that, he was unaware of the latent, or rarely exploited, potency of the hidden seeds; and since they would be brought about 'within the potency' of the things which are involved, they would decidedly not be miraculous, as Aquinas sees it.

A related type of case involves bewitchment, and the 'evil eye'. Aquinas believes that such cases do occur; he says ' . . . when certain souls are strongly stirred by wickedness their looks become spiteful and poisonous, particularly to children with tender and impressionable bodies'.[14] However, he makes it quite clear that his understanding of psycho-physical interactions offers a natural explanation of this kind of case, and that this sort of thing is to be classed neither as miracle nor as magic. And 'no creature' such as a magician, 'can produce any effect in a thing except what is within the potency of that thing'.[15] As we have seen, the potency of something is the potency 'of that thing' not by an inalienable possession, or an unalterable natural necessity which cannot be more fundamentally accounted for; rather, a thing's 'possession' of its potency is by God's will, and, for his

[10] Ibid. ia, 114, 4.   [11] Ibid. ia, 110, 4 and 114, 4.
[12] Aquinas, *Summa Contra Gentiles* iii, 102, title   [13] As above at pp. 13–20.
[14] Aquinas, *Summa Theologiae*, ia, 117, 3.
[15] Aquinas, *Summa Contra Gentiles*, iii, 102, 5.

good purpose, God can and does enable events to occur which could not be brought about by the ordinary natural powers of things. No creature of itself, angel, magician or any other, can overrule the divine imparting of a specific potency to a thing.

Aquinas argues that magic effects are not be attributed to the influence of celestial bodies: of the various specific sorts of magic, when we consider their respective distinctive characters, each turns out to be impossible for celestial bodies to cause. Thus some magic requires the functioning of rational nature, as when information is required (e.g. about stolen property) or when speech, and, it may be, reasoning are employed by apparitions; but 'it is not possible for understanding to be caused by corporeal principles'.[16] Again, inanimate things are (magically) given the power of self-movement, but the possession of a soul is a pre-requisite of the power of self-movement, and (for one thing) celestial power cannot give a soul to, say, copper or other material of which a statue might be made, while the material remains that material, such as copper, which is unable to have a soul.

When he discusses phenomena such as a certain person's, simply by his presence, having bolts of doors open for him or a person's becoming invisible, Aquinas says of these pieces of magic (as he classifies them) that they cannot be caused by celestial powers because celestial powers can only cause in a thing that (form) which is natural to that thing.[17] Since any occurrence in a thing of a power (?deriving from a form) which is not natural to that thing will be miraculous in Aquinas's terms, rather than magic, Aquinas appears to be confused here in his classification because the explanation of magic, which he regards as the correct account, is that magic is due to intellectual substance(s), demons. Yet this will not account for the opening of untouched bolts or people's becoming invisible, as pieces of *magic*, since created intelligence cannot, any more than celestial bodies, cause in other things that which is not natural to these other things.

Intellectual substances must be referred to in order to explain

[16] Ibid. III, 104, 2; Aquinas himself here refers back to ibid. III, 84.
[17] Ibid. III, 104, 6.

magic, because magic involves the use of intelligible signs. We
have seen already that magic cannot be explained by the
operation of celestial bodies when information or a course of
reasoning are magically set before us. Intelligible signs enter
importantly into the practice of magic also in the expressions of
wishes, commands, invocations, adjurations, spells, magic
words or incantations and Aquinas argues that the human
magician who utters the words in question cannot be supposed
to have the power, in himself, to bring about the magical effects,
simply by uttering the words. Where wishes, commands,
invocations or adjurations expressed in an ordinary natural
language are concerned, this is plain because 'the intellect of
men' is not 'able to cause things by its act of conception'
merely.[18] (Rather the other way round, in that the knowledge in
the human intellect is caused by things.) Nor can the respective
specific causal powers to accomplish the effects brought about
by magic be imparted or acquired by study, because study can
only give a knowledge of what to do in order to bring the
magical effect about;[19] the actual bringing about must therefore
be done by something other than the magician who merely
studies to succeed in his work, and this 'other' must itself possess
the particular power without intermediate agency to accomplish the magical effect. 'So, we are left with the conclusion that
effects of this kind are accomplished by some understanding to
which the speech of the person uttering these words is addressed.'[20] An intellectual substance is also to be postulated as
the cause of magically accomplished events when the magicians
have used symbols or figures with a particular shape. Since
shapes cannot of themselves bring about the magical effects,
they must be addressed to, have a significance for, intelligences
which then work the magic.[21]

Aquinas does not seem to make out his argument in relation to
spells, magic words or esoteric incantations which have no
standard generally recognisable meaning in any natural language. He touches on these before he begins to discuss wishes,
commands, adjurations, which are expressed in ordinary lan-

---

[18] Ibid. III, 105, 2.   [19] Ibid. III, 105, 3.   [20] Ibid. III, 105, 6.   [21] Ibid. paras. 7ff.

guage; but what he says about the latter depends on their evident general intelligibility, and the conclusion that all these utterances must be addressed to an intelligence is not made out with respect to spells, magic words and the like. Presumably, however, he could apply to them the sort of arguments which he employs in relation to shapes and figures – as shapes and figures do not have in themselves powers to accomplish magic, neither do particular sounds like the utterances of spells or magic words, and yet magic happens by their employment. By an argument analogous to that which applied to shapes and figures, we should conclude that spells and magic words, otherwise of obscure hidden meaning, must be directed at, addressed to, an intelligence to which these should have significance and which has the power to work the magic.

The intelligence(s) by (appeal to) which the magicians do their work are not evil by nature;[22] but they are not morally good as can be seen from the facts that evil men use the magic arts, that the magic arts are used for evil purposes such as adultery, theft or homicide, that they draw people to the trivial rather than to the goods of reason, that magic practices are sometimes criminal and that they are often inimical to truth.[23] Aquinas holds that where true information *is* given to those who practise divination, it is often given by the demons who seek thereby to win the trust of the enquirer and to lead him on to spiritual loss.[24] That is his principal concern over such truths as may emerge from the practice of magic. Yet he demonstrates that fortune telling can hit on the truth by chance.[25] Astrology, too, can lead us to the truth insofar as it predicts merely what human emotion, which Aquinas believed the heavenly bodies to influence naturally, brings about;[26] in that respect astrology will not be, strictly, magic. Aquinas also deals with a range of practices in which the aimed-for effect cannot be secured by the exercise of the powers of the inanimate objects or human beings obviously involved;[27] the effect can only be had if there is a compact, explicit, or implicit and ill-understood, with demons:

[22] Ibid. III, 107.   [23] Ibid. III, 106.
[24] Aquinas, *Summa Theologiae* IIa, IIae, 95, 4; and similarly, ibid. IIa, IIae, 95, 5.
[25] Ibid. IIa, IIae, 96, 3.   [26] Ibid. IIa, IIae, 95, 5.   [27] Ibid. IIa, IIae, 93, 95 and 96.

e.g. necromancy, soothsaying, geomancy, aurispicy, astrology, augury, sorcery, reliance on omens. All of this is, therefore, forbidden magic.

The occurrence of miracles should serve to support (1) beliefs about the providential ordering and upholding of the world by God, and (2) beliefs about the divine mission of particular people. As to the first, Aquinas says 'it can be manifested in no better way, that the whole of nature is subject to the divine will, than by the fact that sometimes He does something outside the order of nature. Indeed, this makes it evident that the order of things has proceeded from Him, not by natural necessity, but by free will.'[28] As for the second, he says

in matters of divine revelation above human reason, confirmation is provided in ways which are proper to divine power. This is in two ways. Firstly, such that the teacher of sacred teaching should do what God alone can do by performing miracles: this may be for bodily health, and so we have the grace of healing; or it may be for the pure display of divine power, as when the sun stands still or becomes dark, or when the waters are divided; and here we have the working of miracles. Secondly, by being able to display what it belongs to God above to know. These are future contingencies, where we have prophecy, and also the secrets of the heart, for which we find the discernment of spirits.[29]

Aquinas did not suppose that the known occurrence of a miracle would compel anyone's belief in that which the miracle confirms: 'one man believes and another does not, when both have seen the same miracle, heard the same preaching'.[30] Belief and faith require the exercise of the will (of the believer or the person of faith). By contrast, understanding (and acceptance) of the first principles, self-evidently necessary truths, and knowledge of necessary conclusions, which are derived from self-evident first principles, are wholly brought about, caused, in the person who knows or understands, so that there is no need, and indeed no room, for the exercise of will. Miracles are therefore motives which influence but do not override or determine the will of the believer; they are supportive or confirmative of faith,

[28] Aquinas, *Summa Contra Gentiles*, III, 99, 9.
[29] Aquinas, *Summa Theologiae*, Ia, IIae, 111, 4.   [30] Ibid. IIa, IIae, 6, 1.

and they are reasons among other possible reasons, for a believer's faith. The believer regards matters of faith as credible not simply in themselves like self-evident first principles, but by their association with those other factors which lead him to the assent of faith: 'he would not believe unless he saw that they [the matters of faith] are worthy of belief on the basis of evident signs or something of the sort'.[31] The believer requires some basis for his belief-choice (it may be a virtuous glad recognition that the truths of faith are consonant with the good for man, or, perhaps, fulfilment of prophecy as well as the occurrence of miracles); his belief is not properly some arbitary option, and awareness of miracles can constitute or contribute to rational guidance and support in our willing/choosing to believe.

The teaching of Jesus Christ and his very divinity are confirmed for us by the miracles which he worked,[32] miracles which can be performed only by the power of God and which he worked as by his own power.[33] Aquinas suggests that faith in Christ is possible without miraculous attestation, and will be meritorious, but 'signs are given to those who lack faith', whether by their obduracy or other blindness.[34] So while the desire for a sign reflects unfavourably, as Christ said, on those who desire, signs are given by him.[35] The resurrection of Christ in particular confirms our faith in relation to his divinity (and increases our hopes in our own resurrection).[36] Faith in the resurrection itself is in turn supported by proofs which Christ gave the disciples; not by argument based on self-evident premisses, but by angelic testimony and appeal to scripture, by visible evident signs, including his self-manifestation and miraculous post-resurrection activity, he made it clear that he was raised up.[37] Aquinas considers that these arguments taken singly do not suffice to show the resurrection of Christ but all of them taken at once do show the resurrection perfectly.[38] Hence there is what has come to be called a cumulative case for the

---

[31] Ibid. IIa, IIae, 1, 4.   [32] Ibid. IIIa, 43, 1.   [33] Ibid. IIIa, 43, 4.
[34] Ibid. IIIa, 43, 1, quoting 1 Cor. 14.22, and *Summa Theologiae*, IIIa, 55, 5.
[35] See *Summa Theologiae* IIIa, 43, 1 and references there to Matt. 16.4, John 4, 48 and 10.38; 5.36.   [36] *Summa Theologiae*, IIIa, 53, 1.   [37] Ibid. IIIa, 55, 5.
[38] Ibid. IIIa, 55, 6.

resurrection, a good case, of such a kind as should influence wills which are otherwise slow to acknowledge the truth.

In Aquinas, then, we see many of Augustine's views given a sharper, more determinate and worked-out presentation. There are new distinctions, different emphases, and the influence of new theorising (for example, about faith) on important related topics; but there is also a strong central continuity between them.

CHAPTER 3

Locke on the miraculous

Locke agrees with Augustine and Aquinas that miracles can contribute to the reasonableness of Christianity. So miracles may give believers their principal ground for holding that the teaching of Christ is from God and that Jesus is the Messiah. Nevertheless he also affirms that there are other factors which properly have a bearing on the rational exercise of faith. So, for Locke, what purports to be revealed truth can be subjected to at least a negative test: if it conflicts with any of our intuitive knowledge, then it cannot be revealed by the 'Author of our being' because if such a proposition were to be true, this fact would 'overturn all the principles and foundations of knowledge he has given us'.[1] Locke goes on to widen the appeal, so that genuine revelation cannot conflict with anything which is established by the principles of knowledge which he has set forth in the *Essay Concerning Human Understanding*.[2] Yet how, positively, may we recognise a revelation for what it is, from among the claimed revelations which do not actually contradict the deliverances of rational enquiry?

Locke answers that the fulfilment of prophecy and the working of miracles are the principal outward signs by which the true revelation is to be recognised. In relation to the latter he says 'The evidence of our Saviour's mission from heaven is so great, in the multitude of miracles he did, before all sorts of people, that what he delivered cannot but be received as the oracles of God and unquestionable verity'.[3] There is no more important reason for

---

[1] John Locke, *Essay Concerning Human Understanding*, ed. P. H. Nidditch, Oxford, 1975, Book IV, Ch. 18.5.   [2] Ibid. Book IV, Ch. 18.6.
[3] Locke, *The Reasonableness of Christianity*, in *The Works of John Locke in Ten Volumes*, London, 1823.

the belief that Jesus is the Messiah, as Locke sets out the matter in many places.[4] In this he gives miracles a more prominent role in his theological writing and scheme than either Augustine or Aquinas did. Locke can say of miracles that they are 'the basis on which divine mission is always established, and consequently that foundation on which the believers of any divine revelation must ultimately bottom their faith'.[5]

Relatedly, he does not see our need for miraculous attestation of revelation as reflecting ill on us. Locke does not regard us, because we have such need, as lacking either in a wisdom which loves and seeks the unseen heavenly eternal God, or in virtue which moves our will to a ready embracing of God's good will as it has been revealed to us. Locke's concern rather is that we should have good reasons before we accept anything and in particular anything which is proposed as divine revelation. Otherwise our believings will be irresponsible; they will lack a proper basis. In matters of religion, irresponsibility in believing without basis is the error of Enthusiasm.[6] In the case of the Christian revelation, the outward signs accompanying it do in fact provide us with the required rational support, and we are to make use of this confirmation without any thought that a faith so based will be, morally or epistemologically, second-best. Locke's conception of belief leaves no gap between evidence and belief which requires to be bridged by the will; rather he proposes that belief has degrees and that our belief is justified if it is of the degree or intensity appropriate to the available grounds for it. He regards our grounds for treating the Christian revelation as coming from God to be so strong as to justify firm belief, and miraculous attestation of the revelation is the ground on which Locke sets most reliance.

A further shift from the treatments by Augustine and Aquinas arises in Locke's more evident concern about miracles of the remote past, or about accounts of such miracles of long ago. Aquinas was, no doubt, less concerned about miracles in his own day than about the miracles of Christ and of the Apostles.

---

[4] For example, Locke, *Reasonableness*, para. 58ff; *A Discourse of Miracles; A Third Letter concerning Toleration*, in *The Works of John Locke*.   [5] Locke, *Essay*, Book IV, Ch. 19.
[6] Locke, *A Discourse of Miracles*, third last paragraph.

However, Locke's concern is manifested especially in his facing up to issues which are raised, by historical enquiry, for his theory of knowledge. As we shall see further, he discusses in his *Essay* the criteria for the credibility of testimony, of historical testimony and of accounts of miracles in particular.[7] His refutation of Proast also serves to bring out his main interest in miracles of ancient times as supporting modern faith and that quite without state coercion. (Proast had claimed that faith is only found either where it is forced by contemporary miracles or enforced by present state power.)[8]

Locke's definition of a miracle appears in *A Discourse of Miracles* and introduces what may be described as a relatively subjectivist conception of the miraculous. He says 'A miracle then I take to be a sensible operation, which, being above the comprehension of the spectator, and in his opinion contrary to the established course of nature, is taken by him to be divine.' (Locke explains that a person who believes the history of the events is in the place of a spectator, as he intends 'spectator'.) This conception is subjectivist, relative to others which we have already seen, in that it holds an event's miraculousness to consist in someone's *thinking* that the established course of nature has been exceeded, and so attributing the event to God's action, rather than in the event's actually going beyond nature's normal course. Accordingly some occurrence which seems to someone to be divinely worked because it appeared to him to be contrary to nature's established course, but which actually does conform to nature's normal course, would be a miracle. Whether nature's normal course is an objective matter, something which is what it is independently of any human attitude or opinion about it, might be questioned. However, what is nature's normal course, and what exceeds it, is not constituted/ determined by the thought or attitude of any individual. It is therefore a more objective issue than what is miraculous on Locke's account because this latter is a matter of what some individual thinks.

---

[7] For example, *Essay* Book IV, Ch. 16, 9, 11, 13.
[8] Locke, *A Third Letter concerning Toleration*, Ch. 10.

If, to adapt one of Locke's own examples,[9] a native of Siam who is of parochial narrowness in his mental horizons was told and so believed that on a particular occasion an elephant had walked on the surface of a Dutch canal in winter he might suppose that this was the work of God; because he has neither seen nor heard of such a thing, he supposes that it goes against nature's usual course and accordingly explains it by invoking God's extraordinary action. On Locke's definition, this case of the elephantine ice-walker will be miraculous in virtue of the attitude of this Siamese 'spectator'. The Dutch spectators to whom such things are known in winter, while enjoying the diversion afforded by the spectacle, will not regard it as contrary to the established course of nature and so their attitude will not call for the event to be described as miraculous. It is not that the event is then both miraculous and non-miraculous in such a way as to provide an easy *reductio ad absurdum* of Locke's view. That would be too easy a refutation of Locke.

On this and other points it may be helpful to draw an analogy between objectivist, and Lockean subjectivist concepts of 'miracle' on the one hand, and parallel objectivist and subjectivist concepts of 'omen' on the other. Consider the question 'Is a red sky in the morning an omen of bad weather?'. On an objectivist understanding of 'omen', the question means 'Does a morning red sky really indicate conditions in which bad weather will occur?' and a professional meteorologist is best fitted to answer it. On a subjectivist conception of 'omen', however, the question means 'Do some people believe that a morning red sky presages bad weather?'. On this subjectivist conception the fact that some people do and some do not treat a morning red sky as boding bad weather does not generate a contradiction to the effect that a red sky in the morning both is and is not an omen. As in the case of Locke's Siamese and Dutch 'spectators' of the ice-walking elephant, we simply have a non-contradictory description of different beliefs of different people.

Locke does not give his grounds for proposing this subjectivist definition, but in his rebuttal of two objections which he thinks

---

[9] Locke, *A Discourse of Miracles*, second sentence.

are likely to be brought against it, there are pointers to his reasons for the definition. Perhaps surprisingly in view of Locke's reputation as the philosopher of the new empirical science, friend of Boyle, Hooke, etc., a principal factor was his belief that human capacity to discover nature's usual course is feeble, and that consequently people cannot but differ over what does and what does not exceed that course. So, in reply to the first objection to his definition, namely that on the definition 'that will be a miracle to one which will not be so to another', Locke adduces the differences which, given human cognitive limitations and peoples' differing experiences of nature, inevitably arise between people about what will count as surpassing natural law and says 'it is unavoidable that that should be a miracle to one which is not so to another'. That is, Locke asserts that no objectivist definition could circumvent the criticism any better than he does.

Our human incompetence to determine nature's course is of importance for more than mere conceptual mapwork. Since miracles are the chief attestation of true revelation, and because our salvation may be at stake, so that we need the strongest assurance about where true revelation addresses us, a view of miracle which leaves us uncertain about which events really are miracles will leave us, especially if we have little scientific education, with insufficient reliable guidance. However, Locke considers the second objection, that his subjectivist conception may 'take in operations that have nothing extraordinary or supernatural in them', and so may mislead us. Locke seeks to answer this objection by appealing to God's providential care that we shall not be misled about where some revelation is to be known if we adopt the subjectivist view of miracle. We also lack understanding of the powers over nature of non-divine angels, spirits or the like, so we cannot tell whether some exceeding of nature's established course is of God or is deceptive.

By contrast, Locke thinks that miracles as defined by him can 'infallibly direct us right in the search of divine revelation'. Moreover, his definition will, he believes, allow miracles to have their due as confirming to learned and unlearned alike that genuine revelation has occurred:

For miracles being the basis on which divine mission is always established, and consequently that foundation on which the believers of any divine revelation must ultimately bottom their faith, this use of them would be lost, if not to all mankind, yet at least to the simple and illiterate (which is the far greatest part) if miracles be defined to be none but such divine operations as are in themselves beyond the power of all created beings, or at least operations contrary to the fixed and established laws of Nature. For as to the latter of those, what are the fixed and established laws of Nature, philosophers alone, if at least they can pretend to determine. And if they are to be operations performable only by divine power, I doubt whether any man, learned or unlearned, can in most cases be able to say of any particular operation, that can fall under his senses, that it is certainly a miracle. Before he can come to that certainty, he must know that no created being has a power to perform it. We know good and bad angels have abilities and excellences exceedingly beyond all our poor performances or narrow comprehensions. But to define what is the utmost extent of power that any of them has, is a bold undertaking for a man in the dark, that pronounces without seeing, and sets bounds to his narrow cell to things at an infinitive distance from his model and comprehension.[10]

Our human limitations certainly do constitute a problem for us in identifying miracles with confidence: our understanding of the usual established course of nature is tentative and provisional, constantly standing to be corrected, and we have no grasp of the powers of demons or the like to affect what happens in the world. Locke has correctly identified difficulties which can in principle arise if miracles are defined as events surpassing the power of nature and if we wish to have confidence about what miracles have happened.[11] Yet Locke himself seems to actually solve these problems in a way which shows the subjectivist definition of miracle to be of no special help to him. What his purpose needs is just that as God works a miracle of attestation it is clear to all who are aware of the event that He has done so. His solution is that when God wishes to attest His revelation, He accompanies that revelation with wonders of such power as to leave the spectator in no doubt that God has acted to confirm His word or His messenger. First, these signs and wonders will exceed anything which demons or other

[10] Locke, *Essay*, Book IV, Ch. 15.5.   [11] Locke, *A Discourse of Miracles*

non-human powers actually do: we can be sure that the God of power will make it plain when his stamp of approval has been given, and He will allow no potentially misleading miracles of others to be left on the record not decisively countered by His supreme attestation. Secondly, Locke seems to be saying that although we might worry, on the basis of his definition, whether we can be confident that something really would be an exceeding of nature's usual course, because of our unsureness what nature's usual course is, in fact God can and does act in such pre-eminently powerful ways as to leave us in no doubt that nature's usual course has been surpassed. (So, Locke might point out, we may suspect some healings of having a psychosomatic and non-miraculous explanation, but a resurrection of a person thirty-six hours dead will be a different case.) Accordingly, difficulties which might in principle arise for recognising miracles do not in fact pose a problem because the conspicuously supreme power of the God who wishes to communicate securely with us will take care of the matter.

The only case then wherein a mission of any one from heaven can be reconciled to the high and awful thoughts men ought to have of the deity, must be the revelation of some supernatural truths relating to the glory of God, and some great concern of men. Supernatural operations attesting such a revelation may, with reason, be taken to be miracles, as carrying the marks of a superior and over-ruling power, as long as no revelation accompanied with marks of a greater power appears against it. Such supernatural signs may justly stand good, and be received for divine, i.e. wrought by a power superior to all, 'till a mission attested by operations of a greater force shall disprove them: because it cannot be supposed, God should suffer his prerogative to be so far usurped by any inferior being, as to permit any creature, depending on him, to set his seals, the marks of his divine authority, to a mission coming from him. For these supernatural signs being the only means God is conceived to have to satisfy men as rational creatures of the certainty of any thing he would reveal, as coming from himself, can never consent that it should be wrested out of his hands, to serve him. His power being known to have no equal, always will, and always may be safely depended on, to show its superiority in vindicating his authority, and maintaining every truth that he hath revealed. So that the marks of a superior power accompanying it, always have been, and always will be a visible and sure guide to divine revelation; by which men may conduct themselves in their examining of revealed religions, and be satisfied which they ought to receive as coming from God; though they have by no means ability precisely to determine what it is, or is not above the force of any created being; or what operations can be performed by none but a divine power, and require the immediate hand of the Almighty.[12]

Already it has been pointed out that this reliance on God's providence to make miracles trustworthy as the attestation of revelation does not require Locke's subjectivist definition of miracles. However, there is a further problem for Locke himself in his subjectivist conception, deriving from his views about responsible believing. On his subjectivist notion of a miracle, a person who thinks that an occurrence is miraculous arrives at that view in concluding that the occurrence exceeds nature's usual course and does so by God's action. Either he reaches this conclusion by careful, responsible use of his cognitive faculties or he does not; almost all that Locke says suggests the former alternative. In a discussion of the ethics of belief which has religion very much in mind, Locke speaks of a person's

obedience due to his Maker, who would have him use those discerning faculties he has given him, to keep him out of mistake and error. He that does not this to the best of his power, however he sometimes lights on truth, is in the right but by chance; and I know not whether the luckiness of the accident will excuse the irregularity of his proceeding. This at least is certain, that he must be accountable for whatever mistakes he runs into; whereas he that makes use of the light and faculties God has given him, and seeks sincerely to discover truth by those helps and abilities he has, may have this satisfaction in doing his duty as a rational creature, that, although he should miss the truth, he will not miss the reward of it.[13]

Anyone who wishes to hold beliefs responsibly (as opposed to irresponsibly) must, it appears, withhold from the opinion that an event has occurred contrary to nature's usual course, unless he has adequate grounds for confidence about what that usual course is.

The trouble for Locke, therefore, is that since human beings cannot, or at least do not, have such good grounds for

[12] Ibid.   [13] Locke, *Essay*, Book IV, Ch. 17.24

confidence about nature's usual course (still less about the capacities of other supernatural beings to intervene in nature's ongoing process) none of us can, responsibly, reach a conclusion that some event exceeds nature's usual course, does so by God's action, and therefore is, to us, a miracle. Thus the considerations which led Locke to his subjectivist conception seem also to render it useless.

Perhaps it may be thought that, on this particular question of the identification of miraculous events, Locke wishes us to rely not on the ordinary discerning faculties but on an extraordinary way of arriving at our belief. Perhaps he thinks that God in his providence will give particular enlightenment to us, so that we may trust our beliefs about miracles. Only the attempt to give point to Locke's subjectivist definition would lead one to suggest this at all. The suggestion might take either of two forms, each of which runs into difficulty. On the first, we would employ our faculties to the best of our ability, exercising our judgement according to the normal criteria in such matters, and God would guarantee the correctness of our conclusions. However, this idea simply raises again the earlier problem that, if we do exercise our cognitive powers responsibly and in accordance with established criteria, our incapacity to determine what the usual course of nature is will lead us to withhold assent from any conclusions about what is beyond nature, and what is beyond the powers of angels, spirits or the like.

On the second suggestion, our human cognitive processes are by-passed by God who, by direct illumination of our minds, secures our right belief about which events truly are miracles. This suggestion raises two problems of its own:

(a) If God were to suspend, or intervene in, normal intellectual processes in order to prevent error on our part about the attestation of revelation, it would seem more economical, and more straightforward, if He simply communicated to us or implanted in our minds what He wanted to reveal, together with the inescapable conviction that this belief is from God.

(b) In the *Essay* (Book IV, Chapter 19) Locke argues against Enthusiasm, the maintaining of groundless opinions in the conviction that they are given by God's inspiration. Locke says that these claims may, as reasonably, be regarded merely as opinions which their possessor finds compelling. In this context, he says that 'there is one unerring mark' of being a lover of truth for truth's sake, namely 'The not entertaining any proposition with greater assurance than the proofs it is built upon will warrant'. This principle would have to be set aside if a person who has no well-founded grasp of nature's usual course is to opine that a surpassing of nature's usual course has occurred. On the line of interpretation which is now being followed through, Locke's own discussion of the definition of miracles will be touched by Enthusiasm, with the qualification that God acts not to inspire belief, but to head off misleading beliefs about what surpasses nature's ordinary powers. This way of taking Locke's discussion of the definition of miracle in his *Discourse* would be Enthusiastic, because, like the Enthusiasts, he thereby says that God wishes us, and gives us to have, beliefs which lack rational grounds.

When Locke deals with the miraculous in Book IV of the *Essay*, there is no suggestion of irrationalism or suprarationalism. Rather he refers to 'the *proper* case of miracles, which, well attested, do not only find credit themselves, but give it also to other truths, which need such confirmation'.[14] Nor in the *Essay* is there any suggestion of a subjective definition of miracle. We do Locke and ourselves a favour if we regard his treatment in the *Discourse* as unhappily, and for Locke untypically, confused, and look soon to the treatment in the *Essay* as providing Locke's more helpful contribution to our thoughts about the miraculous. Still some more modern writers, who have advocated subjectivist conceptions of miracle, might well claim for Locke that his error is instructive. Only if we have a (religious) epistemology, which does not base proper belief on *evidence* can belief in miracle, on a subjectivist conception of miracle, be reasonable, and in its way underscore revelation, rather than be a mere private fantasy. Yet while reasonableness is seen as a matter of having adequate evidence and while reasonableness in beliefs is insisted on, if epistemically respectable belief in miracles is to be secured, it will be in miracles as objectivistically

---

[14] Ibid. Ch. 16.13.

conceived of. Reasonable belief in miracles as subjectivistically defined will require a different view of what is epistemically respectable in religion, and indeed of the nature of religious belief, from that which Locke maintains. Such writers will no doubt say, 'so much the worse then, for Locke's religious epistemology and for his understanding of the character of religious faith'. Of this, more will be said in its proper place.

On Locke's definition, the further point is to be noticed that no one can argue from the occurrence of what he properly calls a miracle to its divine cause. In order to be called a miracle the divine cause of the event in view must first be established. Someone like Julian the Apostate could acknowledge that events occurred contrary to nature's usual order, but refuse to acknowledge their divine causation.[15] In such a case Locke's definition requires Julian not to say that a miracle has occurred.

However confusing, and confused, Locke may be in discussing some aspects of the definitional question, he is quite clear that his approach involves the presupposition that God exists. Miracles have their purpose in God's attesting his own revelation, and we can trust that God will attach events of the greatest, most strikingly powerful miraculousness to his own revelation. No argument from, or appeal to, miracles is suggested to establish that there is a God. To establish that, Locke looks elsewhere, to causal argumentation, especially from our own existence.[16] It is at least doubtful whether this argument on its own establishes that God will wish our salvation, and so will not allow us to be deceived in matters which bear on our salvation: a supreme cause of us might, for all Locke argues, have other aims or have no interest in the welfare of his creatures. His arguments here for the divine attributes attend to God's power and intelligence rather than to his providence and benevolence. Whether or not Locke ever justifies the assumption, he does expressly assume the existence of a non-deceiving salvation-imparting powerful God, in his accounts of and appeals to the miraculous attestation of revelation. Locke's appeal to the greatest miracles as confirming true revelation gives much attention to competition in miracle-

---

[15] Locke, *Reasonableness*, para. 240.   [16] Locke, *Essay*, Book IV, Ch. 20.

working, e.g. between Moses and Pharaoh's sorcerers, or between Jesus Christ and other claimants to a decisive divine mission. That the greatest miracle in some context confirms the true revelation is based on the belief that the true God will not allow the wonders which accompany false messages to outdo those signs which accompany the true revelation. So he says 'miracles, as the credentials of a messenger delivering a divine religion, have no place but upon a suppostion of one only true God;[17] Thus, while it would be correct to describe Locke as appealing to miracles in the interest of a Christian apologetic, he does not propose to refute outright atheism by such appeals.

The principal specific use which Locke sought to make of the appeal to miracle was to confirm that Jesus Christ was the Messiah sent from God, and that His teaching was teaching from God. In the *Discourse of Miracles*, he speaks of the many miracles Christ did, which, as Christ Himself said were greater than any other man did and by which the greatness of Jewish unbelief is measured.[18] Jews' belief, on the other hand, was prompted when they asked themselves 'When Christ comes will he do more miracles than those which this man has done?'.[19] Nicodemus is cited as concluding that Christ was a teacher come from God because of the signs which He did.

However, the greater sustained appeal comes in the *Reasonbleness of Christianity* where, again, the primary confirmation of the Messiah is said to be by miracles[20] and where the miracles Christ did,[21] and His own resurrection[22] stamp Him as being the Messiah. It would be possible for God to overdo miracle-working, but He confines miracles to circumstances in which only miracles will accomplish the end which He has in view. So Locke:

his wisdom is not usually at the expense of miracles, (if I may so say) but only in cases that require them, for the evidencing of some

---

[17] Locke, *Discourse of Miracles*, para. 11.   [18] John, 15.24.   [19] John, 7.31.

[20] Locke, *Reasonableness*, para. 58

[21] Ibid. paras. 29, 76, 78, 237 – 'The Evidence of our Saviour's mission from heaven is so great, in the multitude of miracles he did, before all sorts of people, that what he delivered cannot but be received as the oracles of God, and unquestionable verity'.

[22] Ibid. paras. 32 and 33 – where Locke points out that the apostolic preaching of Jesus as the Messiah appeals repeatedly to the resurrection as attesting his Messiahship.

revelation or mission to be from Him. He does constantly (unless where the confirmation of some truth requires it otherwise) bring about His purpose by means operating according to their natures. If it were not so, the course and evidence of things would be confounded, miracles would lose their name and force; and there could be no distinction between natural and supernatural.[23]

If God had worked some kinds of miracles, posterity would not have known what to make of the reported outcome, or perhaps the outcome would not have been reported. If Jesus had more openly asserted himself to be Messiah and done miracles as He did, no doubt He would quickly have gained a large and devoted following, but also have speedily provoked the authorities to proceed decisively against him. (It was because of this danger that, in fact, he did not widely declare his Messiahship, so that he could have time fully to teach and complete his work.) If God had miraculously protected him from arrest, posterity might well have doubted that Christ had made Messianic claims or that he worked Messianic wonders or that the Jews had an expectation of a Messianic deliverer. If He had been arrested and Pilate, having been told of His openly-made Messianic claims, had been miraculously influenced by God to pronounce Him innocent, we would not know whether to believe the story or whether Pilate had been influenced improperly to gain the verdict.[24] Of course, his vocation as the Messiah who must suffer required that, in the end, the miraculous rescue which God could effect, would not take place.

Locke's *Essay Concerning Human Understanding* is, as its title indicates, a work about the nature and credentials of human knowledge and justified belief, i.e. about general epistemology. Since a principal motive in setting out on the enterprise was to consider the competence of the human mind over 'the principles of morality and revealed religion',[25] it is not surprising that in

[23] Ibid. para. 143. [24] Ibid. para. 144.
[25] The quotation is from a note written, in his own copy of the *Essay*, by one James Tyrrell of the group of friends of whom Locke speaks in his 'Epistle to the Reader'; Locke tells us that their puzzles in what they were discussing prompted him to embark on an enquiry into the powers of the human mind. Given the occasion of these puzzles, as made explicit by Tyrrell, those who have recently discussed, edited and abridged Locke's *Essay* have surely given too little attention to his application of his epistemology to religion.

the final book Locke specifically relates the epistemological discussion to the credentials of revealed religion. Already we have had occasion to notice Locke's attitude to 'Enthusiasm' which he deals with in the context of his general epistemology, and we saw how the lover of truth for its own sake will not hold any proposition with a greater assurance that its grounds will justify. Historical claims constitute one class of propositions when, conspicuously, probabilities require to be estimated so that the appropriate degree of assurance may be given to each such claim, and Locke attempts to set out principles according to which we form sound judgements. Thus, where some matter of a nature which accords with common experience (as that a person has acted to his own advantage) is reported, and reported by many witnesses, our confidence in the reports is proper. Our assent will and should also follow where some event is unanimously reported by many witnesses, even though the event is not in itself of a kind on whose likelihood common experience can comment one way or the other. These are events which, as Locke says, happen 'indifferently, as that a bird should fly this or that way'.[26]

So far, so straightforward. However, historians' judgements are often required where witnesses or authorities or evidence conflict or are sparse, or where what is reported is, by comparison with common experience, unusual, strange. In those cases, probability, with its proportional assent, 'rises and falls, according as those two foundations of credibility, viz. *common observation in like cases*, and *particular testimonies in that particular instance*, favour or contradict it'. Many are the ways in which these two types of considerations may vary in particular cases. The authors of reports will vary in temperament, motivation, purpose and competence and access to the events reported; and these events may variously conflict with common experience. So 'This only may be said in general, that as the arguments and proof *pro* and *con*, upon due examination, nicely weighing every particular circumstance, shall to any one appear, upon the whole matter, in a greater or less degree to

---

[26] Locke, *Essay*, Book IV, Ch. 16.8.

preponderate on either side; so they are fitted to produce in the mind such different entertainments, as we call belief, conjecture, guess, doubt, wavering, distrust, disbelief, etc.'[27] In his view of historical material, Locke distances himself from those who have supposed 'opinions to gain force by growing older', and lays down '*That any testimony, the further off it is from the original truth, the less force and proof it has*'[28]. Moreover, 'what in one age was affirmed upon slight grounds, can never after come to be more valid in future ages by being often repeated'.[29] History is of great value, then, but it requires a proper caution, and we should be aware of the limited weight which can be attached to its claims.

Yet, further, and importantly, guidance is given to our believings by the use of Analogy which is based on but also goes beyond common human experience. His earlier point, which was supported by elephantine perambulations on the frozen canals of Holland, parochial Siamese and native Dutch, is extended: the guide to probability in those matters, supernatural or natural, of sorts on which our sense experience, on its own and unextrapolated, furnishes no information, is by analogy with what is subject to common, or discovered in unextended, experience. 'A wary reasoning from Analogy' can open up otherwise inaccessible truths.[30]

If common experience, that is common experience of the usual course of nature, is so valuable a guide to right belief, what of miracles and our belief in them? Locke has anticipated the question:

Though the common experience and the ordinary course of things have justly a mighty influence on the minds of men, to make them give or refuse credit to anything proposed to their belief; yet there is one case wherein the strangeness of the fact lessens not the assent to a fair testimony of it. For where such supernatural events are suitable to ends aimed at by Him who has the power to change the course of nature, there, *under such circumstances*, that may be fitter to procure belief, by

[27] Ibid. Ch. 16.9
[28] Ibid. Ch. 16.10 – but it is not easy to reconcile with this what he says in para. 8: that when historians of credit tell us something in whose nature in itself there is nothing for or against belief, 'a man can as little doubt of it as he does of the being and actions of his own acquaintance whereof he himself is a witness'.   [29] Ibid. Ch. 16.11.
[30] Ibid. Ch. 16.12.

how much the more they are beyond or contrary to ordinary observation. This is the proper case of *miracles*, which, well attested, do not only find credit themselves, but give it also to other truths, which need such confirmation.[31]

The elements of Locke's arguments, and some of his phraseology and illustrations, are strikingly echoed in Hume's discussion of reported miracles and their credibility, but a very different conclusion is reached there. How different we shall shortly consider when we look at Hume.

Before we do that, however, we should note that Locke leaves some further explanation/discussion to be desired where he says, on the one hand, that God's revelation, as coming from God, calls for our utmost trust and confidence, but, on the other that 'our assent can be rationally no higher than the evidence of its being a revelation'; and if that 'be only on probable proofs our assent can reach no higher' than such grounds warrant.[32] His references to Faith strongly suggest that he thinks that in practice we can and should rise to the utmost confidence. Yet he does not explain how or on what basis the all-important appeal to miracle-reports can justify our high confidence that miracles, and, consequently, that trustworthy revelations, have occurred. Ordinary canons for historical evaluations may perhaps be suspended if the God, whose existence is presupposed, may have acted extraordinarily. Yet may we not look for, indeed, require, further canons to protect ourselves against false beliefs in false claims that miracles have occurred? Also, what sort of canons would they be, by satisfying which we might justifiably arrive at the utmost confidence? If our believings in revelation are to be responsible, rational, as Locke wishes, we surely need from him further help, more light. Just possibly Locke may have confused the certainty which he attaches to the demonstrable (that is, deducible from self-evident premisses) belief in God's existence with the degree of assurance which is to be attached to beliefs in revelations; but to account in this way for what he says, or fails to say, about high credentials of revelations is to accuse Locke of glaring slackness which is quite foreign to him.

[31] Ibid. 16, 13.   [32] Ibid. Ch. 16.14.

CHAPTER 4

Hume on the miraculous

The chapter entitled 'Of Miracles' is Section x of Hume's *First Enquiry*,[1] but before he presents this specific treatment of belief in miracles, he has already asserted our fundamental reliance on *experience* as the proper guide to what should be believed. For instance, there is his discussion of human action and what we believe when historians treat of it.

Should a traveller, returning from a far country, bring us an account of men, wholly different from any with whom we were ever acquainted; men, who were entirely divested of avarice, ambition, or revenge; who knew no pleasure but friendship, generosity, and public spirit; we should immediately, from these circumstances, detect the falsehood, and prove him a liar, with the same certainty as if he had stuffed his narration with stories of centaurs and dragons, miracles and prodigies. And if we would explode any forgery in history, we cannot make use of a more convincing argument, than to prove, that the actions ascribed to any person are directly contrary to the course of nature, and that no human motives, in such circumstances, could ever induce him to such a conduct. The veracity of Quintus Curtius is as much to be suspected, when he describes the supernatural courage of Alexander, by which he was hurried on singly to attack multitudes, as when he describes his supernatural force and activity, by which he was able to resist them. So readily and universally do we acknowledge a uniformity in human motives and actions as well as in the operations of body.[2]

In this quotation, there is some agreement expressed with Locke's earlier reflections about the historian's criteria for assessing the reports which come to him. More determinate and

[1] D. Hume, Section x, 'Of Miracles', in *An Enquiry concerning Human Understanding*, ed. L. A. Selby-Bigge, Oxford, 1902, pp. 109ff. This is Hume's *First Enquiry*.
[2] Ibid. Section viii, 'Of Liberty and Necessity', p. 84.

exact parallels between Hume and Locke emerge in what Hume goes on to say specifically about miracles. Indeed Hume's argument can be seen as exposing as arbitrary Locke's *ad hoc* excepting of the miraculous from being subject to the criteria for evidence-weighing which are applicable generally. Locke's bold, even barefaced or brazen, setting aside of the standards for evaluating historical evidence generally in those cases where miracles are supposed to have happened, can be called 'special pleading', so long as that expression is not taken to suggest that Locke actually argues the point. In fact, he baldly asserts it.[3]

Commentators on Hume have noted his remark in a letter dated 1762 that his own contention about miracle reports occurred to him when he was in France (from 1735–7) and was discussing the topic with a Jesuit.[4] Perhaps his own distinctive solution did come to him as he describes it a quarter of a century later, but the many echoes of Locke in Hume's chapter, 'Of Miracles' strongly suggest that it is Locke who set up the problematic for Hume and even, by this obviously *ad hoc* and arbitrary exempting of miracle reports from assessment by generally applicable standards, that Locke pointed the way to Hume's way of dealing with the issue.

His concurrence with Locke continues as he discusses how *experience* should be brought to bear in determining contentious matters: we should weigh the evidence on the one side against the evidence on the other, giving our assent to the side with preponderant evidence, proportioning our belief to the size of the preponderance.[5] However, the character of some contended issues is such that reflection on them should, Hume thinks, lead us to declare: 'No contest'.

'Of Miracles' begins with an example of what was, in Hume's eyes, just such a case, set forth in the writing of Tillotson.[6] The debated doctrine of the real presence has in its favour that it comes to us in scripture and/or tradition, which derives

[3] See Locke, *Essay*, Book IV; 16:9, 11, 13.
[4] For example, R. Wollheim in his editor's introduction to *Hume on Religion*, London, 1963, p. 10; N. Pike in his 'Editor's Note' for *Hume: Dialogues Concerning Natural Religion*, Indianapolis, 1970, p. xii.   [5] Hume, *First Enquiry*, Section x, pp. 110–12.
[6] J. Tillotson – Archbishop of Canterbury, 1691 – 'Discourse Against Transubstantiation', 1684, in *Works*, ed. T. Birch, London, 1820, vol. II, pp. 448ff.

authority from 'the testimony of the apostles, who were eye-witnesses to those miracles of our Saviour, by which he proved his divine mission'.[7] In the weighing of evidence, in which weighing our assessment of this doctrine consists, we have to put it against the doctrine that our senses deny it. When we reflect on this weighing-up, we should see that the verdict must go against the doctrine: the sense experience of the first apostles can have had no greater authority (for them) than ours has (for us), and as their witness is transmitted, so the authority of their affirmation (for people of subsequent generations, including us) diminishes. Accordingly, in the nature of the issue, we have to find against the doctrine. Whether Hume actually thought that the real presence of Christ in the sacrament ought to be available to sense experience and whether he endorses Tillotson only for tactical reasons, to ingratiate himself with some readers or to amuse others, does not much matter. His principal concern, what he mainly cares about, is to introduce the notion of a sort or class of question, such as he thought the credibility of any miracle report to be, where evidence-weighing can lead to only one sort of outcome: here also as we are guided by experience our decision *must*, by the nature of miracle reports, go against any such report.

In developing this argument in 'Of Miracles' there are further resonances of Locke, for example in the instances of an Indian prince and of inhabitants of Sumatra whose experience will lead them to treat reports of freezing water, or of freezing Muscovite rivers, with suspension of judgement.[8] Rightly so, because the reports describe a state of nature which, to take the case of the prince, bears so little analogy to those events of which he has had constant and uniform experience.[9] The same proper respect for the regulation of our believings by past experience is applied to the case of miracle reports, so as to exhibit the general case not merely against accepting any such report (and perhaps suspending judgement) but for believing it not to be true. What experience does Hume have in mind, and how does it bear on miracle claims?

---

[7] Hume, *First Enquiry*, Section x, p. 109.
[8] Ibid. pp. 113–14, and footnote on p. 114.   [9] Ibid.

First, any law of nature is established on the strong basis of the unanimous testimony of a considerable, even vast, body of human experience; one essential feature of a miracle will be that it runs counter to a law of nature; so it will be reasonable to believe a claim that a miracle has happened only if the evidence in favour of the claim outweighs the huge weight of evidence for the law of nature which is, allegedly, violated. Given that there is such a tonnage of uniform experience and testimony in favour of a law of nature, only a unanimously well-attested, evidentially powerfully supported case for an alleged miracle's having happened can be made good; only such enormously strong evidence for a reported miracle will be able to outweigh the evidence for the relevant natural law.

The evidence for a claimed miracle will consist of testimony and report. Could this kind of evidence be sufficient to outweigh the evidence for a natural law? How do we generally assess the veracity of testimony? Common experience, Hume says once again, is our guide. We judge a testimony or report which has particular features according to previous experiences of the reliability of testimonies and reports which have had those features. So we trust the reports of people, for example, according to their 'character or number' or 'the manner of their delivering their testimony',[10] or according to their unanimity, or whether they have their own interests to maintain in saying what they do. In addition, and especially pertinent to our present concern, the content, what is said, guides our proper assessment of any report:

Suppose, for instance, that the fact, which the testimony endeavours to establish, partakes of the extraordinary and the marvellous; in that case, the evidence resulting from the testimony, admits of a diminution, greater or less, in proportion as the fact is more or less unusual. The reason why we place any credit in witnesses and historians, is not derived from any *connexion*, which we perceive *a priori*, between testimony and reality, but because we are accustomed to find a conformity between them. . . . The very same principle of experience, which gives us a certain degree of assurance in the testimony of witnesses, gives us also, in this case, another degree of assurance against the fact, which they endeavour to establish; from which contradiction

[10] Ibid. p. 112

there necessarily arises a counterpoize, and mutual destruction of belief and authority.[11]

So some testimony about a particular alleged occurrence is to be assessed by asking, in the light of our experience of the reliability of various sorts of testimony, what credibility attaches to a testimony with specifically these features. If an event is reported of a kind which our experience teaches us is improbable, we should believe the report only if, in view of the report's features, and in view of our experience of reports which have those features, its falsehood would be more improbable than the reported event. As applied to the strictly miraculous, this generates the maxim which Hume enunciates, 'That no testimony is sufficient to establish a miracle, unless the testimony be of such a kind, that its falsehood would be more miraculous, than the fact, which it endeavours to establish; and even in that case there is a mutual destruction of arguments, and the superior only gives us an assurance suitable to that degree of force, which remains, after deducting the inferior.'[12]

Hume therefore subsumes under one concept what Locke distinguished as two distinct 'foundations of credibility, viz. Common observation in like cases, and particular testimonies in that particular instance'.[13] For Hume, particular testimonies are to be given such weight as common observation of like testimonies confers on them. This is important not so much because it is conceptually economical or tidy; it is significant rather more because Hume is bringing out that those who appeal to testimony (as the basis of belief in miracles or anything else) themselves require to hold, to assume, that common experience and observations are generally trustworthy guides, in order then to argue that they can reliably determine what kinds of testimony are dependable and what kinds are unreliable. This presumption, which is needed to enable us to assess testimonies as likely to be reliable, will cause experience to weigh heavily against testimonies about unusual sorts of events. Experience and observation furnish evidence that the unusual is unlikely to have occurred.

This feature of Hume's discussion is relevant when his

[11] Ibid. p. 113.   [12] Ibid. pp. 115–16.   [13] Locke, *Essay*, Book IV Ch. 16, para. 9.

reasoning about miracle reports is alleged to be inconsistent with his well-known scepticism about induction. That scepticism is expounded and defended notably in Section IV of the *First Enquiry* itself,[14] where Hume argues firstly that predictions about matters of fact (such as, for instance, that the sun will rise tomorrow) cannot be established by deductive reasoning, as matters of logical necessity, because their denial is conceivable (we can conceive of the sun's not rising again); the denial of such propositions as can be established by deductive reasonings, will be inconceivable. If it be said, next, that our reasoning about matters of fact can proceed quite properly by making the assumption that the future will be like the past, Hume points out that this assumption cannot itself be justified rationally. It will be invalid to argue that the future will be like the past on the grounds that we have in the past always found later times to be like earlier ones. This assumes that nature's past uniformity is a reason for its continuing and future uniformity, which is to assume that the future will be like the past, the very issue which is at stake. As Hume says, 'It is impossible, therefore, that any arguments from experience can prove this resemblance of the past to the future; since all these arguments are founded on the supposition of that resemblance. Let the course of things be allowed hitherto ever so regular; that alone, without some new argument or inference, proves not that, for the future, it will continue so.'[15]

This discussion about the rationality of taking experience as our guide to what happens in like cases which we do not ourselves experience is conducted with particular reference to prediction. Yet the principles involved are the same with respect to our being directed by experience in our believings about *past* events which we have not experienced (which may be called retrodiction). Hume maintains that this prediction or retrodiction on the basis of past experience is not a matter of reason; rather our use of past experience to guide our beliefs is a matter of 'Custom or Habit.'[16]

A critical reader of Hume's writing about the assessment of

---

[14] Hume, *First Enquiry*, Section IV pp. 25ff   [15] Ibid. p.38
[16] Ibid. Section V, p. 43.

miracle-reports may understandably reckon that Hume there contradicts the scepticism about being guided by experience which he advocates elsewhere. It should be remembered that when Hume speaks about inductive conclusions as not being based on reason, as not being reasonable, he has a specific conception of reason in mind. He is denying that inductive conclusions are reached by means of that faculty of clear and distinct perception which rationalists had seen as the divine image in man. It may not follow, for Hume, that inductive reasoning is altogether worthless. In Hume's eyes, the fact that it has a natural explanation in terms of custom or habit may not have rendered it valueless, though it may well be debated whether this would be the correct view for him to take. It seems that he may actually have been prepared to accept that experience *is* a worthwhile guide to what has happened and what will happen, in cases of which we have no experience but which resemble those of which we do. The negative point he certainly sought to make was that being a worthwhile guide does not rest on that rational insight which was central to the theories of knowledge of rationalist philosophers like Descartes.[17]

Even if Hume really was, as he has also seemed, thoroughly sceptical about inductive reasoning's value, still, for the purpose of the discussion about miracle-reports, Hume could say that he is prepared to set aside the conclusions in which he is sceptical of the rationality of using experience as a guide to our believings, and take it, for the sake of argument, that the appeal to experience does have some rational basis. If so, on the one hand, trusting testimony, in accordance with our experience of that sort of testimony, will be reasonable; but, on the other, where miracles are reported, it will also be reasonable both to treat the reports as being less valuable by reason of their reporting miracles, and to balance against such testimony the gigantic weight of experience in favour of natural law. If, to take the other possibility, Hume were to deny the worth of experience as a rational guide to our believings, then (while Hume would unproblematically retain obvious consistency, as the critical

---

[17] See further: E. Craig, *The Mind of God and the Works of Man*, Oxford, 1987, Ch. 2.

reader sees it) testimony, and evidence generally, would be stripped of any claim to our acceptance; and, with this, our only possible reason for believing that miracles have happened would be removed. So Hume's supposed 'scepticism' about reasoning on the basis of experience regarding matters of fact will not help the would-be-reasonable believer in miracles because such scepticism makes all reports and, particularly, miracle reports, worthless for prediction or retrodiction. However, his point in 'Of Miracles' could, and by the usual canons of charity in interpretation, should be taken to be: if the trustworthiness of experience as a basis for predicting or retrodicting is to be assumed, in order to give rational credibility to reports of witnesses of any kind, that same trustworthiness of experience serves also to check acceptance of miracle reports, both by reducing their value as testimony and by requiring that we set against them the massive evidence for the law(s) of nature allegedly violated.

The gist of the decisive sort of argument against miracle reports, simply as such, upon whose discovery Hume flattered himself, is now obvious; what remains is only to confirm that on the basis of experience no testimony to a miracle can even equal, let alone outweigh, the direct and full proof which unanimous human testimony gives to a law of nature. Once that has been done, we shall have a generally applicable decisive argument for rejecting reports of miracles simply as such, decisive irrespective of the particular features of reports of particular miracles to which, therefore, we need pay no attention as we confidently reject any and all miracle-testimony. The argument to this point (the end of 'Of Miracles', Part I) contends that only, but still possibly, an enormous mass of testimony to a miracle could override the evidence for the relevant natural law, and give some credibility to the miracle. At the beginning of Part II, Hume goes on to claim that the 'but still possibly' goes too far. He says it is easily shown that 'we have been a great deal too liberal in our concession, and that there never was a miraculous event established on so full an evidence.'[18]

[18] Hume, *First Enquiry*, Section x, p. 116.

It is easy to take what follows as having the objective of offering a factual, fair, balanced and rounded account of typical features in accounts of the miraculous, and to go on to complain that, in what is a very negative appreciation of the quality and value of evidence for miracles:

(1) Hume selects partial and inadequate evidence for his unfavourable view of the evidential support for belief in miracles; or

(2) Hume fails to show that these defects must always flaw reports of the miraculous; or

(3) Hume implies in his descriptions of weaknesses discovered in accounts of the miraculous, that there could conceivably be miracle reports which did measure up to his required high standards, but that he subsequently gives examples of very strong attestation of miracles yet still dismisses them as incredible, simply because of their miraculousness. This seems inconsistent or at least confusing: does he or does he not think that evidence for miracles could be good enough to call for belief in miracles?[19]

Hume could have made his purpose plainer; but the principle is a good one that we should try to interpret the author of argumentative discourse as meaning whichever of the range of similarly likely interpretations makes for his strongest argument. According to that charitable maxim, Hume should be taken as meaning simply that experience confers *some* probability that reports of the miraculous will be false; how great this probability is scarcely matters for Hume's point, so long as experience teaches that testimony in general, and testimony about miracles in particular, falls short of being, simply as testimony, wholly and universally reliable. Once he *has* established that the evidence for the miraculous is *somewhat* less weighty than a direct and full proof, his purpose is served: such evidence, by its nature, must be judged less forceful than that which supports a natural law, and so any report of a miracle must be disbelieved by the reasonable person. To achieve this

---

[19] Richard Swinburne in *The Concept of Miracle*, London, 1970, pp. 15–17, makes all of these complaints, and other writers have made some of them.

aim, he naturally does not draw our attention to examples of miracle reports given by educated, honest, reputable, sober, sceptical, disinterested people who are untouched by sensationalism and who attest occurrences which took place publicly in sophisticated and well-documented societies. His aim is not to present a balanced assessment, referring to factors pro and con, of *how* reliable testimony to the miraculous is likely to be. What he does, as he needs to do, is to bring out ways in which testimony to the miraculous has been known to fall short. So our attention is drawn to silly, ignorant or fraudulent, disreputable, gullible or credulous, excitable or impressionable people; to people who are prone to being attracted by the pleasures of hearing and recounting marvels and prodigies, or have something to gain by other people's believing them; to tales of miraculous events alleged to have occurred obscurely among barbarous and little-known people; and to the tendency of miracle-claims, offered in support of different competing religious systems, to weaken one another.[20]

It is a historical question, rather than a strictly philosophical one, whether reports of the miraculous have ever suffered from any of the weakening features which Hume lays out here, and he offers little evidence for some of his allegations. Yet it can hardly be doubted that at least some of them are true and, in view of the variety of competing sects, heresies competing with orthodoxies, and schools of thought, all claiming miraculous attestations, there will surely be few people who will not agree with Hume that sometimes some of these weaknesses have been found in miracle-claims. Since experience reveals that, at least sometimes, the attestation of miracles is in one or more of these ways less than reliable, there must be some probability attaching to any testimony or body of testimony to a miracle that, as such, as attesting to a miracle, it too will be flawed; since there is this probability, no testimony for miracle can outweigh the relevant natural law. This being Hume's gist, the complaints 1 to 3 listed above are of no consequence, and a testimony to miracle, as such, must therefore call forth the rational response of disbelief.

---

[20] Hume, *First Enquiry*, Section x, pp. 116–22.

If we are confronted by an account of a miracle, since it is somewhat probable that the evidence for the miracle suffers from some such weakness as Hume has listed, we should always reject the account because the law of nature in question has a direct and full proof in its favour.

Although Hume can give 'the absolute impossibility or miraculous nature'[21] of alleged events as the clinching reason for denying their occurrence, this is not to be read as a departure from the previous argument[22] which is in terms of what it is reasonable to believe, as directed by experience-based probabilities. By their having 'absolute impossibility', he means that these events have against them the unanimous testimony of experience which supports the appropriate law of nature. Experience attaches a probability of zero to such events, and they are therefore impossible, not as being inconceivable but as going against all experience. Sometimes this has been called natural as contrasted with logical impossibility. A judgement of impossibility like this could only be so much as equalled, but not overthrown, by a mass of equally weighty evidence – in this case testimony whose falsehood would also have to be 'impossible', in having an experience-based probability of zero. Yet experience establishes that there is some probability, how great Hume neither says nor needs to say, that testimony to a miracle will be false. So the 'absolute improbability' of the reported miraculous event prevails.

Perhaps Hume's language is open to criticism in that his policy of balancing evidence for and against, of weighing the 'opposite experiments'[23] could lead us, in a case where a miraculous occurrence is attested by evidence which has some value, to subtract the force of that evidence from absolute improbability. To be sure, on Hume's argument we shall still be required to disbelieve the relating of the miracle because it will still be highly, overwhelmingly improbable, but it will no longer be quite impossible. Yet there is something unsatisfactory about calling something 'absolutely impossible' which, it is conceded, may turn out to be only highly improbable. The point which

[21] Ibid. p. 125.   [22] Cf. pp. 49–56 above, and Part i of Hume's 'Of Miracles'.
[23] Hume, *First Enquiry* Section x, p. 111.

Hume is making, and which remains even when some conceptual awkwardness, or unapt expression, is acknowledged, is that
an event of a sort, for example a person's walking on water,
which simply as that sort of event runs counter to some natural
law, has, as a kind of event which is contrary to a law of nature, a
probability of zero. This same event may also be describable,
and may come to be described, quite truly, as having a property
which will give it some probability by virtue of its having *that*
property, for example being reported by a careful and sensible
witness whose testimony is confirmed by five more careful,
shrewd witnesses. Nevertheless, purely in respect of its having a
property which sets it contrary to a natural law, an event has a
probability of zero, which is the same, in Hume's terms, as being
factually (albeit not logically) impossible.

Three examples are rather comprehensively set out by Hume
of very well-substantiated miracles, vouched for by large
numbers of judicious and veracious people and supposed to have
happened in places, both well-known and comparatively accessible to our enquiries. First, the Emperor Vespasian is reported
by Tacitus to have cured a blind man by means of his spittle;
second, Cardinal de Retz tells of a miracle, widely reputed by its
inhabitants to have taken place in Saragossa, and involving the
growth of a man's leg from its stump after holy oil was rubbed on
it; and third, the many miracles worked in Paris on the tomb of
Abbé Paris, well-attested and not able to be discredited by those
who most wished to debunk them.[24] It is with reference to the
third of these that Hume uses the locution 'absolute impossibility', as follows: 'And what have we left to oppose to such a cloud
of witnesses, *but the absolute impossibility or miraculous nature* of the
events, which they relate? And this surely, in the eyes of all
reasonable people, will alone be regarded as a sufficient
refutation.'[25]

In relation to the second example, the miraculous character
of what is reported is invoked not (as in the third example) to
bring against the account of the miracle the overwhelming force
of the evidence for the natural law, but to diminish the force of

---

[24] Ibid. pp. 122–5.   [25] Ibid. p. 125.

the evidence for the miracle. So, of the Cardinal de Retz, Hume says that he 'concluded, like a just reasoner, that such an evidence carried falsehood upon the very face of it, and that a miracle, supported by any human testimony, was more properly a subject of derision than of argument'.[26] The first example of Vespasian's restoring sight to a blind man, makes neither of these points specifically. It simply points the moral of Hume's discussion by reminding us that obvious falsehoods may be supported by the strongest of evidence. Because Hume has explained how obvious falsehoods can have very strong evidence in their favour, and yet be obvious falsehoods because they have overwhelming evidence against them, the giving of an otherwise puzzling example is now presented to underscore the power of his thesis and spell out its significance.

Hume's case against these miracle reports which are offered in support of a religious view is not yet complete because, while any testimony to violations of the usual course of nature is by its own nature very weak, the attestation of a miracle which, specifically, is supposed to have religious impact will be weaker still. Hume reiterates the earlier contention that miracle-claims which are made in the interests of competing religious systems are themselves in competition; and in his eyes, the remote and shadowy antiquity of the circumstances and first recounting of the alleged miracles make the evidence yet poorer. Referring to the battles of Philippi or Pharsalia, Hume says:

Suppose that the Caesarean and Pompeian factions had, each of them claimed the victory in these battles, and that the historians of each party had uniformly ascribed the advantage to their own side; how could mankind, at this distance, have been able to determine between them? The contrariety is equally strong between the miracles related by Herodotus or Plutarch, and those delivered by Mariana, Bede, or any monkish historian.[27]

Again, even law courts which sit at a relatively short distance in time from the matters which they investigate have difficulty in disentangling truth from falsehood; how much more difficult to do so when a religion is no longer new so that records and

---

[26] Ibid. p. 124.   [27] Ibid. p. 125.

witnesses of its originating circumstances are not available.
Since many stories of miracles which were told to support
religious belief have been exploded in their infancy, and since
religious zealotry does not scruple to perpetrate pious frauds,
hearers of allegedly religiously significant miracle-stories should
attach rather low probability to such accounts. Rather than
accept them and so believe that something has occurred to
violate established laws of nature, we should be guided by
experience and account for the stories 'by the known and
natural principles of credulity and delusion'.[28] Also, 'As the
violations of truth are more common in the testimony concerning religious miracles, than in that concerning any other matter
of fact; this must diminish very much the authority of the former
testimony and make us form a general resolution, never to lend
any attention to it, with whatever specious pretence it may be
covered.'[29] So, because claims about anomalous events which
are made in a religious interest are particularly dubious, Hume
says 'we may establish it as a maxim, that no human testimony
can have such force as to prove a miracle, and make it a just
foundation for any such system of religion'.[30]

He asks us to note this qualification about founding systems of
religions, because he wishes to concede that human testimony
might possibly suffice to establish that a violation of natural law
has occurred, and gives an example of universal terrestrial
darkness for the first eight days of 1600, attested in all countries
(as travellers confirm); this event would be of no help to religious
axe-grinders. Yet Hume goes on to say that experience-based
analogy leads us to suppose such a thing somewhat likely, as part
of a general decay in nature; and so it emerges that he is ready to
admit such a report as possibly believable by a reasonable
person, in part because experience suggests that the event
reported might well not violate natural law at all. Hume's
confusing treatment of this example leaves us in doubt whether
he really intends that a genuine violation of natural law could,
even if it had no religious implications, be properly believed in,
and this doubt is deepened by another case which he postulates

---

[28] Ibid. p. 126.   [29] Ibid. p. 129.   [30] Ibid. p. 127.

wherein Queen Elizabeth's resurrection from the dead was as well attested as such a thing could be. Yet, he concludes that 'the knavery and folly of men are such common phenomena, that I should rather believe the most extraordinary events to arise from their concurrence, than admit of so signal a violation of the laws of nature'.[31] This sentiment so coheres with the central movement of his argument that we should set aside, as an aberration, his apparent concession that a violation of natural law might possibly be believed in, on the basis of human testimony. Perhaps we can take from Hume's different attitudes to the two hypothetical cases that it is possible to judge that, of two events which both seem contrary to natural law, as our current yet developing experience-based understanding has it, one may quite reasonably be regarded as more likely to turn out to accord to natural law than the other. In this confused phase of the discussion, Hume may well be pointing out in effect that, when we are confronted by a report of an event which seems contrary to natural law, we may reasonably react in one or other of two ways: either (1) we shall conclude that natural law may not be as we have thought, and look for a better hypothesis about nature so as to be able to accommodate the reported anomaly – this alternative will be the more attractive, the stronger is the evidence for the puzzling event and the more closely analogous to previous experience is the proposed new revised hypothesis – or (2) we shall treat our view of the natural law as so well-established, and unlikely to be revised so as to accommodate the reported anomaly, that we shall reject the report and attribute its emergence to 'the known and natural principles of credulity and delusion', in accordance with experience. This alternative has been called 'Hume's fork'[32], and although he does not present it explicitly and without confusion, it does seem likely that he would have endorsed it.

Greater care in sticking to his deliberate official definition of miracle would have saved Hume from his aberration. He defines a miracle not merely as a transgression of a law of nature, but, further, as such a transgression 'by a particular volition of the

---

[31] Ibid. p. 128.   [32] See, for example, Mackie, *The Miracle of Theism*, p. 26.

Deity, or by the interposition of some invisible agent'.[33] On this definition there can be no miracles which altogether lack relevance to our view of God, so Hume should have had yet another reason for denying that the eight days' darkness was a miracle: he should have thought it would be no miracle not only (as he did) because the proper view of natural processes might turn out to accommodate it, but also because he thought it would have no religious significance.

In fact, Hume makes no use of the qualification quoted above ('by a particular volition . . .' etc.) and so gives no attention to the problem, for the would-be religious apologist who wishes to appeal to miraculous events, that we know little or nothing about the possible or likely effects of 'invisible agents', such as angels or demons, on the natural world. Locke, as we saw, devotes considerable thought to the problem of identifying the authentically God-worked wonders. No doubt it can be said for Hume that from his point of view, the problem does not arise: his 'check' has stopped the apologist in his tracks before transgressions of natural law can be identified, so there is no problem of accounting for the transgressions of natural law, for example, by attributing them to the proper invisible agents.

Perhaps with an admixture of irony, wit, epistemological naturalism and circumspection, Hume concludes that his undermining of any appeal to reported miracles as part of a rational apologetic actually serves to establish Christianity on its proper foundation, namely Faith, rather than Reason. It is not 'fitted to endure' rational appraisal and

upon the whole, we may conclude, that the Christian Religion not only was at first attended with miracles, but even at this day cannot be believed by any reasonable person without one. Mere reason is insufficient to convince us of its veracity: And whoever is moved by Faith to assent to it, is conscious of a continued miracle in his own person, which subverts all the principles of his understanding, and gives him a determination to believe what is most contrary to custom and experience.[34]

We shall see that the concept of analogy plays a large part in the

[33] Hume, *First Enquiry*, Section x, p. 115 footnote.   [34] Ibid. pp. 130 and 131.

thought of Bradley and Troeltsch (and many others) about the miraculous. (We also saw that the same was true of Locke.) However, before we pass over to give an account of them, it will be helpful to see something of what Hume's thesis is in respect of the 'test of analogy'. Clearly, he agrees with Locke in seeing analogy as allowing an inference from what we experience such that the more often certain sorts of features have been found together, the more likely it is that, in cases unknown to us, when features of most of these sorts are present then features of the remaining sort(s) will be present also; and the stronger the likeness between the circumstances from which we project and those which we know about in the situation to which we infer, the more reliable will be the inference. Hume speaks of the Indian prince's inability to form conclusions about circumstances to which his experience bore insufficient analogy,[35] and says of the eight days' darkness that *it* seems somewhat likely to be in conformity to natural law because it bears analogies to what we know of nature's dissolution.[36] Miracle reports are to be rejected because they cannot be accommodated by any experience-based analogical extension of relevant experience, which is the only principle on which reasonable formation of beliefs about the unknown can proceed.

---

[35] Ibid. p. 114, text and footnote.   [36] Ibid. p. 128.

CHAPTER 5

Bradley and Troeltsch on the miraculous

It was Hume's interest in the nature of human knowing and believing and in the proper limits of human cognitive capacities which motivated his attention to the particular topics dealt with in his *Enquiry Concerning Human Understanding*;[1] and Section x, 'Of Miracles', has its place in this wider project. Hume sees his argument about the credibility of reports of miracles primarily as undercutting those pretensions to knowledge about God which claim to derive from God's miracle-attested self-revelation. At the same time it prescribes limits to historical understanding, and C. S. Peirce can say 'The whole of modern "higher criticism" of ancient history in general . . . is based upon the same logic as is used by Hume'.[2] We shall shortly see that there are some more things to be said about the most respected historiography than those which Hume mentions; but we shall also see how thought about proper or 'critical' history has treated at least one aspect of Hume's appeal to experience as an essential and fundamental criterion of what historians may or may not affirm when confronted by the unusual or amazing.

In spite of Hume some Christian apologists such as Paley[3] continued to account for miracle reports as having been prompted by miraculous events whose best or only explanation is theistic. Yet also, during the nineteenth century, there was

---

[1] Even if Hume is perhaps also defending himself against accusations which had been current against him when he failed to secure the Edinburgh Chair.

[2] C. S. Peirce, *Values in a Universe of Chance*, edited by P. P. Wiener, New York, 1958, pp. 292–3.

[3] W. Paley, *A View of the Evidences of Christianity* in *The Works of William Paley*, Edinburgh, 1830.

more conspicuously a great flourishing of history-writing, careful and cautious in its claims, self-aware in its care. For one of the greatest of nineteenth-century historians, L. von Ranke, God's transcendence was such that his will and purpose at work in history was inscrutable to us. So von Ranke urged that historiography should be concerned to set out precisely what happened, without trying to learn, let alone teach, moral, political or religious lessons. Thus his religious commitment led him to seek out and rely precisely on documentary evidence contemporary with the period which was being studied.[4] By contrast there were other historians whose philosophical commitment (broadly 'positivist') affirmed that the significance of historical statements about the so-called past is wholly given in accounts of presently available experience. Historians like this were unwilling to go beyond accounts of the available 'evidence', in order to construct a thesis about a past; for positivists the past is unavailable and if statements apparently about the past have any significance it is only as a way of talking about present experience.

Sometimes historians (not necessarily positivists) of the ancient world or the early church, writing about aspects which are difficult to assimilate to our modern experience, carried their care to the extent of refusing to offer any account, merely suspending judgement, when others thought that some sort of view should be attempted. So the Tubingen school of historians of the early church could be suspected of positivism or of a dereliction of historians' duty when they declined to express a view on some matters which were pertinent to Christian origins. Understandably, therefore, many thinkers saw a need for deliberate reflection about the character and methods of good historiography. Bradley[5] and Troeltsch[6] offered their essays as contributions to this reflection, Bradley's pamphlet being more original and argumentative, Troeltsch's (later) encyclopaedia

[4] See further, e.g., P. Geyl, *Debates with Historians*, London, 1955.
[5] Bradley, *Essays*, pp. 1–70.
[6] E. Troeltsch, 'Historiography' in *Encyclopaedia of Religion and Ethics*, ed. J. Hastings, New York, 1913. This article is in vol. VI, pp. 716–23. References in these notes are to the more accessible reprinting in J. MacQuarrie (ed.) *Contemporary Religious Thinkers*, London, 1968.

article more an attempt to summarise and indicate the rationale for the, by then, accepted wisdom.

Bradley insists that history is not the reception by us of mediated 'outward impressions' which were once received, and were then 'simply and honestly written down';[7] nor will Paley's view that 'Testimony is a phenomenon, and the truth of the fact solves the phenomenon'[8] survive inspection. For Bradley, a testimony or other single piece of evidence is not to be considered as an independent revealer of the past now brought to our modern awareness. Bradley points out that there will be a whole range of considerations and factors in view of which any single piece of evidence will have to be interpreted. Where we are presented with, say, a report, R, of an event, E, there may well exist other accounts apparently of E; or there may be other reports, from the source of R, of other events about which we may think we already know something. There will be evidence about the sorts of events which these various reporters may respectively have expected to occur, or have believed to be possible. Our mind will have before it an accumulating mass of such factors, and it will seek to frame an interpretation which will accommodate them within a self-consistent overall account. Frequently, an occurrence will be described by several sources which will not precisely agree with one another, and the historian's business will not only be to arrive at a true account of the event, but also (at the same time, as part of the same enterprise) to account for the differences between the sources. The views which are respectively taken of the event, and of the varying accounts of it which have reached us, will be parts of a wider self-consistent version of what has happened in which each element is intelligibly accounted for.

By 'intelligibly accounted for' is meant 'causally explained, in terms of known patterns of causal connexion'. In addition, each causal factor which is invoked to explain the reported event, or to explain the diverse reports of it, will itself require causal explanation, as will that explanation in turn. The historian is therefore engaged in developing a self-consistent causal ac-

---

[7] Bradley, *Essays*, p. 9.   [8] Ibid. pp. 50–1.

count, from which nothing is in principle excluded. The wide scope of this network of inter-related things or events, which provide explanation and are explained, should not lead us to think that the historian is not interested in individuals: 'the object of historical record is the world of human individuality and the course of its development in time'.[9] An individual cannot however be understood except in the context(s) of the causal networks which make that individual what or who they are. Such networks can never be completely grasped by any historian; and Bradley's general philosophical conviction that to properly understand anything one must grasp it in its connexion with everything applies to historical understanding in particular.[10] It is Troeltsch who, in effect, brings out the implication, that there are limitations in the practice of historical enquiry: presumably nobody can effect the historians' ideal rational self-consistent synoptic appropriation of everything. So there are 'several isolated subjects of enquiry', 'historical aggregates', such as human life, a nation, the spirit of an age, a legal constitution or a school of art. A historian can hope to achieve some grasp of such a limited totality. Yet Troeltsch, at least as explicitly as Bradley, has as his ideal a quite comprehensive account. He says 'These aggregates . . . may be recombined, till at length the highest concept of historical totality, i.e. humanity itself, is reached'.[11]

Hume is not discussed by either Bradley or Troeltsch but even if they had known nothing else about his philosophy than 'Of Miracles' his manner of exposition in that chapter would have aroused their suspicions, particularly if Hume was supposed to be offering a view of historical methodology in general. The assessment of a particular single testimony seems to be Hume's concern, and the suspicion would have suggested itself that he is insufficiently interested in the development of that comprehensive account of a wider range of data which is the historian's business, and within which Bradley or Troeltsch would seek to

---

[9] Ibid. p. 36.
[10] See R. Wollheim, *F. H. Bradley*, London, 1959, Chapters 2 and 3; towards the end of the latter chapter there is an account of his particular application of Bradley's metaphysics to historiography.   [11] Troeltsch in MacQuarrie, p. 89.

set some particular report or event. For Hume, two things might be said in reply. First, the whole movement of his thought is from the particular item of testimony to precisely the question of its coherence with our consistent wider view of the world's process, the ways in which events occur. It is exactly in this way that experience is invoked to guide us. Second, he is only concerned about the character of the historian's work insofar as it relates to the assessment of reports of miracles; and it is this specific interest which leads to the order of the exposition of his views in 'Of Miracles'. Thus, he begins by asking how a particular report of a miracle should properly be taken.

Still, the approach of Bradley or Troeltsch may well lead some to wonder whether Hume sufficiently considers the bearing on the assessment of one particular report of a miracle, M, of, for example, reports of other miracles supposedly accomplished by, or on, or in some relation to the same person as is alleged to have worked M. Does Hume cast his net sufficiently widely in looking for those factors which have some bearing on the credibility of his original testimony to the miraculous? We shall take up this question later, in the evaluative discussion.

Whether Bradley or Troeltsch would have raised that issue, they would surely have disagreed with Hume insofar as his view was that our arguing from experience is a matter of custom and habit and that the appeal to experience is to be employed as the test of rational credibility only as an assumption which is made *ad hominem* against the religious apologist, who has to make this assumption in order that it be rational to trust testimony. The *ad hominem* purpose of Hume's taking up the assumption emerges, on this interpretation of Hume, as he goes on to argue that the making of this assumption puts a severe check in the way of any rational believing of a miracle report. For Bradley and Troeltsch, our arguing from experience and believing in the uniformity of nature and the universal applicability of natural law, is no mere habit of mind, nor yet something whose rationality we affect to accept, only for the sake of revealing the inconsistency in the Christian apologist's case. Rather, when we recognise that critical history (as also physical science, each sort of enquiry in its proper way) renders the world intelligible, effecting an understanding of that which could not otherwise count as, nor be comprehended as, a historical fact, we are constrained to accept whatever is a presupposition of the intelligibility-giving activity. The success of our historical intelligence in making sense of what is given to it, working the given into a self-consistent account which also embraces our prior self-critically held belief and experience, argues for the rationality of the presuppositions of critical history. So Bradley writes: 'the inevitability of law, and what loosely may be termed as causal connexion, is the condition which makes history possible, and which, though not for her to prove, she must nonetheless presuppose as a principle and demonstrate as a result worked out in the whole field of her activity'.[12]

We have here a kind of confrontation which is common in philosophy, where a sceptic questions the rational justifiability of claims to knowledge or understanding in some field of enquiry because, he says, investigators in this field must base their enquiries or their conclusions on some presupposition which is not, or cannot be, justified. (In the present case, the presupposition is that what we have experienced, and what we most reliably know, will be a reliable guide to what sorts of events are possible in circumstances about which there is some question about what did take place.) The reply of the anti-sceptic is that since the field of investigation incontestably does provide knowledge and understanding, its presuppositions are thereby vindicated.

Bradley's monograph reveals that the practice of critical history involves philosophical commitments and implications, of a philosophically controversial kind. He is obviously well aware that philosophical commitments different from his own, such as that of the positivists, will lead to different ways of practising critical historical enquiry.

The impression to this point may have been conveyed that he regards critical history as a given, which has a quite uncontentious character whose philosophical implications can be definitively worked out. However, his attitude is more subtle. There is

---

[12] Bradley, *Essays*, p. 21.

an interplay between historical practice and philosophical viewpoint. Thus, for example, positivism calls in question the historian's going beyond or behind present evidence to construct a past world. Bradley not only points out that critical history as it is widely practised does in fact go beyond and behind the evidence to construct its historical accounts. He also tries to show how it does so and why this is justifiable: sympathetic imagination which is constrained by the test of analogy with our own critically assessed experience enables the historian to do more than is licensed by the positivist (for whom so much the worse). Again, what counts as critical history cannot simply be read off the practice of historians. Some of the more naive of them speak as if the facts are to be recognised simply as the subjects of testimony or other evidence which can be assumed to be inerrant or unambiguous, and thereafter as if such facts are unalterably to be reckoned with. Better, more critical, historians do justice to the existence of conflicting evidence, the need to incorporate it in a single account, in which the existence of the various, varying pieces of evidence is explained. In the light of these considerations, historical and philosophical, a better view of facthood emerges, and the more critical type of history is demonstrated to *be* better. Bradley's purpose in his own discussion is the same sort of purpose as that which he attributes to the critical historian: by a process of reflection to arrive at an account which is self-consistent, and which best does justice to the data. The critical historian *qua* historian is concerned to offer an historical account. Bradley as the philosopher of history is concerned to offer an account in which the philosophical claims are consistent with, rise out of, and also in some controversies serve to prescribe, the best kind of history.

Troeltsch, although he is well aware of disputes over the philosophy of history, is confident that we can reliably identify scientific history when we see it, even if much philosophical work needs to be done to analyse its nature. He thinks that metaphysical considerations do not figure in modern historiography except in the occasional aphorism or expression of attitude. He says that this is 'what we find in so purely empirical a historian as Ranke. Modern historiography, as contrasted with the medieval and theological types, has certainly in principle wrenched itself free from the metaphysical element, whatever the personal views of the historian regarding the latter may be.'

Allowances should perhaps be made for the fact that Troeltsch was writing an encyclopaedia article on historiography and that a clear broad descriptive outline may have been more important than careful qualifications and nuances.[13] However, as Bradley makes clear in his exploring of the inter-relation between our conception of the best ('critical' or 'scientific') history and our philosophical view, philosophical or metaphysical standpoints will and should affect our practice of historiography (and vice versa). When Troeltsch seems to take the character of scientific history to be established securely, beyond serious controversy, the related suspicions must be prompted: (1) that his metaphysical or philosophical commitments must thereby also be supposed by Troeltsch to be secure beyond serious question, and (2) that Troeltsch's metaphysics are being implicitly adopted, even foisted upon us, when they should be open to be examined and discussed, in their bearing on the practice of the best historiography. If it should turn out that some prescriptive conception (such as Troeltsch's) of scientific history depends on dubious philosophy, then however well-entrenched the practice of this sort of history may be, the question of its legitimacy should be able to be raised or it can hardly continue to claim to be rational. Insofar, then, as Troeltsch conveys the idea that a dissenter from his view of what scientific history is could only be denying the well-established essence of scientific history, we have to protest that philosophical commitments are involved. And these are not of a firmly established incontestable kind.

Troeltsch gives little attention, as compared with Bradley, to

---

[13] Although Troeltsch can himself find excuse in this, his article has been treated and reproduced as having a significance beyond the mere description of a widely favoured conception of historiography. He has been thought of as setting out its rationale, and reprinted and discussed as having that kind of value, as will emerge in subsequent chapters. The quotation is from p. 93 of Troeltsch in MacQuarrie.

specified false conceptions of historiography, or other erroneous philosophies. Rather, he picks out historical work which he considers scientific, and by contrast, history which falls short of that standard. The great Greek historians (Herodotus, Thucydides, Polybius), 'laid the foundations of modern history as an explanation of public movements by material or psychological causes', and 'took account of analogies and uniformities' and organised their material around the focal ideas of Hellenic civilisation or the civilised Roman State.[14] Christianity, although it did provide focal themes, and utilised some universal conceptions, extinguished history proper and produced 'not a scientific but a revived mythological representation of history'.[15] Humanism and the Renaissance laid the foundations of modern historiography, with the enlarged range of factors which the Enlightenment brought to bear in its search for causes opening the way to the 'enormously enlarged intricately intersecting web of causality'[16] which modern historiography traces. 'On the analogy of the events known to us we seek by conjecture and sympathetic understanding to explain and reconstruct the past.'[17] The 'Biblico-theological views of later antiquity',[18] are in absolute contrast to this modern 'scientific mode of representing man and his development'[19] because the desire to explain was regarded as a mark of the profane mind, because miracles figured so frequently in the story. Troeltsch takes it to be obvious that miracles would be events disanalogous to any in our experience, and relatedly that no causal account of them could be given in terms of causal connexions of any kinds which are found in our experience. Since psychological causality plays a large part in historical explanation, the historian's capacity for sympathy and the direction of his own sympathies will affect the value of his reconstructions.[20] Natural causal explanation also plays a part, Troeltsch argues, giving as an example the destruction of Napoleon's army by the Russian winter.[21]

Bradley gives accounts of the 'prejudication' which history assumes, of the universal scope and uniformity of natural law.

[14] Troeltsch, in MacQuarrie, p. 78.   [15] Ibid. p. 79.   [16] Ibid. p. 80.
[17] Ibid. p. 81.   [18] Ibid.   [19] Ibid.   [20] Ibid. p. 84.
[21] Ibid. p. 87, and Bradley, *Essays*, p. 35.

Freedom of the human will might be supposed to constitute an objection to this, particularly forceful because history engages so extensively in explanations involving human motivation. Yet in practice everyone assumes that we can count on consistency in human action correlated with desire and character: law courts arrive at their view of what occurred, and sentence people accordingly, on this assumption, without, presumably, calling human freedom into question. Critical history asks no more.

Employing this prejudication, the historian extrapolates from his present world. This is how he may construct (something of) the past, embodying in his account the materials, the pieces of evidence, which come to him. This present world is itself subject to critical appropriation; it is not merely the experience of the historian himself, even with the addition of others' testimonies of their experiences. Bradley says 'The experience . . . which is to be the foundation of historical criticism must itself be a critical experience',[22] by which he means that it has to participate in the intelligible unity of a rational system. Only what can be fitted into the system will be acceptable as part of that present world out of which we may then seek to make sense of historical data, employing the same intelligibility-giving principles as those which make sense of our present world. Pre-eminent amongst these is the principle of the universality and uniformity of nature. Nothing can be appropriated into the one intelligible system which we make of our world, whether as part of the present world or as something absorbed by the extension of that present world when part of the past is reconstructed, unless it is compatible with the uniformity of nature, unless, that is, it is analogous to the present world.

Bradley more fully defines what he thinks of the analogy requirement. There are some circumstances in which he thinks it is proper to accept that some events have occurred even though they have no analogy in our present world. He does not mean to speak here of events which actually violate patterns of occurrences which we have established in our present world. Rather he is thinking of events which have neither analogy nor

[22] Bradley, *Essays*, p. 26.

disanalogy in present experience, and he gives as an example what he calls 'mesmeric' phenomena.[23] If we have experience, scrutinised and repeated, of such things, we may claim to know them. This evidence will have to be better than would be called for if we were claiming to know something which does have analogy in our present world. He says 'if we are left to our own observation, and have nothing analogous to support us, we can indeed learn new facts with certainty, but on one condition only, namely that of the most careful examination often repeated'.[24]

We may even secure knowledge of non-analogous events on the basis of others' testimony, provided we can be confident that these 'others' share our world, a world which is subject to the same laws as our world, that the standpoint by which they estimate that which they encounter is the same as ours. The testimony of these others must, in this fashion, 'be equal in validity to our own most careful observations'.[25]

However, where a witness of an alleged event which would be non-analogous to anything in our world is not known to share our present world, and therefore our standards of judgement, we cannot accept his testimony. Bradley applies the general principle to our specific interest when he says 'any narrative of "facts" which involves judgement proceeding from a religious consciousness or a view of the world which, as a whole or in respect of the part in question, differs from ours, cannot have such force as to assure us of any event un-analogous to present experience'.[26] Even if the witnesses do turn out to share our present world, we cannot accept their testimony to the non-analogous unless we can also be confident of their integrity and care in conducting the enqury, as it were, for us.

In summarising his attitude at this point, Bradley reiterates that a witness and his testimony have force for us only because we assimilate then into our critical world:

We have seen that testimony, even without analogy, can be made part of our present critical object; but we have seen also on what condition. Testimony goes beyond individual experience, but not beyond *our* experience; or it takes us beyond our experience if it takes *us* with it. It

---

[23] Ibid. pp. 28ff. By 'mesmeric', he means pertaining to what we would call 'hypnotism'.   [24] Ibid. p. 28.   [25] Ibid. p. 29.   [26] Ibid. p. 31.

is not uncriticized; it stands, if at all, on the basis of our world. It has been made subject to the laws and has been connected with and become part of our personal experience, not in its own right *as* testimony, not in the right of the witness *as* witness, but in the right of and on the guarantee of our own intelligence.[27]

So, again, testimony can 'enlarge our experience, where analogy fails . . . where identification of consciousness is possible; but, where it is not possible, Never'. He continues 'by a mere analogical argument you cannot conclude to a non-analogous fact'.[28] Here he means an argument whose strength, if it has any, derives only from analogy, induction, because we do not share the outlook, the present world of witnesses.

Distinctively historical enquiry does not allow of the identification of the modern historian's standpoint with the standpoints of any of those witnesses whose testimonies reach us from the past. With the passage of time, the views and beliefs of human beings, especially about themselves, develop as human beings themselves change and develop. Moreover, history concentrates on aspects of human life which derive their features from the 'special and characteristic life of an individual epoch', namely their own;[29] and these features will be understood by the people of that time, who are the witnesses to us for their epoch, in ways distinctive of the epoch. Accordingly, we cannot hope to identify with the mind of these witnesses of past periods.

If our interest is scientific, rather than historical, it is possible in the present to identify with the mind of witnesses of past occurrences. We can take observation by people of the past, for example about solar eclipses, or about mesmeric phenomena, as our own because 'we are able so to reconstruct the observers and the conditions of their observations, as to possess ourselves entirely of their faculties, and use them as our own'.[30] Science treats occurrences abstracted from the whole network of their many relationships in time and space, and deals with them only under one particular description and as resembling other occurrences which share that description. To observe and comprehend the occurrence simply under that description requires of a witness the use of only limited intellectual powers,

---

[27] Ibid. p. 30.   [28] Ibid. p. 32.   [29] Ibid. p. 40.   [30] Ibid. p. 41.

and it is possible for a modern investigator to have sufficient
confidence that such powers will have been reliably enough
employed. By contrast, history is interested in particular events
in their particular times, in their individuality as they are set in
complexes of relations which the historian aims to grasp as
whole intertextures of causal and human connexions. To secure
some grasp of a total complex of relations like this both involves
judgements about many more kinds of matters than the making
of a scientifically useful judgement may need, and, typically,
these judgements will be about the very kinds of human matters
whose comprehension will be most affected by the changing and
developing human self-understandings of successive periods.
Hence, those who bear witness to a later age about events of
their own day cannot act as judicious reporters simply observing
in the place of later historians and reporting to the later age as its
representatives, precisely because they cannot grasp a totality of
causal and human relations in their own day with the mind of
the later age which wishes to study the totality in question.

Since distinctively historical research does commonly issue in
conclusions, rather than mere surmises or speculations or
tentative guesses leaving only open questions, and since modern
historical researchers cannot identify with the thought of those
who variously leave records of the historical complex which is
being investigated, some other bases for historians' conclusions
must exist. The only such basis is analogy, between our critically
appropriated present world and the complex which the modern
historian studies. No other ground exists for historical
(re)construction.

Analogy being the nature of all historical reasoning, it is quite
impossible for any past events or past constellations or totalities
of events, which bear no analogy to anything in our present
world, to be established by historical inference. Putting the
matter positively: 'the material of history must hence be subject
to analogy'.[31] Although historians' hypotheses cannot be
checked against specially constructed or repeated experiment,
as the scientists' can, and although the historians' conclusions

[31] Ibid. p. 45.

will also be more tentative and provisional than the verdicts of
law courts, where the givers of evidence can be cross-examined
as the authors of historians' sources cannot,[32] the outcome of
Bradley's account of history is, he states, 'the reverse of sceptical.
The present experience, which is open to our research, is so wide
in its extent, is so infinitely rich in its manifold details, that to
expect an event in the past to which nothing analogous now
corresponds may fairly be considered a mere extravagance.'[33]

There may be some evidence of, or testimony to, the
non-analogous about which historians must simply suspend
judgement. In this, historians are in the position of a law court
where some technical matter which is central to the case is
outwith the experience of judge and jury and where, without an
authoritative expert witness, the issue before the court cannot be
settled.[34] However, it may be that when we are presented with a
testimony to the non-analogous we can readily account for the
existence and character of the evidence or testimony itself
without requiring to postulate any event to which no analogy is
known; this may be the most satisfactory way of appropriating
the evidential raw material into our critical world.[35]

The analogy requirement, which Bradley has argued at
length to be a leading presupposition of historical construction,
would be sufficient to make us set aside the disanalogous along
with the non-analogous, including neither of them in the
attempt to re-weave history's fabric. Yet, although Bradley
deals relatively briefly with the issue, he vigorously advances
distinct reasons for going further with the disanalogous than
merely setting it aside, as one should do with the non-analogous,
possibly to take the latter up later for appropriation into our
scheme if a critical world enlarged by enlightenment comes to
provide the needed analogy. However, where there is in our
critically considered experiences a well-established disanalogy
to some suggested occurrence, the critical historian must dismiss
the 'unassimilated crudity',[36] holding confidently that it has not
happened, because to entertain any other course would be to
propose 'a fact which, when taken as historical, contradicts the

[32] Ibid. p. 42. [33] Ibid. p. 43. [34] Ibid. p. 62, note C. [35] Ibid. p. 50.
[36] Ibid. p. 51.

very notion of history'.[37] We can construe Bradley's contention
as first echoing what he has earlier said is the ground of critical
history: 'the ground of criticism is that which is the justification
of inference; and an inference, it will be admitted, is justified
solely on the assumption of the essential uniformity of nature
and the course of events'.[38] So if we cannot assume the
uniformity of nature, all factual inferences will lack a basis; in
particular, the historians' attempts to reconstitute the past will
be unfounded. In addition to this Humean point, Bradley
secondly insists on there being one truth, such that nobody
should accept that the historical truth contradicts the scientific
truth. If a traditional history presents as reality something
which conflicts with science, then:

One course or another must be taken. Either against the scientific
conscience, and to the loss of science, the historical reality must become
the scientific reality; and that means that the traditional facts must be
received into science as verified certainties, with their consequences
developed in every direction, to provide a collision at each new
discovery – or else (and this must be the better alternative) scientific
evidence is made the criterion, and historical testimony subjected
throughout and in all its details to analogy from that.[39]

At the end of his monograph, Bradley's philosophisings are
applied to the precepts of F. C. Baur as these arose from Baur's
own researches in early church history. Baur speaks less than
clearly of what lies outwith the sphere of historical interpretation, and some had taken this most distinguished historian to be
setting very narrow limits to the competence of history. Bradley
rejects as Baur's intention the suggestion of a positivist-like
denial that any historical event can be properly grasped and
goes on to propose that Baur has in mind the impossibility of
giving a genetic account of the emergence of the new, specifically in spiritual matters. Just as in art, creativity cannot be
accounted for in terms of known causal connexions, so it in the
spiritual world. Bradley concedes this and sees it as posing no
new restriction on the practice of critical history. Artistic
creativity is cited here precisely as providing, from within the

present world, an analogy to the spiritually individual.[40] These remarks of Bradley's may seem to run counter to his earlier insistences on the universality of causal connexion as a presupposition of critical history.[41] The inconsistency appears particularly striking when we note this strong version of his view: 'a fact which asserts itself as (loosely speaking) without cause, or without a consequence, is no fact at all, and no better than a self-contradiction, for the reason that, while professing to exist, it abjures the sole ground of actual existence.'[42] When he considers the spiritually new, which interested Baur, we should take Bradley as qualifying, but not contradicting, these earlier affirmations. He is recognising 'a higher region' than critical history, a higher region whose existence is not claimed as a mere *ad hoc* expedient, but can be grasped on analogy with cases of artistic creativity.[43] Such spiritual novelty cannot be accounted for, nor can its reason be given, in terms of any genetic developmental account which we can ourselves construct, and we have thus some justification for calling it a miracle. Bradley still thought that the novelty had a cause (even though the construction of an adequate genetic account is beyond us) as we can see from his mentioning of transmuted combined ingredients which are taken up into artistic, and by analogy, spiritual novelty. Such novelties certainly had consequences, as nobody would deny. Accordingly, they do enter into causal relationships in ways which comply with Bradley's 'causal connexion' requirement for critical history, even if the *character* of some of the causal connectedness is obscure to us. Bradley is not, therefore, inconsistent in what he says of Baur. Our discussion of this matter has also brought out that the 'causal connexion' requirement does not demand that causes and effects should, in critical history, be able to be expounded to any particular standard of detail. The requirement is simply that an event in a critical history must have cause(s) and effect(s).

So, beginning with the critically appropriated and constructed present world, the world of our experience (including the history which we have already reconstructed) we move out

[40] Ibid. pp. 51–2 and extended footnote.   [41] Ibid. p. 21.   [42] Ibid. p. 23.
[43] Ibid. p. 52.

looking for analogies to our present world in the (as yet) unassimilated historical matter which confronts us. Where analogies are recognised, they enable appropriation and assimilation of the hitherto uncomprehended into our self-consistent critical world. By way of analogy, therefore, and constrained by the demand for consistency, the human world is re-made in critical history. In moving towards this goal it may be that within one's present world inconsistencies or disanalogies lurk, or it may be that weaker analogies have been pursued and stronger ones overlooked. The assimilation of new matter may strengthen one part of the system which is the present world and weaken some other part whose inconsistency with the rest of the system may come to be seen. Elimination of inconsistency and the identifying of the strongest analogies is a continuing process which Bradley describes in his Appendix Note E.[44] This can come to involve the painful discarding of what had once been one's present world, now supplanted by a world where consistency and the illumination of analogy are differently and better (perhaps more widely) achieved. The most acceptable critical account of the world which we can construct will be the one which most comprehensively and uniformly (a) satisfies the demands of consistency, and (b) enjoys the enlightenment which analogy affords.

[44] Ibid. espec. pp. 67–70.

CHAPTER 6

The concept of a miracle – 1

The authors whose thoughts about the miraculous were studied in the earlier part of this book have varying interests to pursue in their dealings with the topic, and they have different things to say about it. However, they are agreed that a miracle will be an evident exception to nature's usual regular course. When they are relatively confident that human beings, by their scientific researches, do properly grasp the causal explanations of events, they will tend, further, to regard miracles as events which lack a (normal) natural cause. They are agreed, finally, that miraculous events, if they occur, will not be merely freakish eccentricities; rather, miracles will be actions of God, done for his purposes in ways which deviate from nature's normal patterns of sequence.[1]

Modern writers have often proposed quite different conceptions of the miraculous. John MacQuarrie (in his *Principles of Christian Theology*) insists that the 'traditional view', that is, that miracles as conceived of above do occur, or have occurred, is 'irreconcilable with our modern understanding of both science and history', and is 'also objectionable theologically'.[2] He goes on to say that the true distinctiveness of a miracle lies in its focussing and disclosing God's presence. It is a mistake to try 'to express this distinctiveness by making the event itself something magical or supernatural, divorced from the natural sequence of events'. To do this is to shift attention 'away from the essence of

---

[1] In saying that all agreed, I have smoothed out the difficulties which were noticed in Locke's attempt to define miracles. However, as was indicated in the chapter about Locke, I have smoothed him out in the way which makes him most consistent.

[2] John MacQuarrie, *Principles of Christian Theology* London, 1966, pp. 226–8.

miracle (the divine presence and self-manifestation) to the discredited and mistaken idea of miracle as a magic sign'.[3]

What MacQuarrie appears to mean by 'our modern understanding of . . . science and history' is a view which the critical discussion about Hume, Troeltsch and Bradley, in the next few chapters, sets out to assess. However, it might be thought that there is little point in thus pursuing those enquiries if there are strong theological reasons for immediately rejecting the traditional conception of miracle. MacQuarrie himself represents a view, which has been widespread amongst theological writers, that there is a compelling and well-understood theological case, about whose main components there is a broad agreement, for rejecting this traditional conception; so it is appropriate now, before pressing on further, to consider that case (as presented by him and some other well-known writers) as a reason, at least *prima facie*, to give up as pointless any further concern about miracles as traditionally conceived of. If no informed theologian would, or should *qua* theologian, be interested in the possibility of miracles as conceived of according to this traditional notion, it may seem scarcely worthwhile engaging in the further less specifically theological discussion, which is the main aim of this study.

MacQuarrie argues for the theological objectionableness of the traditional conception (presenting a conventional wisdom in his text book/reference book treatment) with scriptural support or illustration (it is not always clear which). First is cited Christ's refusal to throw himself from the Temple in such a way that God's rescue of him would turn the amazed onlookers to faith. Then, Christ's condemnation of the 'mentality which looks for such "signs"' is noted,[4] together with the warning that those who reject Moses and the prophets will not be convinced by a resurrection.[5] He goes on to say that biblical criticism enables us sometimes to observe the development of the account of a genuine (on MacQuarrie's understanding of it) miracle into an account of a supernatural sign. This 'inflation' is an unsatisfactory way, typical of a mythological cast of mind, of

---

[3] Ibid. pp. 228–9.   [4] The reference is to Matthew 12, verse 39.
[5] Luke 16, verse 31.

attempting to express the significance of the god-disclosing event.[6] Other writers have spoken of the invention (rather than inflation) of stories about non-natural miracles;[7] the invented stories are said to express the significance of Jesus.

A further consideration is commonly advanced to show that miracles, traditionally understood, are in particular unacceptable as attestations of genuine revelation, namely that a free response of faith to God's self-disclosure will be difficult or impossible if God makes himself known in a conspicuously extraordinary way, acting apart from nature's usual course. In that event we should be overwhelmed or co-erced, no freedom being left to us.[8]

Having now sketched the main points of the theological case against the traditional conception of miracles, we can take them up more fully, and respond to them in turn.

Already we have seen, in Locke, some reasons proposed for God's, or Christ's, refraining from working miracles in some situations. Twentieth-century biblical scholarship has widely, albeit not unanimously, spoken further of the 'messianic secret' for the sake of which Christ asks that his wonder-working be not widely reported:[9] his messiahship is of an unexpected kind and he needs time to fulfil his vocation, time to enable others to grasp its character and (in some versions) time to come to understand it himself. Accordingly, particular episodes where signs and wonders are eschewed, or their significance as attesting the person of Jesus Christ is played down, cannot simply (that is,

---

[6] MacQuarrie, *Principles*, p. 229.

[7] Such as D. Nineham, in *The Use and Abuse of the Bible*, London, 1976, pp. 169 and 187–8. Nineham's refrain, that in the biblical writers 'Theories of the present were . . . represented as the facts of the past', applies widely in the Bible, he believes, miracle stories not excepted. The refrain is drawn from Sir Richard Southern's writings. Southern is quoted at some length (see Nineham p. 123). I have argued that by selective quotation Nineham seriously misrepresents Southern's view. See *Objective Knowledge*, ed. P. Helm, Leicester, 1987, pp. 158–60.

[8] See R. H. Fuller, *Interpreting Miracles*, London, 1963, p. 9 and p. 44, for examples of this: '. . . if Jesus had offered his miracles as proofs either of his messiahship or of the coming Reign of God he would have completely contradicted his own conception of faith as free decision rather than co-erced opinion' (p. 44). Underpinning this argument, which is applied here specifically to miracle-reports, is Kierkegaard's contention, which will be addressed later in the chapter, that properly, christian faith has no objective support.   [9] Mark 1, verse 44.

without argument which would exclude these other possibilities) be taken as ruling out any propriety in any possible appeal to signs and wonders as revealing his significance.

MacQuarrie's case, which many would echo, is further weakened when we attend to the contexts of his biblical citations. The temptation to throw himself from the Temple may (perhaps best) be understood as a temptation, whether it was experienced at one decisive time or whether the narrative should be taken less literally as telling of temptation which he experienced recurrently, throughout his ministry, about the whole character of his mission and work: was it to be simply or principally a demonstration of amazing power or Power? According to this interpretation, Jesus Christ chooses rather a way which involves suffering and weakness, sharing the life of his people and relating to them person to person in intense compassion, mercy and love. To take this way does not, however, necessarily exclude signs and wonders altogether. Indeed, some signs and wonders could attest that the way he has taken is God's way for him; they will set a seal on something else (besides the miracle-working) which has been going on, and also perhaps contribute (for example, by compassionate healings) to some larger whole than the mere working of miracles. The overall impression of his work will not be that he was, fundamentally or merely, a miracle-worker or one who principally effected his purposes and fulfilled his vocation by miraculous exhibitions of power. Alternatively, the temptation may be understood as coming at the outset of his ministry and as being a temptation about the first phase of that ministry: is he to *begin* with a show of power? His resisting this idea may then accord with the 'messianic secret' theories and be an avoidance of premature (mis)understanding of the nature of his ministry. Again, it will not follow that all signs and wonders must be avoided.

The remark about a resurrection failing to convince those who spurn Moses and the prophets occurs at the end of the parable of the rich man who has neglected Lazarus, the poor man at his gate. This context suggests the meaning that (typically) rich people who in their greed fail to attend to the teaching of the law and prophets about their attitude to the poor will not be moved even by a resurrection. Even so powerful a sign will not break the possessiveness in the heart of people like this. Accordingly, no general rejection of the value of signs as attestations of God's servant can confidently be derived from this parabolic saying.

Nor is the 'mentality which looks for "signs"', as such, necessarily Jesus Christ's target in Matthew 12.39. The apparent parallel in Mark has him say in a quite unqualified way that no sign will be given to 'this generation',[10] whereas the Matthew passage (cited by MacQuarrie) says that no sign will be given except the 'sign of the prophet Jonah', by which he means to speak of his resurrection.[11] These are puzzling passages whatever our view of the nature of signs, since Jesus Christ reportedly gave other signs after these sayings. In trying to resolve the puzzle, it is helpful to notice that in each case the people whom Christ addresses are hostile argumentative Scribes and Pharisees; in the Matthew 12 context they have recently placed a perversely antagonistic construction on his healing of the blind and dumb demoniac (verses 22–32). May the meaning of Jesus Christ's remark be that this group of people, or they and those like them, are not going to be allowed to dictate the giving of signs only for their contrary wilfulness then to dispose of them? If so, Jesus Christ's condemnation may have been of the captious hostile claiming to seek for a sign, whose real significance cannot in fact be grasped because of the vested interests of the 'seekers' (in this like the rich who have paid no attention to law and prophets, and will not heed even a resurrection), rather than condemnation of a seeking for signs as such.

The ordinary sense of the word 'generation' might seem to constitute a continuing awkwardness, in that the plainest meaning of what Jesus said seems to be that, of all those born at that time, none would be given a sign of any sort. That would be to take 'generation' to apply to each member of the generation, distributively. Yet it could be taken instead, collectively, as a single body of people. When Churchill died, it may truly have

---

[10] Mark 8, verse 12.   [11] Matthew 16, verse 1ff. echoes the remarks of chapter 12.

been said, in Britain, 'The Nation mourns', even though some
people with memories of Churchill's role in putting down strikes
and strikers earlier in the century did not mourn at all. Here
'The Nation' is taken collectively. When Jesus Christ spoke of
'this generation' he can be taken to be speaking collectively of
the (Jewish) people of his time and those who laid official or
public claim to understanding its destiny. So, when he says that
no sign is to be given to this generation, he means no large public
generally convincing sign which will, by report and authoritative endorsement, convince the body of people taken as a whole.
Such an interpretation of his meaning is consistent with the fact
that usually, when he speaks in this way, he is addressing
precisely those who take the lead in establishing the self-
understanding of the present generation in the unfolding of
God's purpose. Yet, of course, because no signs will be given to
the generation-as-a-whole, it does not follow that signs will not
be given to, or be available to be recognised by, individuals or,
even, crowds to whom, at first, he reveals himself. (Crowds will
not constitute the generation, in this sense of a convinced
synchronous quasi-institution.)

The crowd, the multitude of thousands who were fed,
apparently tried to make Jesus Christ King, which may suggest
that they saw the miraculous feeding as one of those signs,
echoing Old Testament signs which pointed to, and brought,
God's salvation, and which were to be expected as attesting the
coming of the Messiah. Jesus resists their attempt to make him
King because they had misunderstood the significance of the
sign, and by so acting, as the true Messiah would not be
expected to act, he balks their interpretation of the sign, and tells
them, in effect, that they should not take the event as a sign
because they did not understand what was going on. To them,
with their view, it could not be a sign. It is possible that, when he
explicitly says no sign will be given to this generation, the point
is that their fixed misconceptions as to God's purposes and the
vocation of the Messiah make it impossible for them to see the
proper significance of a real sign; yet without the proper
significance there is no true sign; so this generation cannot be
given a sign.

Accordingly, a respectable case exists for, at the least, questioning the widely held views which MacQuarrie presents, and for doubting the strength of his general contention. If, further, we take as historical (as many would not) the account of Christ's reply to those who came from John the Baptist, asking whether Jesus is 'he who is to come', or should they 'look for another',[12] the standpoint of MacQuarrie will be in even greater need of ingenious qualification, if it is to command any conviction.

Recent leading scholarly treatments of these matters have both (a) accounted for the persuasiveness of some aspects of the MacQuarrie view, and yet (b) argued for conclusions which are importantly (for our concerns) at variance from it.

As to (a), there is little hint in the Gospels' presentations of miracles of Jesus that either the evangelist, the spectators, or Jesus himself, thought of the miracle as, *first*, attesting the status or authority of Jesus Christ, the miracle-worker, the thaumaturge. According to Harvey,[13] the miraculous activity of Jesus conforms to no (previously) known pattern, and the various motives variously attributed to Jesus do not include the confirming of his own power or status.[14] Those who witnessed the miracles frequently express amazed puzzlement, not knowing what to make of what they have seen; and they are given little help in their confusion. The disciples are reported in Mark (8.17–21) as slow to grasp the significance of what they have seen, and when we notice this together with the varieties of interpretation of the purpose of miracles which the evangelists present, we can conclude 'that the miracles of Jesus were not, or not all, so obviously intelligible that those who witnessed them *must* have known always what their meaning was'.[15] In this, the miracles were like sayings of Jesus, including notably the parables whose point not all hearers grasp, and those who do grasp it are like the good soil in which the good seed takes root and grows (Mark 4.1–20). Harvey argues that the miracles of Jesus are best understood as signs of the new age which God was

---

[12] Matthew 11, verses 2–6.
[13] A. E. Harvey, *Jesus and the Constraints of History* London, 1982, p. 113.
[14] Ibid. p. 118.   [15] Ibid. p. 114.

expected to bring in,[16] and that, in the Jewish tradition, workers of miracles from Moses, Elijah and Elisha to the time of Jesus did what they did to bring glory to God rather than to try to underscore their own standing, which would be a suspect thing for someone to do.[17]

All of this seems well said; and it gives reasons for the plausibility of MacQuarrie's views. But, as to (b), it is entirely consistent with Harvey's discussion to hold that the miracles of Jesus Christ, when reflected upon, did come to be seen as signifying something about the authority or status of the one who proclaimed the new age and effected the intimations of its coming. Moreover, if it was the expectation of Jesus that people who saw his miracles would move towards some high conclusion about him personally, Harvey brings out reasons why, in his tradition, Jesus would not have overtly affirmed that significance for his miracles. Certainly there is nothing in what Harvey says against the likelihood that witnesses of the miracles of Jesus could and often did move on from their wondering puzzlement, to form some more determinate understanding of their experience, which could well involve some view about the person of Jesus. This conclusion squares with that of E. P. Sanders (whether or not he would accept all of my reasoning) who concludes a chapter which takes appreciative account of Harvey's discussions by saying (inter alia) 'it is reasonable to think that he [Jesus], as well as his followers, saw his miracles as testifying to his being a true messenger from or agent of God'.[18]

As to the claim that stories which report contrary-to-nature miracles have developed as attempts to express God's being focussed or disclosed in particular events, several things should be said. Firstly, how far do biblical critics who claim to trace this sort of development share Hume-/Troeltsch-style presuppositions which then make necessary the acceptance of an otherwise improbable account of the origin of the reports which we have received of contrary-to-nature miracles? To the extent that such presuppositions do operate in that way, a questioning of these presuppositions will be a questioning of these critics' case; in the following chapters, that questioning is to proceed, provided that

---

[16] Ibid. p. 115.   [17] Ibid. p. 112.
[18] E. P. Sanders, *Jesus and Judaism* London, 1985, p. 173.

powerful, more specifically theological, reasons are not uncovered now for taking no further interest in miracles as traditionally conceived of. In the few cases where there exist two accounts arguably of one event, one account (A) telling of a contrary-to-nature miracle, the other (a) of an event which accords with nature's usual course, *should* we take it that the direction of development is inflationary, from (a) to (A)? Perhaps general incredulity resulted rather in the deflation, from (A) to (a).

The theory that non-natural-miracle stories were invented to express the significance of Jesus will be somewhat confirmed if there is some evidence of the existence of a convention whereby this sort of significance would standardly be set forth by that sort of story.[19] However, those attempts which are made to supply the evidence (for example, by claiming that much of the relevant gospel material is Haggadic) have not gained any general acceptance.

In parallel fashion, the inflation theory requires evidence, if it is to command credence or acceptance. MacQuarrie offers, as illustration and evidence, the double account (which is what many mainstream biblical scholars have supposed it to be) of the Israelites' Red Sea crossing (Exodus 14).[20] A widely favoured analysis of this passage resulted in one account (from the so-called J source) of the crossing in which God causes a wind to blow, so that the sea recedes for the crossing Israelites and then returns to engulf pursuing Egyptians, and a second account (from the so-called P source) in which Moses stretches out his hand and lifts up his rod and the sea is divided, with walls of water first standing up on either side for the Israelites to pass through and then collapsing to engulf the Egyptians. The conventional critical wisdom, relying hardly or not at all on Humean/Troeltschian assumptions, dated the entire block of pentateuchal material (called J) to which the former story is assigned much earlier than that (called P) in which the second

---

[19] See M. Dummett, 'A Remarkable Consensus', *New Blackfriars*, vol. 68, no. 809 (1987), pp. 429–30; J. Houston, 'Objectivity and the Gospels' in Helm, *Objective Knowledge*, pp. 147–65. I do not wish to deny that some invention or evolution of miracle-stories, to express the significance of Jesus Christ, may have occurred. However, if we are to conclude that it did, we surely ought to have more evidence than the existence of a mere possibility.   [20] MacQuarrie, *Principles*, p. 229.

story is located. Since MacQuarrie wrote, the critical orthodoxy regarding these supposed blocks of material has dissolved.[21] There is now little critical confidence that the larger blocks of distinct material were properly distinguished into two sources yielding two accounts; consequently, hypotheses about the datings of the respective accounts do not now arise. In addition, confident dating of any pentateuchal material is not now at all generally agreed. Moreover, the J version (on the older analysis) is actually in some ways more miraculous than the P account, in that the pillar of cloud and fire figures prominently in the former whereas it does not in the latter. Better evidence is needed if a general inflationary tendency of the sort alleged by MacQuarrie is to be believed in.

The 'mythological mentality' which envisages inflations is objectionable in MacQuarrie's view because it fails to recognise that, properly interpreted, religious discourse is concerned with questions of human self-understanding, and with Being. That is, the mythological stories should be seen as significant existentially and ontologically, and it will be to conceal rather than reveal religious truth if we try to express, for example, the existentially significant disclosure of Being by telling a story apparently about extraordinary events in the public world, events which do not conform to natural law. (MacQuarrie thinks that the view of religious discourse which he endorses and the approach to its interpretation which is involved carry conviction because a 'coherent and convincing picture' of human existence emerges when the interpretive method is employed, in particular by Bultmann.)[22] Clearly, the supposedly decisive merits of a conception of religious truth as concerned with self-understanding and with Being are here being employed to argue away traditional conceptions, to force re-interpretation of mythological elements of the biblical message in general and of miracle-stories in particular. Full appraisal of the merits of this conception of religious truth is impossible here, and our conclusion must therefore be somewhat provisional. However, one of the merits most emphasised by Bultmann is that modern man takes it 'for granted that the course of nature

[21] For an account of, and good reasons for, this dissolution, see R. N. Whybray, *The Making of the Pentateuch*, Sheffield, 1987.   [22] MacQuarrie, *Principles*, p. 121.

and of history . . . is nowhere interrupted by supernatural powers'.[23] Bultmann's interpretation of the Gospel enables modern man to hear the Gospel without inappropriate obstacles. Strictly, Bultmann goes beyond Hume and Troeltsch and Bradley; but if these three luminaries are mistaken in what they have said about miracle reports, modern man may well be wrong if (as Bultmann, without offering evidence, says he does) he takes it for granted that miracles as traditionally understood do not happen. So, if Hume and Bradley and Troeltsch are unjustified in their view, a major merit which is supposed to attach to the Bultmann/MacQuarrie understanding of the nature of religious truths will be removed. The chapters ahead will set out to deal with this question, if no prior theological consideration blocks the way.

The MacQuarrie-out-of-Bultmann school of thought appeals to a fourth factor in commending its interpretation of the New Testament message. (The first factor is the alleged attitude of Jesus Christ, or of the New Testament authors, to the performing of miracles as traditionally understood. The second factor is the process of 'inflation' which is allegedly observable in the biblical material. The third is that miracle-reports as traditionally received, are unacceptable, broadly for those reasons which were treated as cogent by Hume, Bradley and Troeltsch, reasons to which modern man attaches due weight.) The fourth factor is that this version of the New Testament message can illuminate our human condition, inspire action which, in the world as it is, is creative of good, and in the doing of which we can find ourselves enabled beyond the powers of our own resources; and it is by the disclosure of holy Being that these possibilities open to us. Miracles are particular events in which Being is focussed and significantly disclosed to the person of faith. Bultmann and MacQuarrie wish to acknowledge the value of modern philosophy (notably that of Heidegger) in enabling us to express the New Testament message so as to make it accessible to modern people by using concepts which the philosophy has forged. It is true that, if the proposed philosophical interpretation (Heideggerian Christianity) has these merits, someone who is disposed

---

[23] R. Bultmann, *Jesus Christ and Mythology*, New York, 1958, p. 16.

to want to respect or revere the New Testament, or who adheres to the normal principles of interpretative charity, will rightly look on these merits as a reason for favouring the interpretation offered in Heideggerian Christianity as compared with some other interpretation which lacks such merits. Considerations of this kind will come to weigh significantly only where basic philological and synonymy-establishing techniques, normal in translation or exegesis, leave us with an obscure meaning, or a meaning which, there is other good reason to think, cannot be the correct meaning.

It is noteworthy that some modern men and women have, upon giving attention to it, found the philosophy which Bultmann and MacQuarrie commend for their own purpose of interpreting the Gospel to be far from acceptable. Paul Edwards has articulated an attack, maybe unsympathetic but surely not baseless, gratuitous or unprovoked, on the obscurity of Heideggerian philosophising;[24] many others have expressed reservation of a similar sort, if less caustically or rumbustiously, and little attempt is made by Heideggerians to effect a reply. However, let us suppose that they are fully justified in the claims which they make for their philosophy. If the first three reasons for commending Heideggerian Christianity are to be set aside, either because they have no force, or because their force has yet to be assessed (as for the third factor), the grounds for proposing an 'interpretation' which is not what the New Testament writers appear to intend, are much reduced. If it should turn out that the third factor also provides no reason to reject traditional understandings of what the New Testament writers meant, then the proposal to attribute an implicit or unarticulated Heideggerian Christianity to these writers will not be the exercise of interpretative respect or charity so much as a patronising imposition. The merits of Heideggerian Christianity will commend it as an interpretation of the New Testament, only if there *are* good reasons for rejecting the meanings which are arrived at (elusive as these can, admittedly, be) by normal exegesis.

In this brief review of a modern theological outlook, so far, the rejection of traditional views of miracles supposedly on specifi-

---

[24] Paul Edwards, 'Heidegger's Quest for Being', *Philosophy*, vol. 64 (1989), pp. 437–70.

cally *theological* grounds turns out to rely largely on argumentation which is intended shortly to be our explicit concern; and
those theological arguments which are independent of a Hume-,
Bradley- and Troeltsch-like attitude turn out so far to be less
than compelling. One further theological reason must be
discussed before we can proceed with a good conscience.

In his answer to the question of what it is about the traditional
understanding of a miracle-story which, apart from Hume/
Troeltsch assumptions, renders the traditional understanding
unacceptable, MacQuarrie does not appeal, as others have
appealed, to our faith's being properly risky, insecure, authentically looking for no objective assurances. In this, MacQuarrie is
being self-consistent because he has argued that if miracles are
offered to confirm or attest, they will still leave people free to
believe or reject what the miracle attests. (See his use of the idea
that 'even a resurrection will not convince them'.) Miracles can,
therefore, not give such a security in believing as excludes all
possible doubt. If rationally sufficient evidence does not determine or compel belief in those who know it, we can have no total
assurance of our rightness in belief on the basis of such evidence.
Others, however, have argued in the way which is avoided by
MacQuarrie (see note 8 above). What, then, should we make of
it when a theologian does advance the freedom, and/or objective
insecurity, of genuine faith, as reasons for rejecting the traditional view of miracles?

There must be some doubt, firstly, whether anyone ever has
freedom-to-believe, of the required sort; many philosophers
have contended, at least with plausibility, that our believings
are not under our control.[25] No doubt over the conative
components of religious faith, such as trust or obedience,

---

[25] Notably D. Hume, *A Treatise of Human Nature*, edited by L. A. Selby-Bigge, second
edition, with textual revision by P. H. Nidditch, Oxford, 1978, appendix. pp. 623–7.
See especially 'We may, therefore, conclude that belief consist merely in a certain
feeling or sentiment; in something, that depends not on the will, but must arise from
certain determinate causes and principles, of which we are not masters' (p. 624). Even
those who doubt some elements of Hume's account, perhaps over whether belief is a
feeling or sentiment, often agree that belief is not at the command of our will. Bernard
Williams takes the issue further, and gives further reason for agreeing with Hume,
though he leaves open the possibility, which he does not address, of there being freely
chosen avowedly or recognisedly irrational beliefs. (B. Williams, 'Deciding to Believe'
in *Problems of the Self*, Cambridge, 1972).

freedom is sometimes possible and desirable; but over the essential cognitive component, this, at the very least, needs to be argued. However, secondly, even if a striking contrary-to-nature miracle were to happen in such a way that, for us, the only rational account of it is that it is divine attestation of a prophet and/or his message, it will still be possible for us to reject that message and/or to deny the miracle's occurrence. We may be unreasonable in our assessment; but obtuseness or bloodymindedness are common enough, and, often, people cannot be sure that they are not victims of it. Since it is possible to get things wrong even without bloodymindedness, it becomes clear that security in anyone's believings cannot ever be total, and that the possibility of unbelief exists even where rationally compelling grounds for belief are known.

However, in view of the pervasiveness in Protestant theology of anti-objectivist conceptions of religious belief, it is appropriate to devote some, more particular, attention to the views of such as Bultmann and, in greater depth (because there are greater depths to plumb), of Kierkegaard.

Bultmann explains his view of faith by emphasising that faith is non-theoretical, but practical, issuing in attitude and action, and in this way tries to place faith firmly on the value side of the fact/value distinction. He writes, 'For man is not asked whether he will accept a theory about God that may possibly be false, but whether he is willing to obey God's will.'[26] Bultmann repudiates the quest for rational support for faith; one of his advocates says, of Bultmann's understanding of faith: 'There can be faith only as decision without assurance.'[27] Those who think of faith in such ways rule out any appeal to miracles as giving grounds for, or proofs of, faith.

Theologians who, like Bultmann, extrude the factual from the concern of faith, and for that reason deny that faith requires grounds, have to face the problem that evaluative attitudes generally require or presuppose factual beliefs: the person who has (Bultmannian) faith, and is 'willing to obey God's will' must surely believe at least that there is such a being as God, and that

[26] R. Bultmann, *Existence and Faith*, edited by S. M. Ogden, London, 1961, p. 57.
[27] W. Schmitals, *An Introduction to the Theology of Rudolf Bultmann*, London, 1967, p. 144.

God does will one somewhat specific act or sort of action or lifestyle rather than another. So avoidance of questions about the grounds of factual, truth-claiming beliefs cannot be achieved by an attempted move to the purely, exclusively conative or emotive, evaluative commitment. Further, many (Kantian moralists, for example) would say that the evaluative may be itself factual, truth-claiming, anyhow; while others would say that commitments which are non-factual may properly call for support. If, as is now plain, these ways of representing faith as, properly, groundless, encounter large difficulties, what of the arguments of Kierkegaard?

To understand his repudiation of objective assurance for Christian faith we must grasp Kierkegaard's conception of faith. Faith is costly infinite passion; it is unconditional commitment; and any objective assurance could not be complete or final. So, by argument which has several strands, Kierkegaard concludes that it is inappropriate to look for objective assurance for faith.

First, for Kierkegaard, the intensity of a passion will be shown, even put to the test, by the size of the risk which it (strictly 'its possessor') takes, or, which is the same thing, the smallness of the chance of success in action; and an infinite passion will be seen where the risk is infinite, where the passion is exercised on a probability which is infinitesimal, or zero. The intensity of a passion will also be measured by the sacrifice made in pursuance of the passion, by the passion's costliness; and a passion which lacks objective appropriateness will be more costly, in respect of anxiety and/or rational autonomy, than a passion which has some objective basis. So runs one strand of Kierkegaard's reflections. However, it is at least questionable whether an infinite and maximally costly passion is (a) conceptually possible, and (b) whether (whatever the answer to (a)) a most costly possible passion is religiously, or in any other way, desirable. As to (b), while it can contribute to the value of a religious commitment that it involves cost in respect of many ordinary finite goods (including costs attendant on risk-taking), so that St. Paul's glad loss of many good things in his service of Jesus Christ (Philippians 3.4–8) enhances his discipleship, the most costly possible passion, giving up available goods such as loving beauty, seeking the truth, loving and being loved by other people, in favour, say, of solitude, disease and pain, would seem devilish ('evil be thou my good'), perverse (and un-Pauline: see Philippians 4.4–8). The costliness of religious life is not properly seen (in the way which Kierkegaard's account apparently requires) as a quality whose maximisation is an overriding consideration. Other considerations have proper countervailing claims; and rationality, or having a satisfactory objective basis for one's beliefs may be one of them.

Second, in Kierkegaard's understanding, proper religious belief must involve commitment-no-matter-what. In particular, religious belief is to be held no matter what enquiry, or experience, discovers to be the case. It does seem inviting to agree that a quite unprovisional, come-what-may, (including darkness and despair) character does belong to proper faith. Yet, further reflection raises problems; in the Bible people are condemned for cleaving stubbornly to vain traditions, for failing to see what new thing God is doing; and being open to correction, or ready for discovery, is part of the faithful person's attitude. This being so, faith cannot require holding fast to your first commitment in the face of whatever the world turns out to be like. Perhaps what makes Kierkegaard's position plausible is that steadfast trust in God, issuing in unconditional obedience to God, no matter what suffering we have to endure, and no matter how fickle our moods may be, is proper to the Judaeo-Christian believer, but then these appropriate (conative) 'no-matter-whats' get confused with a (cognitive) 'no-matter-what' which unjustifiably lets faith slip its mooring from any objective basis.[28]

A third strand in Kierkegaard appeals to the inevitable failure of evidence or argument to give adequate ground for the infinite commitment which faith involves. This is because evidence or argument which is offered as justification for some conclusion, however strong it may be, will still leave some finite probability (even though it be a very small one) that the

---

[28] These two paragraphs owe a great deal to Robert M. Adams, 'Kierkegaard's Arguments against Objective Reasoning in Religion', in *The Virtue of Faith*, Oxford, 1987, pp. 25–41. Basil Mitchell's book *The Justification of Religious Belief*, London, 1973, also argues for a view of faith alternative to Kierkegaard's.

conclusion is false: the point is pressed as being particularly obvious, and relevant to Christian concerns where historical questions are at stake. If the believer's interest were merely finite, then the probability might be small enough to be set aside, being too small to worth worrying about; but an infinite interest cannot set aside, as insignificant, any finite probability of error. Where an infinite interest is at stake no probability of error is so small as to be ignorable. So Kierkegaard.

Although this was a prestigiously pedigreed argument when Kierkegaard adopted and endorsed it,[29] and although it has been something of a theological commonplace, it remains at best unclear what, precisely, the course of argument is supposed to be and what, if any, its force is. No doubt it is a matter of psychological fact that many people are made anxious by the tiniest probability of error over their religious convictions and that the intensity of their passion and/or the enormity of what is at stake, and/or the comprehensive import of what is at issue contribute(s) to this anxiety. However, first, it is not clear that anxiety, deriving from an awareness of some probability that the religious conviction is false, is a psychological necessity for the person who has that conviction; some reasonable and informed people seem, actually to have joy and peace in their believing. Also, whatever may be true about psychological necessity, here, the issue centrally at stake is whether religious belief, infinite interest notwithstanding, may be justified (whatever psychological necessities or tendencies towards anxiety may obtain) even when some finite probability of error exists. Does infiniteness of passion or interest, attaching to the truth of some proposition impose an unattainable standard for the strength of the supporting case which must be provided, if the proposition is justifiably to be believed?

There is, surely, one important sort of justification of beliefs where, if a person is justified in believing something by a given body of evidence, or a case of some particular strength, he will be justified irrespective of his interest, intensity of passion, or what

---

[29] He knew it, or its close kin, in the writings of Lessing and Strauss.

is at stake for him. If person A does not much care whether proposition p is true or not, and for him there is little at stake in the question of p's truth, while person B cares a lot and has a great deal riding on whether p is true, there is a concept of justification according to which A and B will nevertheless be justified in accepting, believing, p on the same strength of supporting case. B is less likely to be careless, perhaps in evaluating the strength of a case, readier to see weakness in it. Yet the same (strength of) case ought to justify belief in either person, where this *epistemic* type of justification is concerned. It may take confidence or self-confidence or courage for a person to act on a belief where much is at stake for him, and it may be that he will only acquire such confidence etc., if the case is stronger than is actually needed to justify the belief, and so he may only be able (psychologically) to act on the belief if the case is stronger than is needed to justify it. It may be, in that circumstance, that, presented with the weaker, but still justifying, argument he would not believe, or that he would believe, but (being unwilling to act accordingly) inconsistently. The fact of these common psychological traits does not undermine the claim that the epistemic justification of a belief stands irrespective of the interests, feelings or wishes of the believer.

Perhaps the counter-picture most likely to be proposed is that, when much is at stake, and action called for on the basis of a belief, a greater *degree* of belief is or may properly be necessary, calling for stronger justification, than if the believer has little or nothing at stake in the matter of the belief's truth. According to this suggestion, a greater degree of belief is not merely a greater degree of confidence in the belief, as judged by willingness to act costingly upon the belief, or say, to maintain the belief in the face of the disagreement or mockery of others (of whose qualifications to judge, the believer has no knowledge). Rather, when greater or lesser degrees of belief are spoken of, what is intended is expressed quite literally, that is to say, beliefs of greater or lesser intensity in respect of belief (and not beliefs which are greater or lesser in respect of the pleasure, confidence, duration or other manner or mode of their being held).

On that construction, a belief on which there depended something which was of infinite concern would have to be a correspondingly strong belief, and the justification of such a belief would call for an immensely strong case. Perhaps a maximally strong belief will require, for its support, a maximally strong case. The Kierkegaardian argument may then point out that a maximally strong case for Christianity cannot be had, and the demand that, if there is to be proper Christian faith, Christian belief should be justified, will lead to the impossibility of proper Christian faith. If we once recognise that, and if we are ourselves believing, we shall be led to see that faith is not to be rationally justified; and Kierkegaard appears to offer these arguments against rational support for Christianity in order to free us to see that Christian faith is actually the appropriation of the absurd.

Yet that counter-picture, offered in support of Kierkegaard's claim, is at least questionable. The doctrine of degrees of belief is contentious: Locke advocated it, and Newman criticised it. Quite apart from Newman's own particular arguments, there is a fact which tells strongly on his side of this dispute and which enables us to see that according to our usual concept of belief, belief does not have degrees. This is the fact that, in the immense philosophical literature about the analysis of knowledge as justified, true, belief (an analysis which has a long tradition), no one raises the question as to what *degree* of belief is being spoken of. The principal questions which have been addressed in that body of controversy have been about the *justification* which is required if true beliefs are to count as knowledge. Not any true belief will count as knowledge, for example if it is no more than a convinced hunch or if it is based on 'reading' tea leaves, it will not count. But what kind of justification is needed, for a true belief properly to count as knowledge? That question has been worked over, in print, by hundreds of epistemologists. Now, if there are degrees of belief, it will surely matter what degree of belief is in view. Mere suspicion, to take a Lockean example of a low degree of belief, will just not do for knowledge. Yet nobody asks what degree of belief it is for which justification is being required, in order that the belief, given that it is true, should constitute knowledge. Surely, no one is at fault in this, because it is obvious that the traditional analysis of knowledge as justified true belief employs a conception of belief according to which belief is not greater or lesser, does not have degrees, but is either possessed or not possessed: you either believe or you don't. This conception of belief is simply the usual ordinary notion of belief. Accordingly, the counter-picture which was sketched in order to support Kierkegaard is conceptually vitiated, and that other account of epistemic justification holds the field according to which the epistemic justification of a belief stands, irrespective of the passions or interests of the believer.

Moreover, if Kierkegaard's contention is that costly *action*, including self-commitment, requires particularly well-founded belief, and that the more that is at stake in the action, the better the basis of the belief will be required to be, then, first, the cost in the circumstances of the case, of *not* acting, in particular not acting as a Christian, must also be borne in mind, and then the reflection that it may be entirely reasonable to act on the basis of rather low probabilities where much is at stake. Butler's maxim that probability is the guide of life, and examples such as those of people justifiably risking their lives to save what may, with only a low probability, due, for example, to poor visibility, actually be a drowning person, remind us that costly action and self-commitment do not obviously and generally require proportionately strongly based beliefs. Kierkegaard's view cannot, therefore, command agreement.

This survey of the standard arguments strongly indicates that the alleged freedom and/or insecurity of authentic faith are not a compelling theological reason for rejecting traditional conceptions of miracle; and this conclusion stands: that supposedly theological reasons for dismissing the conception of miracle as violation-of-natural-law turn out either to depend on (or to be) the Hume-Bradley-Troeltsch outlook, the assessment of which is our main concern, or to be at their strongest, so open to question as certainly not to require the abandonment, at this preliminary stage, of any further interest in a traditional conception of miracle. Moreover, the wide extent to which, as it has become clear, the Hume-Bradley-Troeltsch outlook does underlie theologians' attitudes to miracles, actually underscores the need at some point to scrutinise and evaluate that outlook, and not merely accept it *pro more*, as an ineluctable given.

CHAPTER 7

The concept of a miracle − 2

Of those authors whose work was earlier expounded, Hume most clearly and helpfully captures the conception of the miraculous which is their common concern. In this chapter, the point and implications of Hume's definition will be brought out, as possible objections to that definition are considered and assessed.

First, he describes a miracle as 'a violation of the laws of nature',[1] and he goes on, in a substantial footnote, to give his deliberate definition: 'A miracle may be accurately defined, *a transgression of a law of nature by a particular volition of the Deity, or by the interposition of some invisible agent*'. Crisply, in his next sentence, he makes plain that what is, in this way, miraculous is not determined by, or otherwise relative to, human comprehension. He says 'A miracle may either be discoverable by men or not. This alters not its nature and essence.'[2]

It is essential to Hume's purpose that the definition enables us to identify those events which, if they were to happen, would call for exceptional explanation because they cannot be accounted for by usual, natural, explanations. The apologist hopes to argue that extraordinary divine action may then be considered, or invoked, as the explanation. So-called miracles, which are natural-law-conforming, for example a fortuitous coincidence or the surviving of some catastrophe by a 'miracle' escape, or seeing some natural phenomenon as significant, as when the sun breaks through the clouds and assures us that our worrying can

---

[1] D. Hume, *Enquiries*, ed. Selby-Bigge, second edition, Oxford, 1978, p. 114.
[2] Ibid. p. 115, note 1.

and should cease, do not serve the apologist's purpose in at all the way in which miracles as defined by Hume have been thought to do.

Of course, the miraculous according to these other conceptions can be considered also, and the value or significance of such 'miracles' assessed. Hume, however, is out to capture that conception which has principally engaged the mainstream of writers about miracles, who have regarded miracles as confirming signs, attestations of revelation. Some reflection about this definition is called for, because some writers besides those who have favoured quite different conceptions of miracles, such as those indicated in the previous paragraph and those touched on in the previous chapter, have had, at least, reservations about Hume's expressions and it is necessary at several points to try to see what is involved in the adoption of his definition, and to address people's misgivings about it at once, before we try to use it.

First, there are questions prompted by the characterisation of a miracle as a 'violation' or 'transgression' of natural law. One question here is whether his language, suggestive of being at odds with, of contravening, counteracting, working against, natural law, departs from the intention of Augustine and those many followers of his who prefer to speak of miracles as *praeter* or *supra naturam*, rather than *contra naturam*.

St Augustine thought that the normal order of nature is grounded in the dependable constancy or consistency of God. God's purposes do not alter, and so the natural order, which is upheld from moment to moment by this unchanging God, will characteristically exhibit constancy. Nevertheless, it is possible that while these divine purposes remain the same, they may be served by God's acting in an exceptional, anomalous way on particular occasions, and in particular circumstances.

Specifically, his love for us may wish to provide us with both a predictable context, sufficiently consistent for our life and responsible (loving) action to be possible, and a context in which he can also on occasion make known himself and his loving will for us by his self-attestation (the attestation of his self-disclosure) through extraordinary miraculous events. If so, miracles may occur which do not conform to the normal natural ordering of events, and which will be unexpected on the basis of our experience of nature; but such occurrences need not (and Augustine thinks will not) be inconsistent with that unchanging will of God which is also implemented in nature's normal order. All events (with the possible exception of free but disobedient actions of God's free creatures) happen in the working-out of God's will and purpose, whether these events accord with nature's usual course or not.

To describe miracles as *contra naturam* may suggest conflict or at least counteraction between the purpose of miracles and the purpose of those events which accord with nature's usual course. Indeed, the Augustinian theorist might object to Hume that what is said to violate or transgress natural law may seem more difficult to understand as an expression of the consistent mind and faithful purpose of the unchanging God who orders nature than what is said simply to lie outwith natural law, to be unaccounted for by natural law, or to be *praeter* or *supra naturam*. At the centre of this study is the issue of whether this whole Augustinian picture is sustainable, and there is no intention that at this point we should beg the question, assuming the answer. Yet, neither should we adopt a definition which of itself creates problems for any party to the dispute. Augustinians would not wish to accept a definition which might cast doubt upon the immutability of the divine purpose and/or God's competence in carrying it out.

Furthermore the argument can be turned, as it were, in the opposite direction by those who appeal to the orthodox doctrine of God's unchanging, consistent sovereign purpose and his omnicompetent wisdom, and then argue that events which go counter to that purpose are impossible. To suppose that God could not, from the first, build it into nature that his purposes would be consistently and effectively worked out in nature's continuing process, and that he might have to act, on occasion, to alter and correct the course which nature was, of itself, taking, would impugn God's power, or his steadfastness or purpose, or his wisdom.

Leibniz says that those who think otherwise 'must needs have a very mean notion of the wisdom and power of God'. Schleiermacher echoes the point where he says that it suggests imperfection in God or God's work to suppose that he might introduce miraculous changes in what has been ordained. D. F. Strauss (*Christliche Glaubenslehre* I, para. 17) likewise urges that it will be unworthy of God if we take him to have intervened in the natural order which he has created. Leibniz also, tantalisingly, says that while this reasoning applies to God's sovereignty over nature, he may be thought of as working miracles to supply 'the wants . . . of grace', without the impugning of his power or wisdom or consistency of purpose. Leibniz does not make clear *why* he thinks that miracles to meet the wants of grace will not lead to the impugning of God, and why he thinks that the form of argument which applies with respect to nature will not apply with respect to grace. Schleiermacher and Strauss do not even hint at any sort of case to which the line of argument will be relevant.

It has been Schleiermacher's advocacy of this argument which has been most influential in Protestant theology. Yet Leibniz is more perceptive; he recognises or at least suspects that there could be purposes of God, no doubt unchanging, whose implementation might precisely require departures from nature's usual course. C. S. Lewis summarises the Schleiermacher view effectively: 'Only an incompetent workman will produce work which needs to be interfered with.' He goes on to point out, *per contra*, that a poet may with powerful effect introduce an irregularity into verse. The traditional apologists' view of miracles as particularly attesting God's revelation supplies a rationale for God's acting irregularly which need cast no slur whatever on God's power or competence. Leibniz invites us to consider that rationale; the simplistic argument of Schleiermacher gives no good reason not to.[3]

By adopting the terminological preference of Augustinians for 'beyond' or 'above' nature, rather than 'against' nature, we would be able to direct critics away from taking that (too) short

[3] See H. G. Alexander (ed.) *The Leibniz-Clarke Correspondence*, Manchester, 1956, p. 12. F. Schleiermacher, *The Christian Faith*, translators H. R. Mackintosh and J. S. Stewart, I Edinburgh, 1928, section 47, pp. 178ff. C. S. Lewis, *Miracles*, London, 1947, p. 115.

way with the question of whether it is reasonable to believe that miracles have occurred.

Of course, a critic may be arguing more than the surface conceptual point that what is properly called a violation or a transgression involves contrariety of purpose against that which it contravenes, in this case the will which expresses itself in nature's normal course. He may rather be contending for the deeper claim that Augustinianism cannot sustainably hold that the unaltering purposes of God can be effected by a course of nature which is both characteristically ordered, and yet is sometimes miraculous. If this deeper point is what is in mind, the critic will require and wish to make the case out more fully; and assessment of it will call for the fuller discussion which, in the next chapters, follows this proper preliminary concern about definition.

Augustinians might well, therefore, wish, in the definition of miracle, to avoid language which suggests countervailing wills, or one inconsistent will. Accordingly 'violation' and 'transgression', in Hume's treatment, are suspect in Augustinian eyes.

However, the decisive point in response to all this Augustinian unease is that, for Hume, 'violation' and 'transgression' carry no implications about divine purposes. For him, natural laws are descriptive of what happens, and do not necessarily reflect the will of a law-giver. So 'transgression' and 'violation' in Hume's usage carry no implications of inconsistency of purpose or countervailing purposes. (If 'transgression' does contain in its normal usage the idea of deliberate disobeying of a law which expresses a sovereign's will, then Hume's use here should be seen merely as a figure of speech.) Hume starts from a position where 'a system of religion', by which be principally means theistic belief, requires a foundation and we are invited to consider, and reject, attempts to provide a foundation in reported miracles. From this perspective, so-called 'transgressions' only 'break' laws as unusual events 'break' general descriptive rules, as when a flurry of snowflakes 'breaks' the rule 'It never snows in June', or as an unexpected event breaks a patterned sequence; no opposition of wills, or conflict within a single will is involved. We can allow Hume his usage, therefore, as he intended it, so long as we protect the Augustinian's interest. This can be done by insisting, entirely reasonably, that acceptance of Hume's 'violation' or 'transgression' talk in describing miracles does not commit us to any conflict or inconsistency within the will of God, if it should be concluded that miracles can be believed in.

Indeed, where Augustine or his followers sought, as they did, to use accounts of miracles for apologetic purposes, they should have been prepared to accept the initial Humean perspective in which there is no assumption that any purpose whatever is at work in nature's ongoing. From that perspective, Hume's terminology could not be thought to carry any implication of conflict or inconsistency within the will or purpose of God.

Hume's 'violation' or 'transgression' language raises a second question or problem over whether a miracle which is worked by God (to simplify the discussion we can leave aside invisible agents) would actually be a transgression of natural law. If events occur which cannot be accounted for by a covering law (that is, a law of nature) and God is correctly invoked to explain them, it may be argued that no natural law has been violated because no natural law deals with, or attempts to describe, circumstances in which God takes a hand. Natural laws typically say that when circumstances of type C occur, then events of type E also occur; and a violation of a law will consist in the existing of circumstances type C together with the failure of an event of type E to occur. However, no natural law specifies that, amongst the circumstances C with which it is concerned, God is actively present. Accordingly there can be no natural law broken, violated, transgressed when a divinely worked miracle occurs. In the first paragraph of his essay 'The Miracles of Scripture', Newman sets out this point. Speaking of the concept of a miracle he says: 'It does not necessarily imply a violation of nature, as some have supposed, – merely the interposition of an external cause, which, we shall hereafter show, can be no other than the agency of the Deity. And the effect produced is that of unusual or increased action in the parts of the system.'[4]

---

[4] J. H. Newman, *Essays on Miracles*, London, 1890, p. 4.

In trying to assess this charge of incoherence against Hume's definition of miracle, we may first look at one version of the charge which envisages God's action as the introduction of distinct physical factors, such as forces, or energy, where in the usual course of events no such factors would be found. If God is thought of as introducing *de novo*, *ex nihilo*, physical factors such as a force or energy into nature's processes, the emergent event can well be regarded as law-conforming. This will be because there can be a natural law which includes in the description of the circumstances of type C, to which the law relates, some mention of the presence of (God-introduced) force or energy of the directions and/or magnitudes involved (without any reference to its introduction by God); in that light 'transgression' or 'violation' of natural law will be an inappropriate description of the emergent event of type E, where E is just the kind of event the law predicts. The occurrence of event type E will be in accordance with a law of nature which deals with circumstances in which such force or energy act (whether introduced by God or not will be irrelevant to this law).

However, the prior event of the appearance of this extraordinary God-introduced force or energy would occur out of circumstances antecedent to it such that a natural law which related to *these* circumstances would not specify this event (the imparting of power, or the application of force) as emerging. 'Violation' or 'transgression' of natural law does, therefore, seem to be involved, as Hume says, in divinely worked miracles. It is true, no doubt, on this account or construction of God's mode of action, that the event which is usually called miraculous itself emerges from its immediate circumstances in accordance with a natural law, and that the infraction of natural law properly understood happens elsewhere, that is earlier, in the sequence of events. However, if the description of what usually happens, the natural law, is made wide enough to comprehend the circumstances in or from which the extraneous factor (force or energy) extraordinarily appears, it will not predict the emergence of the force or energy, or that which the force or energy brings about, but will anticipate the occurrence of different sorts of events. The event usually called miraculous thus does occur contrary to a sufficiently comprehensive statement of natural law, even if there is also a narrower statement of natural law with which it accords.[5] Hume's conception of a miracle as a transgression of natural law so far does seem to have the application which Hume intends, even if we have to qualify that way in which Hume's conception would most easily be supposed to apply. So, with that possible qualification, Hume's conception stands as an adequate expression of the concept which is dealt with by our authors who argue for or against miraculous attestation of true revelation.

However, Newman's point need not be taken as meaning that God brings about miracles by introducing extraordinary physical factors, such as a force or energy into nature's process. As it was first expressed above, the point might well be, rather, that there are no natural laws which speak of God, or of God's action, as a factor in the course of events; so circumstances in which, supposedly, God has acted, has interposed to act, will neither be in accordance with a natural law nor in violation of one. For this reason, and without any specification of the way by which God might act to work miracles, talk of miracles as 'transgressions' or 'violations' of natural law seems questionable.

This rationale for rejecting Hume's 'transgression' terminology supposes, at least implicitly, that God does not figure in statements of natural law, because God is not present or active in events of the sort which the laws cover. On this assumption, if God were to be actively present in the natural world it would be by an irruption, an interposition, because God is not generally actively present in the world. This view would commend itself to people of a deistic tendency.

People of deistic tendencies, while acknowledging that the physical world depends on God for its Creation at the first and for the causal powers which God then implanted and which are at work within it, affirm that since Creation God has not acted in natural processes but has, rather, left the natural world to proceed in accordance with the causal principles of order initially given to it. On this view, the immanence of God in the course of events is not asserted. By contrast, God's immanence in

[5] Cf. C. S. Lewis, *Miracles*, Ch. VIII.

nature is insisted upon by theists. Nevertheless, many theists hold that God has given causal powers to things in the world and that these things themselves, without God's moment-to-moment activity, act on one another according to their natures. For present purposes, that sort of theism has it significantly in common with deism that the course of natural events proceeds, without God's acting in the events, by the agencies of things as they fulfill their own given causal roles. We shall return to deism, and this sort of theism.

There is also a species of theism which holds that God acts in every event,[6] that there are no causal powers in things such that once they have been given to these things, they enable them to act thereafter without God's involvement. Instead the appearance of consistent causal powers in things derives from God's consistent modes of action in and with the course of nature. For this brand of theism, God is not exceptionally present in miracles, exceptionally interposing himself. God is not an intervening extraneous factor. What is different about a miracle, as compared to the ordinary course of nature, is that God then acts in nature differently. For this theistic viewpoint, then, there will be a point in describing miracles as transgressions of natural law, in that God, in working miracles, acts exceptionally, anomalously, as compared with his normal pattern of action. It is not, as in the supposition of extraneous factors, as, for example, in deism, that miracles will involve a factor which is not normally present and which renders natural laws irrelevant. Rather, the same God who is present alike in law-conforming and anomalous events wills, for his own purposes, to act exceptionally, when miracles happen; and such exceptions to the standard pattern of occurrences are reasonably to be thought of as violations of natural law. Those who are interested in the appeal to miracle reports as (perhaps part of) an apologetic for this sort of theism will not, therefore, endorse the deistic objections, which we have been reviewing, to Hume's 'transgression terminology'.

The deistic objections, and the objection of theists such as

---

[6] R. G. Swinburne has sketched this sort of view. See his *The Existence of God*, Oxford, 1979, Ch. 8; also 'The Argument from Design', in *Philosophy*, vol. 43 (1968), pp. 199–212.

Newman, need not in any case result in outright rejection of Hume's definition, since a qualification of it can take care of the objections while retaining the purpose of Hume's definition in identifying the class of events to which the apologist wishes to draw our attention. What matters is that those events are identified which, if they are not explained by God's action, or that of some other spirit, cannot be accounted for at all, and will lack any explanation. So, where there arise these objections, from deists or theists, that Hume's definition of miracle is incoherent, the definition can be qualified by defining a miracle as 'what would be a transgression of natural law, were it not for extraordinary divine action'.

It would weigh down the subsequent discussion if, over each issue, it is necessary to deal in an additional treatment with the cases where the qualified definition (as it will be called) of miracle applies. Yet this will seldom be needed. For the most part it will be obvious how what is said can be transposed to accommodate the qualified definition, and the views of those deists or theists who advocate it.

A third theme for reflection is raised by Hume's definition when we recognise that a law of nature is supposed to be a statement describing what actually happens. Not just any true statement about what happens will rank as natural law, of course. In addition to fitting the facts, a statement must have, for example, generality and simplicity; that is, it must say 'whenever circumstances C obtain, event or state-of-affairs E will occur' (generality), and the statement will be the more highly valued the simpler the formulation under which it subsumes the phenomena with which it deals, revealing a simple pattern in the phenomena. In addition to its generality, a law of nature will be somewhat comprehensive, and the more comprehensive the better. In its generality, it identifies all members of some class, but the class description might be framed in such a way that there are very few members of the class. A law will be more comprehensive, roughly, as it ranges over more phenomena, describes more events.

Apparently, therefore, a natural law describes the actual course of events. How then, it is an obvious question, can there possibly be transgression, violations, or exceptions to natural laws? How can an event occur which transgresses a description of the actual course of events? The answer appears to be that nothing can take place which violates a statement of what actually takes place, and so there can seemingly be no miracles as Hume has defined miracles.[7]

This conclusion would require us also to conclude that the long and vigorous interest in miracles, notably seen in the authors reviewed in Chapters 1–5 can and should be swiftly undercut: there is simply no conceptual room for miracles as traditionally understood. Perhaps (it can further be argued) the issue has been overlooked because it is common for there to be infractions of what people at the time of the infraction have *thought* the law of nature to be. It is often by peoples' noticing infractions of what has been believed to be a law of nature that the supposed law of nature is seen not to be a law of nature at all. This familiar sort of development in the improvement of scientific understanding may have obscured the conceptual impossibility of there never being a transgression of what truly is (as distinct from what has been widely thought to be) a law of nature.

Can the dilemma be avoided: either some statement does really set out a law of nature, in which case it allows of no exceptions or 'transgressions', or there is a violation, in which case this transgressed-against statement cannot express a genuine law of nature?

One way of trying to escape the dilemma may be to appeal to the fact, already noted, that there are multiple criteria for being a natural law. Comprehensiveness is desirable and simplicity is required as well as generality and being in accord with observations. Suppose that there is what has been widely taken to be a law of nature, very well-established because it has survived many tests against experience. Suppose next that there is now reported a transgression of this supposed law. (For the moment let us set aside the question of whether it will be reasonable to accept the reports of the transgression. This

[7] This conceptual point is basic to the thesis of A. McKinnon in 'Miracle' and 'Paradox' in *The American Philosophical Quarterly*, vol. 4 (1964), pp. 308ff.

(epistemological) question is the major issue in much of the rest of this book, but our immediate present concern is the prior (conceptual) question of whether a transgression of natural law can be conceived of.) Faced with a supposed transgression of a supposed law it can be argued that it is not necessary, as the stark dilemma-posers allege it to be, to choose between rejecting reports of the transgression, and framing a new law to accommodate both these reports and all other relevant experiences which the supposed law described correctly. This is because the best endeavours of the scientific community to produce a new statement of the natural law, countered by no good observations, may result only in a formulation which is very much less comprehensive and/or very much less simple than the violated formulation. If this new proposal is adopted, the loss in comprehensiveness or simplicity in what we have now accepted as the law of nature, as compared to the previous violated formula, will be great. Some writers about science claim that in such a situation it is not at all clear that the scientist will, or should be prepared to, suffer a great loss of simplicity or comprehensiveness.[8] Rather, it is said, he should maintain the theory which is much more comprehensive and simple than the more strictly observation-conforming alternative. The anomalous, transgressing observation will then stand as an exception to the accepted theory which is the most reasonable view available about what the law of nature is. That is, it will be reasonable to regard the non-conforming observation as a transgression of natural law.

On a number of points this attempt to make elbow-room for the notion of a transgression of natural law is questionable. For

---

[8] For example, I. Lakatos, 'Methodology of Scientific Research Programmes', in *Criticism and the Growth of Knowledge*, eds. I. Lakatos and A. Musgrave, Cambridge, 1970, pp. 118ff. T. S. Kuhn repeatedly suggests that accuracy is only one value by which scientists choose theories and that scope, simplicity and fruitfulness are others which have been neglected. Maybe in his controversy with Popper's falsificationism (the doctrine that scientific proposals are replaced if and only if they are disconfirmed in experience), he exaggerates the weight which is to be attached to the other values, besides accuracy. Certainly, he seems to hold that a theory might be accepted for its simplicity and/or scope, even if there existed an isolated, or rare, counter-observation. For one example of Kuhn's writing to this effect, Lakatos and Musgrave, *Criticism* p. 261.

one thing, while scientists do value simplicity and comprehensiveness in theories, many would not treat these qualities as having the sort of importance, compared to accuracy and being in accord with observations, which this argument requires. In their view, ready comprehension of nature will be assisted if the scientist can reduce the buzzing blooming confusion of natural phenomena to simple formulas with wide-ranging applicability. However, is ready understandability something for the sake of which truth can be sacrificed, in this, or any other cognitively significant discourse? Even if, as in our hypothesis, a simple comprehensive formula is true of all events to which it applies, except one, its failure to explain that one event will be total. Again, even if the advancing of understanding is thought of as the goal of the scientist, rather than, or equally with, the acquisition of truth, what sort of understanding, if any, is given by a theory to which there is a known outstanding exception? The answer is so far obscure.

For another thing, it appears that, when Lakatos speaks as he does of retaining the comprehensive, simple theory in the face of a disconfirming instance where no better replacement theory is available, he is talking of theories which are being maintained provisionally, as the best that can be managed, in the course of the progress from worse to better theories. He is not obviously talking here of theories which have proved their predictive worth and survived tests sufficiently to be in line for Law-of-Nature status. As an attempt to formulate a policy for those who try to progress in understanding nature and are in the course of a confusing journey (which is what it is), his recommendation may have value. Yet, seen as that sort of proposal, it is less plainly relevant to the conceptual question about the possibility of transgressions of natural law. Apart from the points just touched upon, so many deep and currently controversial issues about the character of scientific enquiry are raised on either side of this discussion[9] that, until further light is shed on them by the specialists' debate, it is better meanwhile to look elsewhere if we are to discover reasons which will give

[9] See, for example, Ian Hacking (ed.) *Scientific Revolutions*, Oxford, 1981, as well as Lakatos and Musgrave, *Criticism*.

confidence that the notion of a transgression of natural law is coherent. Yet, even though these are controversial issues, their being live controversies makes it unreasonable to conclude confidently that Hume's definition does exclude there ever being miracles.

The generality which belongs to statements of natural law opens up a more telling line of argument. Laws of nature do not describe the actual course of events just in any fashion, but in general terms. (Indeed, it is by their generality that the appropriate simplicity and comprehensiveness of statements which aspire to express natural law are possible.) A principal purpose of a natural law is to say what generally occurs whenever circumstances of certain kinds obtain. Since a natural law aims to capture the patterns which are generally to be found in nature, an event which is an exceptional one-off, and which is not supposed to belong to or indicate a regularly recurrent pattern, is not reasonably to be described in their formulations by those who try to frame natural laws. An anomalous event, when discovered, does not pose a problem for those who see it to be a violation of what appears to them to be natural law. The statement of the natural law will not any longer be a true generalisation, but there may be reason to believe that the violation is not going to return, or that if it were to return, its occurrence need not conform to that statement which sets out the *regularly repeating* pattern of events in nature. If, for example, a violation may best be interpreted as the extraordinary action of a free agent, no covering law will properly apply to it (although there might fairly be some expectation that it is rather likely to recur if the free agent, God, should wish again to pursue similar purposes in similar circumstances). In such a case, the old, albeit violated, generalisation will still be the best guide to what will happen, leaving aside the possibility of extraordinary and in principle unpredictable events. Framing a new, revised generalisation to accomodate the violation will secure the truth of the generalisation as an account of nature's actual course, but it may actually mislead those who take it as a guide to what should be expected in nature. A law of nature is taken, importantly, as a guide to our expectations, and the revision will mislead by apparently treating the not-to-be-repeated counter-instance as if we may expect it to be repeated. Revising the statement of the law accordingly thus leaves open possibilities for the future (or unknown past or present) course of events which we have no reason to believe will ever be (or have been) actualised.

To focus the point: generalisations which aspire to be regarded as natural laws apparently claim to be true descriptive generalisations, and also to be sound guides to what should be expected in those, by us, non-experienced parts of the course of natural events. Being a sound guide may not just be a matter of saying what is true, if this saying what is true leaves open possibilities which will never be actualised. To give sound guidance, it may be better to (re)affirm a generalisation which has been falsified, but falsified in quite extraordinary circumstances. (If I say that someone strolling in our local park will surely encounter dogs or cats or birds or squirrels or timber-wolves, what I say can be true even if no timberwolf ever goes there; but if no timberwolf goes there what I said will be deemed rather poor guidance about what to expect.) So there can be a case for treating as a natural law a generalisation which gives best guidance about nature's usual course, even though there have been violations of that generalisation. When, in these extraordinary circumstances, a conflict arises between the strict truth-securing, and the expectation-forming, functions of natural law, the preference for the latter over the former, in these circumstances, is justified. In that case, the conceptual room is created for a violation of natural law. If, in addition, staying with the old generalisation involves gains in simplicity and/or comprehensiveness as compared with the adoption of a revised, strict truth-seeking generalisation, the argument for retaining the older transgressed-against generalisation is still stronger, and with it the case for the concept of a violation of natural law. To talk of violations or transgressions of laws of nature has a rationale, is not perversely incoherent. William Paley pointed the way here when, referring to the affirmation that miracles were exceptionally and particularly 'wrought on the first promulgation of Christianity, when nothing but miracles could decide its authority', he wrote:

It is not like alleging a new law of nature, or a new experiment in natural philosophy; because, when these are related, it is expected that, under the same circumstances, the same effect will follow universally; and in proportion as this expectation is justly entertained, the want of a corresponding experience negatives the history [he means 'disconfirms, or fails to confirm, the report of the novelty']. But to expect concerning a miracle, that it should succeed upon a repetition, is to expect that which would make it cease to be a miracle, which is contrary to its nature as such, and would totally destroy the use and purpose for which it was wrought.[10]

These defences of Hume's definition of the miraculous have been rebuttals of particular objections to the definition. Yet there is, in addition, an argument *for* Hume's definition, an argument which could not have been considered by Hume. This is because the point derives from developments in twentieth-century physics, according to which there are sub-atomic events, such as the emission of sub-atomic particles from radio-active substances, whose time of occurrence cannot be predicted with precision. Moreover, such rather unpredictable sub-atomic events can even determine events in macroscopic nature. For example, an instrument for detecting such sub-atomic particles may be wired up to a detonator and a large explosion brought about at an unpredictable moment when a sub-atomic particle is emitted and detected. Now, natural laws are used to predict just those events which are in accordance with them; but this example, of the unpredictably produced explosion, brings it out that there can be events which are not predictable, but which are not contrary to, not transgressions of, any natural law. The occurrence of events like these, which are not predicted by natural law but which do not call for any explanation in terms of the will of an agent, such as God, who

---

[10] Paley, *Evidence of Christianity*, 1794, 'Preparatory Considerations'. See, for example, Paley's *Works*, pp. 298–9. By contrast, see the view of Hick, *Philosophy of Religion*, p. 39. For a similar approach to Paley's see (1) Swinburne, *The Concept of Miracle*, Ch. 3; (2) Penelhum, *Religion and Rationality* pp. 274–5. Both of these owe something (as they acknowledge) to N. Smart's *Philosophers and Religious Truth*, London, 1964, Ch. 1.

acts in an extraordinary way, is not of use to the apologist whose case Hume wishes to appraise. The apologist appeals to events which are not merely non-predicted by natural law but are contrary to natural law, have a probability of zero and are ruled out by natural law. Hume's language can, quite naturally, be taken to express the point: a miracle is a *transgression* of a law of nature.

It is time to pass on from the justification of Hume's 'transgression' and 'violation' terminology, to other matters which arise from his definition. We might reasonably be tempted to ignore the last phrase of Hume's definition: '. . . or by the interposition of some invisible agent'. If such an agent is supposed to be an angel and messenger of the monotheistic god, the phrase adds nothing of importance (for our concern or Hume's) to the earlier part of the definition. If, by 'an invisible agent', is meant a member of a number, a pantheon, of deities, or a spirit, ghost or spook operating autonomously, it is rather unclear whether an event attributable to such an agent would be what is generally called a miracle, and it would not in any case be of interest to an apologist for orthodox monotheism. (Interpreted as attributable to a being of that sort, we might today, rather uninformatively, call an anomalous event a paranormal phenomenon, rather than a miracle.) Hume himself gives no attention to this clause of his definition when it is taken as referring to one of a number of independent deities, or to autonomous spooks, and none to any implications which the adoption of this definition will have if this clause is taken that way.

Nevertheless, the presence of this clause reminds us that other explanations of miracle-reports are possible and ought to be considered, besides that (readily compatible with atheism or agnosticism) which interprets a report as a species of deceit or error, and that which offers a monotheistic interpretation according to which the report is a reliable report of a miracle worked by the god of monotheism. That is, we are reminded that an apologist for monotheism must not only counter Hume's conclusion that a report of what would (if it occurred) be a genuine miracle is not reasonably to be accepted as true; but this apologist must also deal with non-monotheistic explanations of genuine miracles which invoke a god, or gods (out of a number which may exist) or a spirit, to account for the miracle.

Already Augustine, Aquinas and Locke, by their attempts to reckon with the diabolical or demonic, have made it clear to us that, if reports of the miraculous were cogent, a monotheistic god is not the only *prima facie* candidate for the role of miracle-working agent, whose action could account for the miracle. Modern interest in 'the occult' suggests that there are people who would wish to see discussion of other possible explanations of miracle reports in addition to the atheistic or agnostic, on the one hand, and the monotheistic, on the other. This clause of Hume's definition therefore opens up a challenge to the apologist for monotheism, which he has to meet not merely in order to produce a better theoretical argument (whether anyone cares about these possibilities or not) but to deal with concerns which have had historical and contemporary expression.

Finally, it should be noticed that Hume's definition requires that a god's (or other interposing spirit's) activity in bringing about an occurrence must be established before the occurrence qualifies as a miracle. A religious apologist will not, according to this definition, first establish that a miracle, as defined by Hume, has occurred and then pass on to argue from the miracle's occurrence to the likelihood of a god's activity (employing the further premises which are likely to be required, and are able to be supported). If we are strictly to conform to Hume's definition we must not yet describe as miracles events, such as walking on the water or a resurrection from the dead, which have not yet been shown to have been brought about by a god. It accords with Hume's usage, therefore, to refer (as henceforth here) to these transgressions of natural law, for those whose bare occurrence the apologist must offer evidence (and whose happening he can then attempt to explain as (a) god's doing) by using provisional locutions such as 'supposed miracles', 'puta-tive miracles', 'conjectural miracles', 'mooted miracles', or 'events widely interpreted as miracles'.

CHAPTER 8

Hume's case – preamble to assessment

In previous chapters, intimations have been made of prominent scientific, philosophical or epistemological objections to claims that miracles, as defined by Hume, have happened. These issues are central to this book's concern; in beginning to square up to them there is the prior question of the proper order to follow. Objections or difficulties which we described as 'scientific' appear to be so called because they are typically posed by people who are, by modern categorisation, scientists. Usually such objections raise problems either on the one hand for particular miracle claims such as that a paralytic was miraculously cured, or that Jesus Christ once turned water into wine, or that a man whose dead body had decomposed so as to smell was restored to full life, or on the other, for the very idea that there can be exceptions to natural laws.

Regarding claims about particular alleged miracles, there are, firstly, scientists' attempted explanations of the events in accordance with known, maybe recently discovered, natural law; if these explanations succeed, then the events under discussion are no longer to be treated as miraculous. (Even some, albeit an undetermined, probability of successful natural explanation, makes it probable to the same degree that the event is no miracle.) Suggestions on the basis of analogous cases of psychosomatic explanation of the cure of a paralytic will be in this category. Scientists who, from their specific expertise, contribute in that way to debate over claims about the miraculous, make a valuable contribution, and do so properly as scientists; and there is little more to be said about that kind of scientific judgement except that it is exceedingly unlikely to account for all alleged or supposed miracles.

Secondly, drawing on their specialist understanding of nature's (normal) processes, scientists have pointed out what would have to be involved for a reported miracle to have occurred. Thus, if water were to be turned into wine (as described in John's Gospel), carbon atoms would have to be produced from oxygen and/or hydrogen atoms; but chemistry is founded on the postulate that matter is composed of atoms of distinct kinds, that those atoms are indestructible and (the relevant point for the present issue) cannot be changed into atoms of another kind.[1] Once again the scientist is contending that no miracle took place, not now because the event described has a natural explanation, but because as described, and as such things are understood by science, the event could not have happened. The scientist here does, certainly, draw on his particularly scientific understanding in advancing his argument. However, in his application of it he requires to make an assumption whose justifiability is not a specifically scientific matter. In saying that as science understands the kinds of events involved, the miracle would, if it were to occur, require an impossibility and therefore that the alleged miraculous event cannot have happened, it is assumed that the scientific understanding of what standardly happens is applicable in this case of the supposed miracle. Yet that assumption will be unjustified if there is reason to think that nature's normal course may have been deviated from. Whether there could be such reason, and what it might be like, are further related issues; as we have seen some authors have thought that they had reason to believe nature's normal course had been violated.

It is at least lacking in imagination for people like Professor Longuet-Higgins who urge this kind of point to think that, for example, assumptions on which 'the whole of chemistry' is founded alone determine such issues. Thus, when the water was

---

[1] D. M. MacKinnon in his *Themes in Theology*, Edinburgh, 1987, pp. 63–4 cites the distinguished scientist, Professor Longuet-Higgins, as making this point, upon which MacKinnon had earlier touched in his *The Problem of Metaphysics*, Cambridge, 1974, pp. 114–5.

reportedly 'turned into' wine, perhaps carbon atoms were created *ex nihilo* by God, or carbon atoms may have been created by the undetected supply of great quantities of energy by God. Professor Longuet-Higgins was, it seems, reflecting on the difficulty of conceiving of, of comprehending, the transformation of just that mass of water, without addition, into wine. By what course of events could it come to pass? As a corrective to too easily assuming that we are thinking clearly when we envisage the occurrences of miracles, Longuet-Higgins' comments are salutary. Other reported miracles also make for the sort of difficulty which he exposes: what, in some detail, are we to think happened if five loaves and two fish multiplied to feed a crowd? Yet scientists' pronouncements about what is possible and what can be understood as scientists understand and describe normal nature, are not decisive arguments against the possibility that a miracle did, however puzzlingly, happen. If it is not normal nature which he is describing, as *ex hypothesi* it may not be, the scientist *qua* scientist is no longer expert. Reasoned judgement about whether the scientist's view of what standardly happens, and what can happen, should be assumed to hold good, is not within the competence of the scientist *qua* scientist, as 'scientist' is nowadays understood. These issues are also philosophical. They can be both what is now called 'scientific' and philosophical; a natural philosopher of yesteryear would have professed the appropriate competence to approach these questions. Today, however, the sciences are pursued as specialist disciplines in such a way that the scientist frequently is not, *qua* scientist, a philosopher.

When it is asked whether there can be exceptions to natural law, it is quite as clear as it is over the previous question that this is a philosophical rather than a narrowly scientific issue. It is, of course, fundamental to scientists' work that nature should exhibit uniformities, patterns of sequence in its processes. Whether anyone can rely on nature's doing so is a question rarely asked by physicists, chemists or biologists; and within universities it is seldom dealt with in courses in faculties of science or technology. It is a philosophical question, as our academic culture now categorises these matters.

Later, a scientist's treatment of an alleged miracle will be examined, but the proper order for the present stage of the investigation has been shown to be: first the philosophical and epistemological. That is because when scientists are speaking strictly within their scientific competence they say relatively unproblematical things about miracle claims. The import, for claims that miracles have happened, of other things which some scientists say will, it should now be plain, depend on the resolutions of prior questions, which are properly philosophical and epistemological.

Hume's critique of appeals to the miraculous, as these appeals are standardly made by apologists, is the proper and major starting point, not only because of its many modern supporters,[2] but because consideration of it will lead on to and greatly shorten the task of assessing those others who have written about the miraculous, making Humean points without necessarily affirming that they are Humean; yet others often transpose parts of Hume's argument so that themes from Hume's case can play important parts in their own systems. In the cases of, for example, Bradley and Troeltsch, these are systems of thought which are significantly different from Hume's but a fair appraisal of Hume will go far towards enabling fair assessments of these later writers, and what is distinctive of them can receive specific attention in due course. Accordingly, Hume's celebrated and notorious views must now be assessed.

At one place, Hume's language perhaps suggests that what he is arguing against are unjustifiably large claims for an apologetic appeal to miracle reports. He defines his aim as being to show 'that a miracle can never be *proved*, so as to be the *foundation* of a system of religion' (my emphasis). Foundations need to be firm and well-established; so it seems fitting that a foundation of a system of religion should have to be *proved*. However, the occurrence of a miracle obviously could not be proved either by deductive proof (that is, as Hume would say, by showing the relations of ideas), or, since what is in question is a miracle, as a

---

[2] For example, P. H. Nowell-Smith, 'Miracles', *New Essays in Philosophical Theology*, edited by A. Flew and A. MacIntyre, London, 1955, pp. 243f.; A. Flew, *Hume's Philosophy of Belief*, London, 1961, Ch. 8; Mackie, *The Miracle of Theism*, Ch. 1.

matter of natural necessity; so, although his usage elsewhere suggests these as the standard types of proof, both the impossibility in relation to miracles of these kinds of proof, and the rest of what he says here, indicate that a miracle will be proved in Hume's view if it is shown to be worthy of belief according to standards of reasonableness. Hume's central discussion of wise men's weighing of the evidence in the determining of their beliefs is concerned about the wise coming to have reasonable beliefs, rather than about their perhaps coming to have proof in Hume's more exact and exacting sense. If Hume had meant to assess the prospects of a proof of miracles, in his more particular conceptions of proof, he could and surely would have taken a much shorter way with the issue.

Early in his discussion Hume sets out his principle for the evaluation of belief as reasonable. While it is unsatisfactory as it is set out, it can be amended so as not to destroy Hume's argument, his check on superstition, over beliefs about putative miracles. If we are confronted by a report that an event which is widely interpreted as a miracle has happened, such as the report that Jesus Christ walked on the water, and we wish to know whether it is reasonable to believe the report, Hume proposed that we weigh the evidence for walking on the water's having occurred against the evidence that nothing of the sort occurred, our assent being given to that side of the question for which there is the greater weight of evidence. Hume says, '. . . when we discover a superiority on any side, we incline to it, but still with a diminution of assurance, in proportion to the force of its antagonist'.

Now, as a proposal in what is commonly called 'the ethics of belief', or as a proposal about the evaluation of beliefs, that is unsatisfactory. It is surely not the case that we ought to believe that for which there is, in some question, simply *somewhat* stronger evidence than for its 'antagonist', nor that a belief based on *somewhat* stronger evidence than its 'antagonist' can claim to be assessed as rational. Mackie says that Hume oversimplifies, and that we must judge not only where the preponderance of evidence is, but also how secure this judgement is (for example, whether new information or better hypotheses are likely). Yet he does not question the rightness of believing on the side on which there is a secure preponderance of firm evidence. However, where there is a small preponderance of the evidence on one side, perhaps against a still substantial weight of evidence on the other, the person who forms no belief and has no assurance whatever about where the truth lies is surely not always obviously to be faulted for that? Moreover, there may well be cases where the secure evidence on one side is very much weightier than that on the other, and seems likely to remain so, but where the issue is still not beyond reasonable doubt, perhaps because there is some firm evidence on the weaker, lighter side of the balance, evidence which is hard to set aside. In such a case, once more the person, perhaps a juryman or historian, who is aware of all of this evidence and its weight will not have to *believe* on the side which the evidence favours in order to be reasonable. Suspensions of belief may well be more appropriate. So, insofar as Hume and Mackie are offering a proposal in either the ethics of belief or the evaluation of belief, what they say is defective.

However, Hume's purpose is to put a check, a block, in the way of supposing that belief in miracles could be reasonable. For that he does not need to develop a view about what will be *sufficient* for rational belief; if he sets out some condition which is necessary for rational belief, and then shows that a miracle report could not satisfy that necessary condition, his aim will be achieved. In particular, Hume's ends will be served if it is agreed that where evidence on each side of an issue is weighed, our acceptance of some claim will be reasonable only if there is a preponderance of evidence in favour of the claim. Whatever might be said further about belief-evaluation (and more might well be said), it is possible to proceed on the basis of acceptance of this as a necessary condition for reasonable believing, and to turn to the main arguments against Hume's principal claims.

His reasoning leads up to the, for him, decisive point that it will never be reasonable, on his condition for reasonable believing, to believe a report of a proposed miracle because the huge weight of evidence in favour of the law of nature which the putative miracle would violate will outweigh, or at least will not be outweighed by, the evidence for the putative miracle.

The target for Hume's attack is, as has been said, the apologist who sets out to supply a rational basis for a system of religion by appealing to miracle reports. This apologist can presuppose no assumed or previously established beliefs in a god, or gods, or other spirits. It is important to bear that in mind since some opponents of Hume have insisted that on theistic assumptions Hume's way of evaluating reports of alleged miracles is quite unsatisfactory because he fails to recognise how theistic assumptions will affect the assessment of credibility of a reported putative miracle. Paley is a particularly clear case. He said

Mr. Hume states the case of miracles to be a contest of opposite improbabilities, that is to say, a question whether it be more improbable that the miracle should be true, or the testimony false; and this I think a fair account of the controversy. But herein I remark a want of argumentative justice, that, in describing the improbability of miracles, he suppresses all those circumstances of power, and disposition of the Deity; his concern in the creation, the end answered by the miracle, the importance of that end, and its subserviency to the plan pursued in the work of nature. As Mr. Hume has represented the question, miracles are alike incredible to him who is previously assured of the constant agency of a Divine Being, and to him who believes that no such being exists in the universe.[3]

Paley is not alone in noticing that theistic assumptions, even of a less full, orthodox character than his own (he assumes all of the following: the power and benevolence of the deity, and the existence of a future state about which God will wish to inform us) would require the modification of what Hume says. Among them are Mill and Mackie who generally strongly support what Hume actually says.[4] What Paley urges might be directed, to some purpose, against those modern believers in God who have accepted Hume's conclusions, that reports of miracles are not credible, as if, notwithstanding their theism they are compelled in reason to concur with Hume's argumentation. Yet as a rejoinder to Hume himself, Paley's remarks have no force. That is because Hume intends specifically to consider whether the apologist, whose non-believing audience makes no theistic

[3] Paley, *Evidences of Christianity*, *Works* p. 229. More recently C. S. Lewis has made the same criticism of Hume: *Miracles*, p. 123.
[4] J. S. Mill, *A System of Logic*, London, Book III, Ch. 25, para. 2.

assumptions, can make a case for his religious system by appealing to reported proposed miracles. As has been fully shown in Chapter 4, Hume thinks that no such case can be made.

There could be stronger or weaker anti-Hume contentions: the strongest would be to hold that a quite decisive certain proof of God's existence and attributes can be founded on reports of miracles, so that miracles provide sufficient 'foundation' for a well-established system of religion. At the other extreme, the weakest or minimalist, contention would maintain that an appeal to reports of proposed miracles could give some reason (whether sufficient or not) for belief in the existence and action of a god, by contributing some probability to a religious system. It will be argued, in what follows, that Hume's check on belief in miracles is unwarranted, that the argument which he gives as his warrant is fallacious, and at least that the minimalist contention has not been shown to be mistaken by anything Hume says. The critique of Hume is therefore no mere tinkering or nit-picking but, with the discrediting and the removal of Hume's check on all such argument, it thoroughly clears the way to the renewed consideration and possible re-employment of an apologetic which comes out of a long Christian tradition of argument.[5]

To effect the refutation of Hume, his weaknesses must be accurately identified. It will be argued *inter alia* that at a vital stage Hume apparently assumes what is at stake, what is in dispute between the disputants. Both Paley and C. S. Lewis have accused Hume of question-begging; but it is not their contention which is decisive. Indeed, that argument of theirs is unsound, and before turning to the strong anti-Hume case, it is necessary to see why the arguments of Paley and Lewis are ineffective.

Paley says about Hume's attitude to some contested report of a supposed miracle, '. . . to state concerning the fact in question, that no such thing was *ever* experienced, or that *universal*

[5] Recent writers, even those most critical of Hume, such as Brian Davies, *An Introduction to the Philosophy of Religion*, Oxford, 1993, or Swinburne, *The Concept of Miracle*, do not overthrow the argument which is offered in support of Hume's check, Hume's essential thwarting of the apologist.

experience is against, is to assume the subject of the contro-versy'.[6] In similar vein, Lewis takes the phrase 'uniform experience' in Hume to refer to all experiences of events of the kind in question, including the experience of whatever, if anything, actually happened to originate the reports of a putative miracle. He remarks, '. . . we must agree with Hume that if there is absolutely "uniform experience" against miracles, if in other words they have never happened, why then they never have. Unfortunately we know the experience against them to be uniform only if we know that all the reports of them are false.'[7]

Paley and Lewis take it, apparently, that Hume regards a law of nature as describing what actually happens in its field, such that there can be no exceptions to a natural law. Hume's argument, taken this way, would be that a law of nature is based on uniform invariable experience, and can allow of no excep-tions if it is to *be* a natural law. Already, in the defence of Hume's definition of miracle, it emerged that he cannot be understood in the Paley/Lewis way, or it would be by definition that there are no miracles. Hume's argument against the credibility of re-ported miracles does not simply explore the implications of his definition, to reach his conclusion; so Paley and Lewis have not engaged with Hume's actual argument.

That argument of Hume's takes the controversial reported occurrence and asks what it is reasonable to suppose has happened in that case, when all experience of other occurrences in relevantly similar circumstances is alike in differing from what is controversially reported. Hume thinks that this weight of, as it were, unanimous experience in accordance with natural law should be weighed against any evidence that there may be that the occurrence was of some other sort than that which is generally experienced. This procedure involves no implicit assumption (included in the premises as an entailment of the natural law) that the contested occurrence was also of the sort generally experienced in those kinds of circumstances; rather, that is likely, as Hume thinks, to be the *conclusion* of an inference.

[6] Paley, *Works*, p. 298.   [7] C. S. Lewis, *Miracles*, p. 123.

If we should speculate, or wonder, what took place or will take place in a particular instance – about which we are uncertain – of a kind of situation, we do move in thought from what is usually experienced in that kind of situation to conclude that what is usually experienced is thereby the likelier to have occurred in the case of which we are uncertain. Nor is the instance about which we are uncertain arbitrarily or unjustifiably excluded from the description of what is usually experienced in such cases. Rather it is the problematical case which must be judged by the *rest* of our relevant experience. If Hume is mistaken in applying that mode of reasoning to possible miracles, it is not because he requires to assume, as an entailment of the natural law, that no miracle happened, nor because he improperly excludes the problematic case, that of the putative miracle, from his descriptive law about what is generally experienced in like cases. Rather, he is engaged in an inductive inference with respect to a problematic case, and the argument of Paley and Lewis does not expose any flaw in this procedure; Paley and Lewis seem not to recognise that this is Hume's procedure.

CHAPTER 9

Hume's case tested – 1

In the previous chapter, fault was found with Hume's contention that a person is justified in believing what has simply a better-than-evens probability of being true. That defect in the development of Hume's case about how people should assess reports of miracles was easily repaired so that his conclusions are not affected. However, other of his contentions about the proper weighing-up of evidence for or against putative miracles are more seriously flawed, and in such ways as to leave his conclusions baseless.

The evidence for a supposed miracle's having happened is mainly, or (usually) entirely, the report which has come down to us, for example that Jesus walked on the water. Its strength or weight will depend on the character and/or interests of those people whose report it was, and on how the report has been transmitted to us; and the sorts of factors which Hume discusses in the second part of 'Of Miracles' will have to be considered. So if it were to be shown that some sceptically inclined people, such as the apostle Thomas seems to have been, were at all responsible for originating the report or for investigating it at an early stage of its currency, then we would have one of the factors which Hume sets out, in the early paragraphs of Part II of 'Of Miracles', as serving to give the report weight. On the other hand, if the report originates amongst undiscriminating credulous people and reports an occurrence which happened at such a time and place as makes it difficult for discriminating enquirers, at that time or later, to check it out, then these circumstances of its origin render the report weaker than it would be if it had first been made by sceptical cosmopolitan sophisticates, and concerned an event which was, in the relevant way, public.

What is to be set against this evidence, this strong or not-so-strong report that the putative miracle occurred? As Hume conceives of the necessary weighing-up, we are not to counter this report principally and most weightily by adducing reports of other people who were present at the time of the alleged walking on water. Such people might claim to have seen whatever it was that took place, or deny that it was a walking on the water, or deny that anyone can be confident about what actually happened because of the overall circumstances: perhaps it was misty; maybe there was reason to think that the boat was off course and/or near a place where there was a known sandbank stretching out, a long finger or promontory, just beneath the surface of the water.

That sort of counter-evidence is not often the sort of counter-evidence which is available, to be weighed against the report; and even if it is available it will not constitute the huge and decisive evidential tonnage against such a report's ever being credible which Hume claims, as his main point, to be able to place in the balance. Rather, what is available, and is to be set against the report of the putative miracle is: all the evidence which exists in support of the laws of nature allegedly violated. In this case there will be substantiation of Archimedes' Principle, together with much *data* about the density of adult human bodies. That, and the evidence which is like it – (1) in not being evidence claiming to derive from eyewitnesses of the circumstances in which the putative miracle is alleged to have happened, and (2) in being evidence for laws of nature – is what has to be put on the scale and weighed against the evidence for an occurrence of a putative miracle, according to Hume, in Part I of the essay. Hume goes on to argue that when this weighing-up takes place the evidence for the putative miracle cannot prevail.

In these same pages Hume also offers a distinguishable further thesis by which he claims to appeal to experience, and by which he seeks to reinforce his conclusion. This thesis relates the likelihood that a report is true to the probability of (the occurrence of) the kind of event which is the subject of the report. Specifically, Hume contends that if an event would in itself and as judged by experience, be very improbable, so also will it be very improbable that a report of that event will be true. Hence, because a miraculous event by its nature as a miracle would be exceedingly improbable, any report of a miracle is exceedingly unlikely to be true. This is Hume's subsidiary argument.

In the critique which follows it will be contended that in the pleading of his case Hume is in error in two important ways, and that the exposure of these errors destroys his case. He is at fault, it will be claimed, in holding: (a) that the evidence for the relevant law(s) of nature is, in the overall dialectical context, undeniably relevant to an assessment of the probability (or improbability) that a reported putative miracle actually took place; (b) that the improbability of an event of some particular sort (setting aside, for this probability-reckoning, the event's having been reported and any features or aspects of its having been reported), simply as that sort of event, itself determines the probability of the truth of an actual report of the event. In this chapter, (a) will be examined; in the next chapter, scrutiny will fall on (b).

As to (a), by 'the overall dialectical context' is meant the context of this debate between a religious apologist and his undecided interlocutor, as they discuss whether some report(s) that a putative miracle has occurred give(s) rational support to the view that a god has acted in the course of events. Consider the case of the reported walking on the water by which an apologist wishes (let us suppose) to support his case. In the overall dialectical context, will evidence for Archimedes' Principle, and evidence that the density of any human body is close to 1, be relevant without question, as Hume assumes that it will, in considering whether the miracle happened?

The problem is this: the adducing of some observations which support Archimedes' Principle, and of others which support generalisations about the density of the human body, as pertinent evidence in the matter of whether Jesus walked on the water, depends on our excluding, at the outset of the evidence-weighing, the possibility that a god may on occasion order or bring about, and particularly on this occasion may have ordered or brought about, events which run counter to our general experience of nature. Suppose that there is any reason to think, or even to consider the possibility, that a god has, on the occasion reported, so acted that generally obtaining patterns in events do not, on that occasion, obtain. On this supposition, a body of evidence, however vast, in favour of Archimedes' Principle and in favour of human bodies always having a density between 0.8 and 1.2, cannot without further argument be taken as relevant to deciding the question of whether on the reported occasion Jesus walked on the water. Perhaps the usual run of events, for which evidence for natural laws would be good evidence, has been departed from. So Hume reaches his conclusion that evidence for a supposed miracle will always be overriden because it will never outweigh the large body of (as Hume sees it) undeniably relevant evidence in favour of natural law, only by *assuming* that no god has acted miraculously in such a way as to produce an event of a kind contrary to natural law. Yet, obviously, the apologist is not bound to recognise that assumption as necessary or well-founded. Hume's check appears to lack a firm anchorage.

Hume seems some of the time to have held that no putative-miracle-report can emerge which is not at least as satisfactorily explained by concluding that it is a species of error (exaggeration, pious invention, misunderstanding maybe) as it is explained by saying that it takes its rise from, and recounts, actual events. Because human experience provides a direct and full proof of natural laws and therefore, in Hume's view, against miracles whose occurrence would violate these laws, the strongest possible evidence for a miracle, being also a direct and full proof, could only at best equal that against. Many writers, including it appears Hume himself, have judged that in so saying Hume overstates. These writers, and the self-amending Hume, say that there could theoretically be natural laws for which, as support for natural laws goes, comparatively little evidence exists and for whose violation there is a huge weight of very powerful evidence, which may outweigh the evidence for the natural law which is allegedly violated.

Yet even on this Hume-amended standpoint, it remains his view that all actual putative-miracle reports will only be rationally believable, only explainable as recounting the facts, if their falsehood would be more miraculous than what they report. The need for a putative miracle-report to surmount that barrier, be unhindered by Hume's check, if it is to be accounted for, and accepted, as recounting facts, makes it immensely unlikely that the proper account and explanation of the occurrence of a putative miracle-report is that it recounts the facts, and makes its explanation as some species of error or insincerity, or as not to be taken as *intending* to state facts, immensely likely. However, the exposure of Hume's unjustified assumption, as the flaw in his reasoning which it is, takes that high barrier out of the way, removes Hume's check.

Whether the fault in the Humean course of argument is strictly a begging of the question will depend on what, exactly, 'the question' is. However, it is obvious that where theism is in dispute, the constellation of arguments, in Part 1 of Hume's 'Essay on Miracles', to establish that it is not reasonable to believe a report that a violation of natural law has occurred such as to invite a theistic explanation was largely redundant if one of the assumptions necessary for the success of the argument is that there is no god who works miracles, or, at least, that on an occasion which is in question no miracle occurred. It is obvious also that those whom Hume addresses, people who are considering whether in assessing religious claims they should give credence to putative miracle-reports reporting anomalous events whose best or only explanation will be theistic or deistic, will surely not make this assumption, because if they do there is no point in their evaluating putative miracle-reports as possible grounds for theism. For people who do make this assumption, the principal argument of Hume's essay, that in Part 1, will be unnecessary, while for those who do not make it the argument has no force.

Defenders of Hume may think that all this is to take too short a way with Hume's argument, that it fails to see the underlying strength of what Hume says. Two lines of Humean defence, or counter-attack, must be considered. The apologist's own dependence on inductive reasoning if he is to bring forward evidence for the occurrence of a miracle prompts the first line of counter-attack. If inductive reasoning, using experience as guidance, may be rendered unreliable by the actual or possible extraordinary action of a god, how can the apologist argue that a miracle has happened by arguing inductively from evidence? Inductive argumentation will be unreliable if the course of nature is subject to god-wrought irregularity. The second line of counter-attack asks what reason anyone, apologist or religious enquirer, could have and could appeal to as a ground for supposing that a violation of natural law might have taken place, without their having assumed some part of the religious system already; maybe it is not Hume who begs the questions here? If an apologist brings 'reason to think . . . that a god has . . . acted' (above p. 134) to the assessment of putative-miracle reports, then the assessment is not, it seems, being carried out from a neutral stance so as to reasonably convince a religiously uncommitted enquirer. It will be the apologist or his defender, rather than a Humean, who is failing to respect the dialectical context. This is the Humean's second counter-claim. These pro-Hume lines of thought can be taken in turn.

In his own writings Hume brought it out that in order to be able to assess and then rely on any evidence or testimony, we have to take it that experience is a reliable guide: it is by our experience that we assess the likelihood that events of one particular kind (such as a particular kind of person, X, reporting Y) are or were accompanied or preceded by events of another particular kind (such as the event Y which the X-type person reported). In particular, the theistic apologist who must place reliance on evidences, including the reporting, of miracles must assume that experience is a trustworthy guide; he must, that is, rely on inductive reasoning. Whether he is arguing that some miracle is strongly attested or, it may be, investigating, as Roman Catholic authorities do, some claim that a miracle has occurred, he must trust induction. This being so, the apologist has a problem. If there is 'the possibility that a god has . . . so acted that generally obtaining patterns in events do not, on that occasion, obtain', (above p. 134) then it appears that we never can rely on the recurrence of any generally experienced correlations. That is we cannot, apparently, put any trust in inductive reasoning. Thus, the notion of 'being evidence for . . .' will, seemingly, be useless. Appeals to evidence, then, seem to require the assumption that there is no miracle-working god. In order to launch his apologetic, the apologist who appeals to putative miracles must exclude that which he is setting out to establish; for, if he allows the possibility of a miracle-working god, he will undermine inductive reasoning and render useless the (for him essential) concept of 'being evidence for . . .'. So, at any rate, says the defender of Hume. Accordingly he will say that neither the apologist who appeals to miracle-reports, nor the Church authority looking into claimed miracles, recognises the dilemma which faces them: either inductive reasoning is consistently applicable, in which case a god cannot be supposed to have brought about events which transgress the usual course of nature, or inductive reasoning cannot be generally relied upon, in which case no apologetic appeal to miracles or Church investigation into reports of miracles, can proceed because no appeal to evidence will be possible. Is the dilemma inescapable? Is this line of defence of Hume cogent?

On an exegetical and *ad hominem* tack the critic of Hume can, as a first response, reiterate that the foregoing can only be thought of as Hume's own argument if Hume was confused about, and uneconomical in setting out, what he was proposing. His discussion of evidence-weighing (of balancing probabilities on the basis of experienced correlations, and of the overwhelming weight of evidence (in the nature of the case) against a report of a violation of natural law) is unnecessary if, on the one hand, any effective adducing of evidence for anything whatever and, on the other, entertaining the possibility of a miracle-working god, are mutually exclusive. The apologist could have been dismissed on this ground without any reference to the weighing against one another of evidence pro and con.

However, the case for the defence of Hume which was sketched above is suggested by what Hume says, and the important issue is not the existence, nature and extent of Hume's shortcomings in clear conception or exposition of his view, how far he may have been confused or uneconomical, but the strength of the best defence case possible. Accordingly, the issues brought out by this renewed Humean argument must now be addressed.

If we do suppose it possible that an invisible agent may at any time or place disrupt the regular, patterned character of events in nature, and if we further suppose it possible that these disturbances of the even tenor of nature's way may be capricious or random, or perhaps systematically designed to mislead us, then the notion of 'being evidence for . . .' will be useless; and we can never, on these suppositions, argue for miraculous intervention of such a being on the basis of evidence or testimony. Equally, if the mind of a miracle-working agent is supposed to be wholly inscrutable to us, possible exceptions to nature's normal course will be capricious or random from our point of view, and once more we will be unable to put any trust in an argument which rests on evidence. (Indeed, if the truth-acquiring capacity of our minds depends on the workings of our physical organisms (especially our brains) according to regular patterns, we shall, on these suppositions of possible capricious or inscrutable intervention, be unable to trust any argument whatever.) If the only alternative possibility to the altogether consistently law-conforming universe is a universe whose processes may be altered at any time by a capricious or wholly inscrutable spirit so as to disrupt the regular pattern, the defence case for Hume would be successful.

Descartes, of course, entertained the thought that our cognitive (or would-be-cognitive) endeavours might be being controlled or affected by an evil demon; whether or not we think that Descartes' argument to eliminate this possibility is sound, we have to proceed with our reflections about any matters whatever on the assumption that no evil demon does influence our truth-seeking enterprises. Unless we discount the possibility of an active evil demon who acts upon the world and/or upon us, we must abandon all scientific, historical, philosophical or other enquiries after truth because we cannot rely on apparent evidential or conceptual connexions about any of these matters. The following are (correlative) presuppostions of our practices of investigation: (1) that the world is such that true and trustworthy beliefs about it are possible for us, and (2) either that God is no deceiver and that he will not permit demons to deceive us, or (if there is no god) that the universe produces and maintains in us such faculties as can form and recognise true, reliable beliefs about the universe. Even if only as presuppositions of practices in which we find ourselves impelled to participate, rather than propositions for which we can find independent rational support, we must maintain these presuppositions in all our enquiries. In particular we shall have to maintain them if we are evaluating a report that a putative miracle has occurred. So, to the extent that the case for the defence of Hume is asserting this point, all must accept it. However, does acceptance of those presuppositions of the practice of enquiry eliminate all possibility of a rational investigation's concluding that a putative miracle has occurred?

Suppose that a god, having no intention to deceive, has acted so that an event has occurred contrary to the usual patterning of nature's processes. This anomalous event is not intended, nor need it have even the tendency, to confuse or deceive us because it is obviously enough made to occur only so as to endorse the god's prophet, or signal the import of significant events.

The endorsement of the prophet may well be the sufficiently obvious point of this putative miracle if, say (1) there are other well-attested reports of supposed miracles associated with the same prophet; (2) his teaching is found, when closely considered and when attempts are made to practise it, to illuminate and open up possibilities for human life and society which are new, and enriching, as judged by the admirable criteria of the prophet himself; (3) the content of the miracle, what is actually done, accords with the prophet's teaching in striking ways so that for him to work the miracle is for him strikingly to practise what he preaches.

The signalling of the import of events may be the obvious point of a supposed miracle if these events fulfil long-held hopes about what God will accomplish in his good purpose and if the supposed miracle strikingly exemplifies what the community expects as a sign of the awaited events, or even what the community has asked for as sign and forerunner of the anticipated fulfilment.

Although putative miracles like these would *ex hypothesi* be contrary to natural law, their obvious intention and purport sets them apart from the merely random, capricious or inscrutable. Putative miracles like these will be events which are neither law-confirming nor quite unintelligibly, inquiry-destroyingly, anomalous; examples like these serve to introduce a third possibility; this is the possibility which the critic of Hume wishes us to note. Once the existence and nature of this third possibility is grasped (and a review of theologians who have advanced it surely makes it easier to grasp) it becomes clear that even though the universe may turn out to be not altogether law-confirming, still, on this third possibility, the presuppositions of the practice of enquiry may nevertheless be maintained. Those regularities upon which we depend in order to assess evidence can be assumed to hold good notwithstanding the occurrence of some transgressions of natural law. Why? Because the god-intended import of these few extraordinary transgressions will readily be recognisable; and the recognition of that import removes any reason to question the presuppositions of the practice of enquiry. An event which is clearly seen by all to transgress natural law is not, by the fact of its anomalousness alone, bound to deceive or confuse people about what the natural law is because they may be aware of the third possibility; and if its point in the purpose of God towards us is seen, not only suspected or speculated about but confidently grasped, then the anomalous event leaves us with no ground for a general fear of the kind of incomprehensible disturbances of nature's usual course which would undermine the presuppositions for, and the possibility of, rational investigation.

If the apologist's view about the purpose of putative miracles is possible, the existence of violations of natural law, or their possibility, will not (it has now been argued) necessitate the abandonment of all inductive reasonings. Nevertheless, inductive reasoners will require to be cautious. They will have to consider whether, in any case which interests them, and about which they attempt to reason, there are any *prima facie* reasons to suspect that violations may have occurred. *Prima facie* reasons would be the existence of hypotheses, about a divine purpose, which are promising-looking, for such reasons as these: (1) because they fit well with what is known about the history of the times apart from any alleged instances of violations of natural law; (2) because they accord with promising-looking interpretations of other reported associated violations; (3) because, and crucially in addition to (1) and (2), they offer to explain why in its circumstances the anomalous event might well occur; a promising-looking hypothesis will provide a rationale for the occurrence of the putative miracle and, so, for the existence of reports of the miracle. Nevertheless, since in this, the apologist's view of the way in which nature's patterned regularity should be understood, natural processes *are* characteristically, usually, patterned in a consistent way, it will still be appropriate generally to trust inductive reasoning which is carried out with proper caution (that is, not having thoughtlessly dismissed any likelihood which might present itself that a god has for his own purposes acted anomalously in the case at hand). The defender of Hume is therefore unjustified when he claims that any possibility of there being a violation of natural law must rule out all value or trustworthiness in inductive reasoning.

Relatedly, it is not only a Christian belief of long standing that it is the same god who upholds nature's ordered course who also works miracles. Reflection on the way by which miracles are usually supposed to serve their purposes discloses that it will only be against the background of a general orderliness that the exceptional, miraculous event can serve its purpose. This further underlines that the apologist's suggested alternative to the Humean conception of the Universe's unvarying orderliness as a brute natural fact is (not that there is no reliable order, but rather) the competing hypothesis about a characteristically order-giving yet occasionally miracle- working god, sketched above. So, once again, there is plainly no need to fear that rejection of Hume's view must lead to abandonment of arguing from experience and analogy, about nature and history. Unless we have reason to think that some divine purpose may be being served by the violation of nature's usual patterns, we may assume uniformity, the apologist with no less justification than the Humean.

Furthermore, the reasoning within theistic hypotheses about what divine purposes may be being served by particular miracles will draw on our understanding of intelligent (human) motivation. That is, we shall, here, still be reasoning by analogy, from experience. As in every analogical argument, there are differences (in this case where we move from man to God) between the analogates. Yet it *is* by analogy, and by appealing to experience, that the theistic hypothesis proceeds, in its attempt to account for strong, weighty reports of putative miracles. So the difference between Hume, on the one hand, and the anti-Humean who wishes to advance theistic hypotheses to account for (probably *inter alia*) reports of putative miracles, on the other, is not that the former appeals to experience and analogy as guides to what we should believe while the latter rejects these utterly. The dispute between them is over how analogy and experience are properly employed. Certainly it is a confused misrepresentation by the Humean to argue that our giving up a picture in which the world's unvarying regularity is given or assumed requires a self-destructive abandonment of all rational criteria, which require an appeal to experience, for the assessment of evidence.

The long-standing Christian belief is, as was pointed out earlier, that the same God who gives and maintains nature's usual regular order is also, on occasion, responsible for miraculous departures from that usual course. The awareness that this is the apologist's viewpoint should, as was also pointed out, surely have alerted defenders of Hume that the alternatives in the dilemma which they pose to the apologist are not exhaustive: either a wholly consistently natural-law-conforming universe, or a universe whose sequence of events is, to us, random, capricious and unreliable. Maybe those who argue on the basis that these are the only alternatives do so because their thinking is shaped, perhaps without their recognising it, by their atheism. If atheism is presupposed, and nature is supposed to be ordered, the order which is possessed by natural processes will be, presumably, a brute inexplicable fact about the world, that is, a fact which cannot be known to depend on any other, or prior, fact. On atheistic presuppositions, if the course of nature were not ordered there would be no basis for any reasonable view about the character or extent of the disorder, or order, no way of understanding any rationale for whatever order or lack of it there turned out to be. On this latter view inductive reasoning, reasoning which appeals to experience, will be of quite unknown worth, will be quite unreliable.

E. J. Craig has suggested that often in technical and/or closely analytical philosophical work a broad world-picture, a Philosophy, with capital P, is articulated or defended even when the analytical philosopher himself hardly realises the relevance of the wider picture to his close reasoning. Sometimes, Craig observes, the complex and ramified defence of the world-picture arrives at its conclusion without satisfying those who do not share the Weltbild. Craig says '. . . it is repeatedly found that content smuggled in from the Weltbild itself is somehow assisting the passage to the conclusion'. This can happen, for example, by his world picture's 'helping a thinker to overlook an alternative which, once seen, is damaging to the cogency of his line of thought'.[1] Whether or not the present overlooking of the opposing alternative which is proposed by the religious apologist is an example in Humean thinking of these tendencies for whose existence Craig convincingly argues, the apologist's alternative *is* suppressed in such a way as might well be attributed to an implicit but illicit assumption of atheism.

More than that, the Humean's underlying atheistic world picture may also have its effect on his thinking when he assumes the indisputable relevance of evidence for the allegedly violated natural law to the issue of whether a miracle happened. If there is no god, the possibility of a god's so acting that there is a departure from nature's usual course can be discounted. Craig speaks of the illegitimate prompting of suppressed premisses as a further way by which Weltbilder question-beggingly assist arguments in their own support. Yet the context of a genuine debate about Weltbilder in which atheism is not common

---

[1] Craig, *The Mind of God and the Works of Man*, p. 3.

ground between contestants, but is disputed, does not permit atheistic assumptions to be made, nor infiltrated, simply because of their being atheistic.

The foregoing full consideration of the first of the two lines of defence of Hume[2] opens the way to a clearer view of the matters which are raised by the second, and in particular to a better grasp of the character or structure of the argument between apologist and uncommitted enquirer.

The defender of Hume has been responding to the charge that Hume's procedure in evidence-weighing improperly rules out the possibility that God might have brought about a violation of nature's usual course. By treating evidence for the natural law as unquestionably relevant to the issue of the occurrence of a miracle, Hume is accused of assuming something which is at issue in the controversy. However, if certain of the conclusions of inductive reasoning are, as the apologist now insists, to be suspended or set aside because there is 'good reason' for thinking that God may have brought about a violation of nature's normal course, the defender of Hume now wishes to know what 'good reason' there could be which would not beg the question on the apologist's side. Hume's advocate agrees that in the debate between an apologist and an uncommitted enquirer neither party may introduce, as if they were agreed premises, matters which are in dispute between them. The enquirer or unbeliever whom the apologist addresses has no religious commitment and requires to be persuaded that a miracle might provide support for a religious system. Yet the apologist is now portrayed as introducing some factor as a reason for thinking that a god might have worked a miracle, as if this factor should be recognised, accepted by the unbeliever or enquirer who as yet has in fact no convictions whatever about religious systems, and is considering what might provide some supportive foundation for a religious system.

The 'foundation' terminology, which is Hume's own terminology, points to the likely conception, as Hume and his defender conceive of it (at least much of the time), of the

---

[2] As identified above at pp. 131–3 of the present chapter.

structure of the apologist's case: first a foundation has to be established presupposing no part of the religious system, requiring nothing which is in dispute to support it. Then, with that foundation block, that premiss firmly in place, something can be built on it, derived from it, together no doubt with other premisses. The apologist, if he is to succeed, is expected to establish the occurrence of a violation of natural law as a well-based foundation block; the occurrence of this putative miracle will then require to be explained, and the apologist will offer an explanation in terms of the action and purpose of God. That, at least, is what is required of him. It is essential to this conception, in particular, that the foundation block is well established without any appeal to any part of a religious system. Non-religious examples can be given, easily enough, of enquiries which reckon with a firm *datum* and move from it, to try to explain it. Suppose that five sober men of good sense are fishing in the sea from a small boat, on a calm evening, two miles out from land. Some forty yards away from them there erupts from the surface of the water a cloudy spout of vaporous water. The column takes several seconds to rise and fall; all five men see it, and one of them is able to photograph it. The fact of the spout is well established. If after enquiry the further premiss can be added that only a whale could cause such an occurrence, the well-founded proposition that the spout happened provides a foundation for the conclusion that there was a whale in these waters. Hume appears to think that the apologist aims in parallel fashion to establish the occurrence of a putative miracle sufficiently firmly to provide a foundation for belief in God.

On this construction, we certainly cannot increase our estimate of the probability that the seeming miracle did happen by arguing, Paley-like, that given God's purposes and character God is likely to have worked such a miracle, without our assuming something which is in question. Hume's defender would be quite correct to object to such question-begging. The argument can be represented in the following schema in respect of logical form, for purposes of logical appraisal, and maybe in respect of the order of coming to know (or recall or recognise), that is, in respect of the epistemic sequence of events:

p; (the well-established foundation)
p only if q; hence q.

If, in order sufficiently firmly to establish p, the supposed
foundation for the argument, it is necessary to be able to affirm
q, or to affirm probably -q, (in the apologist's reasoning the
substitute for q would be: there is a god who may be expected to
act in p-like ways in the circumstances in which p occurred) then
the final conclusion of the argument has not been established on
the basis of p. Rather, the argument is circular.

There are, however, other kinds of enquiry where the
character of what first presents itself is not so certain. A primary
datum may have features about which we are not sure but which
importantly affect the proper interpretation of the *datum*. In
regard to an issue like this, it will be difficult to say which, if any,
propositions should be regarded as premiss(es) relative to some
other proposition which is the conclusion; moreover the truth,
or the likelihood, of some one of these propositions will often not
be established independently of the likelihood or truth of
another of these propositions. There is nothing disreputable
about all of this where, as in the following example, what is
being argued for is an account whose component parts (propositions) taken together make best sense of a range of *data*.

Suppose that a man is seen at 02.00 hours hurrying down the
street and into a car in which he drives speedily away. He is seen
by a couple who each independently are fairly confident that the
man is one Gordon Allan; but they are puzzled as to why he
should be in this industrial part of town, when he lives and works
miles away. The fire brigade comes by shortly afterwards to
fight a warehouse fire nearby. The couple read in next day's
newspaper that the warehouse belongs to William Allan and
Co., and they think 'William' was the name of a brother of
Gordon. One of the couple is a solicitor, and they are able to
discover that Gordon, who has a reputation for less-than-
straightforward practice is a shareholder in William Allan and
Co., a family business which is not prospering. These discoveries
suggest an account of events which would confirm the nocturnal
identification of Gordon Allan, namely that when seen he had

been setting the warehouse on fire, for the insurance money. (If it had further transpired that the warehouse was not insured, that the Allans all knew this and that they were on good terms with one another, the identification would again have become more problematical.) Here is a question, the identification of someone, where what is seen may come to be understood as part of an interpretation involving and making sense of a number of factors taken together. The couple who thought they saw Gordon Allan but were unsure and puzzled had minds open to explanatory interpretations, or further considerations, of the kinds which emerged. That does not mean that they concluded or assumed or believed that Gordon Allan was the torchman who set the warehouse on fire; rather they are open to that possibility, as to others, in trying to establish whether it was Gordon Allen whom they saw. There turns out to be reason to think he may have been an arsonist because there are some facts which fit that interpretation, and so that interpretation comes to be entertained and thought about, perhaps to be believed in due course, perhaps to be rejected. It is at any rate a promising-looking hypothesis. However, 'having reason' in this way to consider an account of something which is problematical (1) does not involve *accepting* that account or even any controversial part of it, prior to considering the account. Also, while it does involve thinking that the account seems, in view of the factors which have so far come to light, to have some probability, it (2) does not involve attaching any firm judgement of determinate probability to the account or to any controversial part of it, prior to evaluating the account taken as a whole. Having a reason to take such an account seriously enough to assess it involves no argumentative circularity.

So, someone who is confronted by a report that nature's usual pattern has been departed from may consider whether the alleged violation might serve some divine purpose, and may go on to think about particular promising-looking explanatory hypotheses to that effect, without *assuming the truth* of any claims about God, without question-begging.

If the fire service say that the fire may have been caused by an electrical fault but that there is no evidence that it actually was so caused, the hypothesis that Gordon Allan lit the blaze, which was promising-looking as soon as it became known whose warehouse it was that went on fire, continues to have promise so long as an accidental explanation (for example, in terms of an electrical fault) of the fire is not rather firmly established. In particular, there does not need to be some judgement of probability that Gordon Allan did it *before* the hypothesis that he was the man who was seen, and that he was a torchman, becomes promising-looking. Rather, tentative identification of him as the person who was seen may well be, for the couple, the leading factor in giving probability to the whole account which identifies Gordon Allan as the torchman. So there need be no *assumption*, even of a probability, that a god has miraculously acted for the apologist to urge that the proposal is promising-looking that a god has acted against nature's usual course. There is no assumption needed even of a probability that there is a god. The proposal that a god has acted miraculously may still be regarded as promising-looking if it would effectively account for a good deal, including a good deal which it is not otherwise easy to account for. The existence of testimony to the putative miracle may be difficult to account for well in any other way, and so may give strength to the apologist's claim to have an at least promising-looking proposal.

Whether a problematical field of enquiry will be explored in one rather than the other of these ways (that illustrated by the case of the spout, and that illustrated by the nocturnal man-in-a-hurry) depends on the evidence or information available to the investigator. Suppose that the couple who saw the nocturnal hurrier had an excellent view of the man, and had taken down the number of the car in which he made off, and that it was Gordon Allan's car and face which they surely saw. Especially if, further, they did not come to know of the warehouse fire (the fire brigade took a different route and the couple did not read the newspapers), the problem becomes more that of explaining a firmly established *datum* than of giving an account of a range of factors, within which a *datum*, whose character is somewhat uncertain, will be explained.

Where an apologist for some religious system appeals to

evidence for a putative miracle, to support the system, his appeal will be more forceful, and his apologetic argument will owe the more to the supposedly miraculous event, the stronger the evidence for the event's occurrence. An understandable concentration on the evidences for the particular events respectively under scrutiny may have helped to encourage some apologists as well as Hume and his supporters to treat the apologetic argument as essentially appealing to a wholly and solidly established *datum* to provide the system's foundation, a *datum* which is, in itself, supposedly proved. Yet once there is a recognition that often the best interpretation of some (piece(s) of) evidence emerges when its place in the most convincing interpretation of a wider range of evidence is seen, and once the relevance of this to apologists' reliance on reports of putative miracles is understood, the way is open to a better grasp of the kinds of argumentation which may be involved. Then it can be seen that exploring proposed interpretations, and having reasons to explore them because they seem to have merits, are perfectly reputable, and require no question-begging assumptions.

Accordingly, the 'having a reason for thinking that God may have acted anomalously' does not necessarily involve the apologist in affirming something, or assuming something, which the non-believer does not accept, and thereby in begging a question that is in dispute between apologist and non-believer. Rather it may be a matter of having a reason for entertaining and investigating a suggestion, a hypothesis, because it seems to fit at least most of the apparently significant factors of which we have information, and so holds out promise of explanatory power. The apologist's suggestion is that a god may, for his own purposes, have acted anomalously; the apologist makes this suggestion because it offers promise of explaining the *data* which have to be reckoned with. His 'reason for thinking that a god may have acted anomalously' is not an intruded, question-begging improper *assumption*, but rather the appearance which the religious system, or that part of it which is relevant to the explanation of reports of putative miracles, presents, of offering, promising or threatening (depending on one's point of view or preference) to account for a good deal which calls for explanation. The reason for pursuing a promising-looking hypothesis may be simply that it is promising-looking, and there need be no assertion or assumption or belief that the hypothesis, or any part or presupposition of it, is true. The apologist whose 'reason' to explore and commend his theistic hypothesis is that sort of reason need not be guilty of making any assumption which the dialectical context rules out, need not be condemned as a question-begger.

CHAPTER 10

Hume's case tested – 2

It is now opportune to look at the second objection to Hume's case, and then to consider further Humean responses to the attempted wholesale elimination of Hume's check.

Hume argued that the improbability of an event, simply as the sort of event it is, is by itself determinative of the probability that a report of that event is true. It is time to examine this issue first for its own sake, but secondarily because at this stage of the enquiry someone might take me to be holding, implausibly, that the fact that it reports something contrary to natural law should never be allowed at all to cast any doubt upon some report that a putative miracle has occurred. As a first step towards a correct view about this question, it is helpful to see that Hume's view is incorrect, and why it is. He holds that the improbability on inductive grounds, of some state of affairs, of itself obviously counts against the likelihood that a report which alleges that that state of affairs has obtained is true. So 'the incredibility of a fact . . . might invalidate so great an authority' (that is, as Cato was).[1]

Might it not be, however, that some people (and Cato perhaps one of them) will take particular care over what they say precisely when what they say seems surprising, questionable or unexpected. Edinburgh solicitors are alleged to be cautious about agreeing, even when flaming June has touched Edinburgh, that it is a fine day; and over points which might possibly be regarded as questionable (if only by the most bizarrely

---

[1] Hume's *Enquiries*, p. 113, or *Of Miracles*, edited by A. Flew, La Salle, Illinois, 1985, p. 29.

ingenious) a categorical statement from an Edinburgh solicitor will be rare. If such a man were to witness a walking on water, we can be sure that he would be carefully circumspect indeed before telling of it. The more *prima facie* unlikely the event, under its obvious descriptions, the more care will be taken by a person of this disposition that any account which he brings himself to give of it is accurate. It is rather likely that among some members of the population more reports of unremarkable, mundane events are erroneous (by reason of carelessness or inattention) than reports of the extraordinary. Edinburgh solicitors in these habits are exhibiting, albeit conspicuously, traits which are found in the human race more widely. (Would Hume himself not have been likely to exhibit them?)

It is therefore clear, now that the above considerations are before us, that Hume is justified in none of the following:

(1) in taking some improbability of some event which is reported, considered apart from the fact of its being reported, as a factor which quite evidently counts towards the improbability of any report of it;

(2) in saying that a report will be very unlikely to be a true report if what is reported is itself, considered apart from the fact of its being reported, very unlikely;

(3) in treating a report's truth as improbable in proportion to the improbability of the kind of event (apart from its reportedness) which is reported. He offers no justification because he seems to think that the thing is obvious. Yet a little care in reflecting about the matter reveals him rather to be obviously wrong.

The point at which Hume slides slack-mindedly from arguing with some cogency that we may assess a report's credibility by weighing those features which are seen to belong to the report under review and which have been associated in our experience with true reports, against those features of the report under review which are generally associated with false reports, occurs on page 113 of the Selby-Bigge, second edition, of Hume's *Enquiries*, and on pages 28–9 of Hume's *Of Miracles*. He has been giving examples of such features, especially (at the end of the previous paragraph) such as have usually been found to belong to false reports: when witnesses are few, of doubtful character, have an interest in the acceptance of what they assert, contradict each other, tell their story too hesitantly, or protesting too much. Then comes the slide. He says 'Suppose, for instance, that the fact which the testimony endeavours to establish, partakes of the extraordinary and the marvellous; in that case, the evidence, resulting from the testimony, admits of a diminution, greater or less, in proportion as the fact is more or less unusual'; and so on.

Now Hume could have continued to reason more soundly if he had continued by treating the improbability of what is reported (taken on its own, and apart from the fact of the reporting) that is, the report's content, as one feature of the report. He should then have asked how, in our experience, a report's having an improbable content correlates with that report's being true. Hume's own view that having an improbable content in itself counts against the report's probability *would* be justified as a conclusion of such an empirical enquiry, if indeed experience were to reveal a correlation between a report's having an improbable content, and that report's being found to be false. However, Hume seems to have thought his view to be self-evident and did not attempt this sort of necessary empirical justification.

A priori it is however impossible to say how far people in general are like the archetypal Edinburgh solicitor, or how far they abandon all discriminatory care, for the pleasures of reporting a 'prodigy'; it is not much easier to determine this *a posteriori*, of course. If we could establish distributions within the human race of degrees of care for, or recklessness about, the truth, where reports of the extraordinary are concerned, that could help us to assess the probability of any one such report, simply *qua* a report made by a human being who reports something extraordinary.[2]

In practice more will usually be known about the testifying human being, which will enable a better estimate to be made of the likelihood that what he says is true. This better estimate will

---

[2] This might well be by establishing the probability that a person falls within a particular range of the spectrum from carelessness to carefulness.

be based on experience of reports of the extraordinary made by people of that particular sort (for example, of a particular culture, or particular education, or as affected for good or ill by others' acceptance of the report). No doubt caution over accepting miracle stories is well justified by the sketchy impressionistic surveys which our random experience makes possible of the human beings who report prodigies, and their backgrounds, characters and dispositions to care for the truth when marvels are recounted. There have been many cases of illusion, hallucination, deception, wishful-thinking, exaggeration and pious fraud where putative miracles have been reported. The fact that a report tells of something which would be contrary to natural law *should* prompt some careful assessment before the report is believed.

However, even such types of more defensible (that is, more defensible than Hume's) reasonings about reports whose content is extraordinary could not provide the general and (in practice) insurmountable difficulty, which Hume is confident that he has produced, for any acceptance of reports of putative miracles. He argues in his unjustified way as he moves towards the conclusion which he seeks; he was perhaps led along (a common human failing) by the attractiveness to him of the thesis he is proposing, but also maybe by the ease with which one can slide from a claim about a state of affairs, S, to the same claim about S-as-reported-by-P, or the report of S by P, as though whatever it is justified to say about S will be justified also of S-as-reported-by-P, or the report of S by P. (A philosophical generation which, post-Frege, is well aware of such distinctions as those between a proposition, on the one hand, and the assertion, or the assertedness of the proposition, or the proposition-having-been-asserted, on the other, has less excuse for following him than Hume had for leading the false way.) In addition, of course, the fact that both of these sorts of arguments, the more defensible and the illicit, can be described, Hume-wise, as appeals to 'experience' does nothing to warn the unwary that they are on slippery ground.

So, where there is a report of an event, and the event would if it occurred run contrary to natural law, that fact about the report (that it reports something which is contrary to natural law) may well have a bearing on our assessment of the report's reliability. Yet the mere fact that what is reported is anomalous will not on its own determine the assessment, as Hume thought it should. Rather that fact, most probably in conjunction with further facts, for example about the disposition or knowledge-ability of the author of the report, may be set against experience of other similar reports of anomalous events. In this way, then, experience can guide the assessment of reports of putative miracles.

We have already looked at defences which are offered against specific attacks upon the Humean view of the reasonable response to reports of putative miracles. Other contentions are likely to be advanced on Hume's behalf and we should consider these, both so that justice may be seen to be done, and so that some truths come to be more clearly seen.

Thus, first, someone might well concede that Hume's argument *appears* to have been shown to be unacceptable by the foregoing discussion, but be reluctant to accept what appears to be the unplausible alternative. This seeming alternative is that one could be justified in holding a theistic world-view on the basis of a report that a single putative miracle has occurred. It is much more likely that, confronted by such a report, the reasonable person should rather look for explanations of the experience of this report which appeal to, for example, the possibility of error over what the natural law is, or to such factors as human gullibility, sensation-mongering, or critical judgement's being set aside by religious enthusiasm, than that she should entertain a religious world-view. Accordingly, it may well be felt that even if Hume's arguments are admittedly, bad, what we should conclude is simply that he has failed to provide an adequate rationale for what seems nevertheless to be the rational view.

For ease of exposition, much of the debate, in this book and elsewhere, has been conducted by discussing the proper response to a report of, or a body of evidence for, some particular putative miracle. It is consequently understandable that the alternatives should come to be thought of as alternative responses to a report of a single miracle, as it were bracketed off from any wider context, and leaving out any other factors which might lend support to a theistic hypothesis. However, as was shown in the previous chapter, what is in question is not whether a strong report of a single putative miracle could alone provide the foundation for a system of religion, a theistic system, but whether a report of a putative miracle may give some support to, contribute some force to, a case for theism.

While Hume's arguments were accepted, there was some justification, *prima facie*, for taking reports of putative miracles one by one, holding of each of them that, because they report violations of natural law they must be unworthy of credence (or be very unlikely to be worthy of credence). They could thus be dispatched one by one. However, having now shown shortcomings in Hume's case, we are free to consider whether reports of putative miracles can contribute to a case for theism and what, if any, their apologetic force could be.

Secondly, it requires to be made plain that, and why, an apologetic which is given force by appealing to reports of putative miracles will not require or presuppose the success of some natural theology (that is, a theology which is supposedly derived by argument from facts about the world which are available to be known by anyone, through observation (as in the case of the Design Argument) or rational reflection (as in the case of the Ontological Argument)). In Section xi of the *First Enquiry*, Hume proceeds from 'Of Miracles' to contend (as he also contends in the *Dialogues Concerning Natural Religion*) that the outcome of the attempted well-known species of natural theology is at best so exceedingly tenuous as to provide inadequate support for the justification of any rather determinate theism. It seems likely to have been Hume's view, and certainly it has been the view of supporters of his,[3] that because (1) the person who is confronted by a report of a putative miracle cannot, in his attempt to account for this report, appeal to any conclusions of natural theology as supporting a theistic explanation of the report's occurrence, or as giving an initial presumption in

---

[3] See for instance, Mackie, *The Miracle of Theism*, pp. 26–7, especially the argument of the introduction, and Chs. 2–8 and 10.

favour of a theistic hypothesis which would account for the report, it follows that (2) for lack of any substantial natural theology this report will have to be rejected, for the reasons given in 'Of Miracles', whereas with the support of a substantial natural theology a miracle report *might* best be interpreted theistically. Familiarity with this line of argument may well prompt Humean sympathisers and other readers to suspect that the sort of theistic hypothesis to whose acceptability, it has been suggested, reports of putative miracles might give support, requires also the support of a successful natural theology. Reasonably enough, they may wish to see the issue explored.

The exact course of this Humean line of reflection needs to be more carefully considered in order clear-sightedly to assess it. At least two possibilities seem to be open when we ask exactly *how* the assumption, justified by natural theology, that there is (at least some probability that there is) a god would affect the reasonable assessment of reports of putative miracles. On the Humean view, as we have seen, no report of a putative miracle can of itself furnish evidential support which is sufficient to outweigh the evidence in favour of the supposedly violated law of nature. Now, that assessment of a report of a putative miracle might be thought by the Humean to require revision if there is a justified presumption of theism's having some probability (1) because that presumption will cause evidence for the law of nature to have no clear bearing on the question of the putative miracle's occurrence: if there is or may be a god who *may* cause events to occur in an anomalous way, then evidence about how nature usually behaves will not necessarily have a bearing on what actually occurred in the case in question.

Alternatively, (2), some justification of belief in the existence of a god (who would necessarily have some characteristics about which the argument for his existence would give us guidance) could contribute probability to a proposition that he has altered nature's usual course in particular ways, ways which accord with his character or purposes. The report of any putative miracle will have evidence in its favour and a great deal of evidence against it. So the Humean claims. On the side of the report will be, for example, evidence consisting in some witnesses' testimony or behaviour, and other circumstantial factors, but even when these are taken together they will not outweigh the, as the Humean thinks, massive and pertinent evidence which is on the other side; and on the balancing of this evidence the putative miracle must be judged insufficiently probable to be credible. However, if, from the deliverances of a natural theology, there can properly be added to the probability-enhancing evidence for the putative miracle a probability that such an event as is reported would occur in the prevailing circumstances, because there is a god whose known purposes or attributes entitle us, in these circumstances, to expect just that anomalous action from him, then the probability-balance may be shifted so that the miracle is now credible. Without the contribution made by natural theology, the Humean who pursues this version of the argument thinks, the evidence in favour of the law of nature will always be a balk which is insurmountable by the apologist who appeals to reports of putative miracles.

So a theism which is based on some natural theology might be supposed favourably to affect the assessment about the truth of a report of a putative miracle in either, or both, of the ways (1) and (2) which have now been described. However, as against the Humean camp, the contention of this book is that even in the absence of any natural theology, putative miracle reports can have apologetic value. That is, however the import of a theistic presupposition on the assessment of a report of a putative miracle may be understood, such a report can give weight to a theistic hypothesis, can support a case for theism, even when no theistic presupposition whatever (resting on natural theology) is made.

Different reflections will be relevant according to whether the Humean supposes that a successful natural theology might, if it existed, open the way to a religious apologist to appeal with some hope of argumentative success to reports of putative miracles along the lines of (1), or along the lines of (2), above. Let us first take the case where the Humean thinks natural theology could help after the fashion of (1).

It seems at least possible that it is because of an easily made confusion that he will deny to reports of putative miracles any possible value to an apologetic appeal, which is made without any support from natural theology. It is easy to confuse (A) not presupposing that theism is true, with (B) presupposing that theism is not true. In the absence of any cogent natural theology, an apologist (or an uncommitted enquirer into the credentials of religion) who explores arguments for theism which appeal to reports of putative miracles should have the attitude set out in (A). Having this attitude he wishes to determine whether the occurrence of the report of the putative miracle is best explained theistically. So he will be evaluating and/or constructing and/or amending the kind of promising-looking account, which was somewhat characterised in the previous chapter, by which it seems possible that a range of *data* can be explained. Now exploring and assessing a theistic explanation which deals *inter alia* with the occurrence of a putative miracle is, surely, compatible with (A). Explanatory accounts are normally evaluated without its being presupposed that they or any part of them are, or are probably, true.

The Humean view, as we saw, thinks that the evidence for a law of nature counts very heavily against a report that the law has been violated. It has been argued as a primary point of the previous chapter that if a theistic explanation of the report's existence is an open possibility it is unjustified without any further reflection to admit evidence for the natural law, in Hume's way, as counting against the report of the putative miracle. Now (and here, maybe, the confusion creates error) if (B) obtains, the situation is otherwise and it *will* be justified, in trying to establish what happened, to weigh evidence for a natural law against a report of a putative miracle. Can it be that the Humean view involves a slide from (A) to (B), thinking confusedly that the absence of a cogent natural theology must involve (B), when in fact it does not involve (B), and is entirely compatible with the necessarily to-be-maintained (A)?

That is, perhaps the Humean supposes that there are just these alternatives: either there is a successful natural theology, in which case evidence for laws of nature cannot without ado be taken to be evidence against reported seeming miracles, or there is no successful natural theology, so that we must adopt (B), presuppose that theism is not true, and without hesitation treat evidence for nature's laws as evidence against putative-miracle reports. Yet one does not have to choose between presupposing that theism is true and presupposing that it is not true. One can, and in the dialectical context here, one should, refrain from either presupposition, and should have the attitude of (A).

Whether or not these considerations provide a psychological explanation for the Humean error, they do help to bring out both that there is a Humean error, and what that error is if a natural theology is held to be necessary in the manner of (1) before a miracle report can give support to theism. Indeed Hume's own urging that evidence for a law of nature counts without question against the report of a putative miracle may well involve confusing (A) and (B); such a confusion would explain why Hume thinks himself justified in urging this without offering any support, or reasoned justification for it. If we do assume that there is no god, particular inductive projections cannot be rendered unsound by divine miracle-working, so no doubts need arise about the relevance of evidence for natural law to cases of reported claimed miracles.

As for the Humean whose thinking is represented by (2) above (and this is more likely to be the reasoning present in the usual Humean train of thought), he still relies on the relevance of evidence for natural law against reports of putative miracles. For him the absence of a substantial natural theology means that the evidence for a putative miracle on its own, and unsupplemented by reasoning about a god's likely purposes and actions, stands no chance in practice of outweighing the evidence for the relevant law(s) of nature; hence the religious apologist will have no rationally believable putative miracle of which to attempt a theistic interpretation. The argument against this Humean, therefore, returns to the issue of the admissibility of evidence which is in favour of the allegedly violated law(s) of nature against reports of putative miracles. Once more what requires to be brought out is that, in a context in which the truth of theism is in question, and in which it has neither been presupposed nor rejected (that is, (A) above obtains), the possibility of a divine bringing-about of anomalous occurrences cannot be ruled out. Accordingly, the evidence for the allegedly violated natural law(s) is not admissible, without any reflection or question, against reports of putative miracles; and the case of this Humean against any possible apology which, notwithstanding the absence of support from natural theology, attempts a theistic account of putative miracles, is unsuccessful.

In a particular case, of course, it may be that an event which would violate a law of nature may be reported, but no reason exist for anyone to entertain the smallest suspicion that a god could have had some purpose in bringing about an event of the particular sort in question. Natural explanations of the existence of the report will be sought, and it will be accepted that inductive projection is appropriate in this case and that the evidence in favour of natural law is a good guide to what took place. In yet other cases, reasonable people may suspend judgement about whether a god has acted anomalously and whether evidence for natural laws has a bearing on what occurred. However, take the case of a teacher whose words sublimely illuminate the human condition and who has previously been the subject of well-attested reports saying he was involved in events contrary to natural law in ways which suggest that he may thereby be divinely approved. Then suppose that this person is further reported, by reports of some weight, as having been resurrected, putatively miraculously, after having been put to death by his enemies. In such circumstances reasonable people may perhaps be justified without further aid from natural theology, in concluding that God may well have raised him up, so that in this instance evidence for natural law may be no guide to what occurred. In such circumstances, the report of the resurrection contributes to the believers' case without support from natural theology. Even if the reports of putative miracles are not so strong as to justify belief, they may still give some support, add some probability, to the theistic hypothesis.

One consequence of the foregoing is that Mackie is evidently mistaken when he is discussing what difference different presuppositions, different world-views, will make to our assessment of putative-miracle reports. Mackie says that whereas someone with an already-established theistic belief might, sometimes at least, and properly, on the basis of his assumptions, regard miracle-reports as true, the agnostic or atheist must regard reports of putative miracles, because they report violations of natural law, as very improbable indeed (*The Miracle of Theism*, pages 26–7).[4] This is what he says about the explanation of reports of putative miracles where 'the context is that of fundamental debate about the truth of theism itself':

Here one party to the debate is initially at least agnostic, and does not yet concede that there is a supernatural power at all. From this point of view the intrinsic improbability of a genuine miracle, as defined above, is very great, and one or other of the alternative explanations in our fork will always be much more likely – that is, either that the alleged event is not miraculous, or that it did not occur, that the testimony is faulty in some way. This entails that it is pretty well impossible that reported miracles should provide a worthwhile argument for theism addressed to those who are initially inclined to atheism or even to agnosticism.

As against Mackie's position, it should now be clear, firstly, that it is only by presupposing a conclusively justified *atheism*, or presupposing belief in a non-miracle-working god[5] (as some theologians, such as R. Bultmann have thought that they had good reason to do),[6] that you are entitled to adduce with any cogency, say, evidence for Archimedes' Principle and evidence supporting generalisations about human body-density, as evidence against Christ's having walked on the water. *Agnosticism*, by contrast, leaves it open whether there is a god who works miracles, and so does not rule out the possibility that, for example, Archimedes' Principle may be an unsound guide to

---

[4] Ibid. pp. 26–7. Mackie follows Mill in this. See Mill, *A System of Logic*, Book III, Ch. 25.2.

[5] The description of God as 'intervening' (Mackie uses this way of speaking on p. 21 of *The Miracle of Theism*) would not be accepted by theists, as opposed to deists. Yet the theistic apologist can challenge most atheists or agnostics as to how apparently well-attested, apparently anomalous events are to be explained, except in theistic terms, in terms of God's actions in the world, since ordinary scientific explanation is apparently impossible. Couched in this way, an apologetic appeal to putative-miracle reports, otherwise of the sort which Hume and Mackie consider, is possible, without the talk of supernatural intervention into a closed system.

[6] See Chapter 6, note 23, above.

what occurred on some particular occasion. Agnosticism may be shifted by some well-attested putative-miracle report (probably, in practice, taken with some further considerations) which counts in favour of theism.

Atheism which is held for some reason or reasons may, however, also be vulnerable to reports of putative miracles. A person who denies that a miracle-working god exists might find that well-attested, weighty reports of violations of natural law properly require him to review the force of his reasons for his atheism, or his belief that there is no miracle-working God, and to consider revising his world-view accordingly, especially where some point which those miracles would have in the purpose of a divine worker of the miracles can reasonably be suggested. His denial that there is a god who works miracles, is, presumably, either an empirically defeasible hypothesis or is proposed as a necessary truth for which supporting reasoning may be mistaken. (It is unlikely to be thought simply self-evident.) Either way, the emergence of putative-miracle reports which cannot satisfactorily be accounted for as species of error puts a strain on this world-view. One possible, to-be-contemplated, way of removing such a strain will be to give up the world-view and allow that sometimes miracles have occurred, reasonably to be attributed to the actions of a god who has certain specifiable consistent purposes. In this way, there *is* a possible cogency in putative-miracle reports as counting against the belief that there is no god who works miracles. (If the non-theistic world-view is held as a necessary truth, identification of the error in reasoning involved will obviously make this change in world-view more satisfactory, just as location of unrecognised weakness in the evidence for the hypothesis that there is no miracle-working god will also render the change from *that* world-view more satisfactory.)

What if the unbeliever is an atheist not on the ground either of deductive argument which has atheism as a conclusion, or of evidence for atheism, but what we might call a methodological atheist? If this is regarded as justified by Occam's razor (to the effect that we ought not to multiply entities without necessity), then the occurrence of powerful, weighty putative-miracle reports, not readily set aside as exemplifying some of Hume's (see part II of his essay) species of error, may surely constitute a *necessitas* which will make postulating the entity, god, appropriate? The occurrence of putative-miracle reports like these will constitute a *necessitas* not, of course, because it is the basis for a knock-down proof of God's existence whose conclusion follows with apodeictic necessity, but because it necessitates the postulating of a god in order to construct the most satisfactory account of the universe.

Stratonician atheism, being the doctrine 'that whatever characteristics we think ourselves able to discern in the universe as a whole are the underivative characteristics of the universe itself', is introduced by A. Flew in response to the theist's argument that the universe's orderly (scientific-)law-conforming character calls for theistic explanation.[7] If the occurrence of each particular event within the universe is only to be explained, and understood, as exemplifying some regularly occurring pattern which belongs underivatively to the universe's functioning, and so given a covering-law explanation, then any events which occur contrary to natural law will not *be* explained or understood. Of course, the reasonable view about what the natural law is which covers a particular case may well change, so that what it would be reasonable, at one time, to regard as anomalous, might later come, as reasonably, to be seen as law-conforming. Further, an event which appears to go against natural law, as the laws of nature are then supposed to be, may reasonably be suspected of being really in *accordance* with natural law, because, for any of a variety of possible reasons, it may reasonably be suspected that the current view about what the law of nature is should be revised. Indeed the occurrence of the seemingly anomalous event may properly support such a suspicion.

However, there may be seemingly anomalous occurrences of another kind such that there is no reasonable prospect of any revision in our understanding of natural law which will accommodate them, and the reasonable view to take of them will be that they are or were violations of natural law.

[7] A. Flew, *God and Philosophy*, London, 1966, p. 69.

Hume's own examples of the (hypothetical) reports of eight days' darkness, and of Queen Elizabeth of England's *post mortem* three years' rule, respectively constitute instances, as Hume understands and presents them, of these sorts of case.[8] The former, Hume thinks, may reasonably be suspected of being really in accordance with natural law, whereas with respect to the latter there is no reasonable prospect of any revision in our understanding of natural law which will accommodate it. (Of course he thinks we should conclude that the reports of the latter must be in error.) It would obviously also be possible to exemplify this distinction as it would be made in the light of modern comprehensions of natural law.

Suppose that we receive an extremely well-attested report of an event which we reasonably (as explained above) take to have been, if it occurred as reported, a violation of natural law; and suppose that its occurrence, like the occurrence of other reported violations, and other non-anomalous events such as the teaching of a prophet (which may be accompanied by putative miracles) or significant patterns in history, or religious experiences, would serve the postulated purposes of a god; then theism, in regarding this alleged and very powerfully evidenced event as a miracle, may be able to offer an explanation of this weighty testimony, and of what it reports, more satisfactorily in the light of experience and analogy than Stratonician atheism can. So long as Hume's argument of Part I of his essay stood, it seemed at best enormously unlikely that evidence for any event which occurred or occurs contrary to what we take to be natural law could ever be sufficient to justify reasonable belief that the event had occurred. To be sufficient, on Hume's view, the evidence would have to be more rationally cogent than the body of evidence which supports the allegedly violated law of nature. If the argument of the preceding chapter is correct, this requirement, which is argued for by Hume, is unsoundly argued-for; as a consequence, the prospect of overcoming Stratonician atheism by an appeal to reports of putative miracles (and probably, in practice, to other considerations at the same time) is enhanced.

---

[8] Hume, *First Enquiry*, pp. 127–8.

Some account requires to be taken of the Humean contention, here, that it will *always* be preferable, unless one already has other grounds for theism, to respond to reports of phenomena which apparently constitute counter-instances to natural laws by looking for other and better, or new, natural laws, which may explain the troublesome reported phenomena, rather than postulate the action of a deity as the explanation. Now no one can sensibly deny that it will be reasonable to look for, and expect, the explanation of some seemingly anomalous phenomena (for example, possible phychosomatic healings) by appeal to as yet undiscovered natural laws. However, other kinds of anomalous phenomena will seem very unlikely indeed to be explained in such a way. Examples would be: the complete growth within five minutes of sweet blood-oranges on a cactus; the restoration in a few seconds of all limb functions of a paralysed polio victim; restoration to full life of a dead person, such as Elizabeth of England in Hume's own imaginary example. It is hard to see on what rational basis the Humean can now (in the light of what has been argued above) properly insist that a theistic explanation of reported occurrences such as these cannot possibly be preferable, no matter how strong the evidence for these occurrences.

Humeans have said, of course, that precisely those reported events which are unlikeliest to find an explanation in terms of natural law are, because of the weighty evidence for natural law, most likely to be wrongly reported and least worthy to be accepted as actual; but the weakness of that move has by now been sufficiently exposed. Only what one might call a fideistic atheism which refuses to consider its rational credentials will refuse to countenance the possibility that a theistic explanation may account *better* for the range of phenomena, including some putatively miraculous phenomena, than atheism. Moreover, a rational agnosticism or atheism (or theism) will require to confront the question as to where the preferable explanation lies, by reference to argumentation from analogy and experience, argumentation which is not arbitrarily restricted by rationally indefensible Humean constraints.

A Stratonician atheist might deny that any explanation (even of the covering-law kind), or understanding, of any event is possible; Hume, possibly advancing scepticism about the value of inductive reasoning, just might take this line on the grounds that no justified view about what are the laws of nature can be obtained. In 'Of Miracles' he makes no use of any such scepticism, possibly because he thinks that he can show how the apologist who appeals to reports of putative miracles, and who must accept inductive reasoning, must also come to accept that no report of a putative miracle will have apologetic value. The principal argument of the 'Essay on miracles' having now been refuted, a Stratonician might revert to scepticism about induction and claim that theism and atheism have equal explanatory power, namely none, but that atheism is ontologically more economical. The scepticism about explanation and understanding associated with this inductive-reasoning-rejecting Stratonician atheism will be shared by very few, and involves the rejection of reasoning which most people regard as acceptable. *This* Stratonician atheism has, therefore, a very high cost.

Some philosophers are reluctant to allow talk of causes which are not empirically identifiable. Such people will not readily entertain 'seemingly anomalous occurrences . . . such that there is no reasonable prospect of any revision in our understanding of natural law which will accommodate them',(pages 164–5 above) and for which it will be preferable to postulate empirically unidentifiable causes. Better, in their view, to assume that a revision of accepted natural law, albeit a revision of whose character we do not yet know, is called for and will turn out to be possible.

This refusal to countenance entities which cannot be picked out by us in space and time, and which, in principle, could not be pointed out to anyone, may rest, as in the case of S. Hampshire it appears to rest, on a descriptive metaphysics which sets up standards of explanation or even of significance, on the basis of what is in fact said or thought.[9] If the basic discourse or common, shared, conceptuality from which the standards are derived excludes God from the start, it ought scarcely to trouble the theistic apologist (nor to impress the enquirer to whom he addresses himself) that his theism fails to fit

[9] S. Hampshire, 'Identification and Existence' in H. D. Lewis (ed.) *Contemporary British Philosophy*, third series, London and New York, 1956.

the standards proposed. The standards laid out in a descriptive metaphysics which is founded on a significantly incomplete sample of thought and discourse (as, on a theistic view, this one is), have no claim on the theist.[10]

A refusal to countenance what cannot in principle be ostensively picked out may derive from a more ambitious explanatory metaphysics, such as that of Kant. In the context of this chapter, a general treatment of all the implications of this possibility is (plainly) not possible. What can be said, however, (and germanely to the pretentions of both descriptive and explanatory metaphysics) is that where such a metaphysics fails comfortably to accommodate weightily evidenced reports that putative miracles have occurred and can only give an implausible account of these reports, or no account at all, the adequacy of the metaphysics is somewhat called in question.

If there are methodological atheisms which are altogether indefeasible presuppositions, no apologetic considerations *could* touch *them*. Yet a Humean like, for example, Mackie, is clearly wide of the mark in saying that appeals to reports of putative miracles can have no apologetic value for the theist who confronts the atheist. Mackie, and Mill, are therefore at fault in what they say about the bearing of reports of putative miracles on the maintenance of atheism, as we earlier saw them to be in error in their assessment of the bearing of such reports on the maintaining of agnosticism.

Someone who acknowledges that the Hume/Mackie criterion for assessing the credit-worthiness of reports of anomalous events (for all but those who hold atheism as an indefeasible presupposition) has now been undermined is of course not therefore bound to accept all such reports. The main conclusion reached so far is that Hume has not formulated a necessary condition which any report of a putative miracle would, to be believable by a reasonable person, have to satisfy, yet in practice be unable ever to satisfy. His check has come loose from its anchorage. Therefore, it has not been shown by Hume to be impossible for there to be apologetic force in reports of miracles.

[10] For fuller discussion of this issue, see Mitchell's *The Justification of Religious Belief*, pp. 16–19.

Reported miracles and epistemology

As this debate between apologist and Humean has developed, two views of the character of explanatory or interpretive accounts have at different times and for different purposes been hinted at or partially sketched. On the one hand, Hume employs an image which has become standard in epistemology, when he speaks of people's setting forth a miracle to provide a foundation of a system of religion. Apologists who have advanced a case like Paley's are in Hume's mind here. The apologist treats the event, inescapably strongly evidenced as he believes it is by the report of the miracle, as a *given* whose character is both firmly established and in need of an explanation. The explanation is then so to speak erected, founded on this established undeniable given which comes to us by way of testimony and report, and is mediately given rather than immediately, such as our own subjective experience would be. It is in its character as contrary to natural law that it calls for explanation and comes, in the apologist's eyes, to serve as foundational for the account which explains it, the system of religion. If that significance is to be seen, there must be an awareness of what the relevant laws of nature are, or seem to be, together with the reports based on witnesses' testimony and experience; only then can a *datum* come to be recognised as being miraculous. Still, once its actual occurrence, as an event contrary to natural law, is admitted, accepted, acknowledged as fact, there is before us something which has to be reckoned with, a given (strictly, at this stage, putative) miracle which calls for explanation. In the apologist's eyes it constitutes the factor peculiarly requiring and justifying an account along the theistic lines which the apologist advocates; the anomalous event is the particular factor which compels that interpretation.

On the other hand, for himself, Hume rather treats reports of putative miracles as open to challenge and open to being accounted for, under the guidance of other human experience, as not being what they seem *prima facie* to be. Accordingly, what has come to possess the experience-based standing of a natural law may require us to account for even an immensely well-confirmed, evidentially cogent report of an anomalous event as some species of error rather than a given to be reckoned with. Hume does not himself deal with the case where we ourselves experience or seem to ourselves to experience, an event contrary to natural law; but Hume's latter-day supporter Mackie has continued the direction of this sequence of thought.[1] For Mackie the expression 'the testimony of experience' has significance in suggesting that as a sort of testimony, our experience is likewise properly to be interpreted as error in the face of an incompatible natural law. On this view, *data* might perhaps be accepted without further reflection, in their obvious-seeming character only where there is no reason, which should be known, to take them at other than face value. Even in such cases it will be proper to consider whether the *data* should be accepted as they present themselves or whether there is, or may be, reason to account for them, assimilate them into the body of beliefs, as being other than they appear, other than as *prima facie* they present themselves. No *data* need, quite without thought, to be accepted and reckoned with simply as they are given, mediately or immediately. If, as given, they are difficult to fit into the rest of our body of beliefs, then our first preliminary grasp of them may have to be modified, or else the prior body of beliefs altered, to accomodate the new thing.

These alternative pictures roughly correspond to, or exemplify, alternative accounts which philosophers have offered of the body of our respectable beliefs. Epistemologists who have been most ready to speak of justified belief as having foundations in experience have believed in, or looked for and hoped for

---

[1] Mackie, *The Miracle of Theism*, p. 28.

undeniable, immovable, unmalleable givens whose character is so evident as not to be in question, upon which an edifice (or several of them) of human beliefs is then secure.[2] These givens are usually supposed to be sense experiences, sense-data. Paley with his confident talk of testimony as being a phenomenon which is explained by the fact which must then be reckoned with, is no doubt a relatively unsophisticated foundationalist in that he does not spell out, as a more modern epistemologist would try to do, whether his foundation is the event of the giving or coming to know the testimony, or the experience which was had by the witness testifying, or the fact of the putative miracle. Modern foundationalists have become sensitive to such questions because advocates of other ways of epistemological thinking have pressed the dilemma: whenever you characterise the foundational given as being some sort of thing rather than another, do you not inevitably and at once lay its character open to question in as much as the appropriation and characterisation may at least in principle be open to question in respect of accuracy? Yet if you treat it as a bare uncharacterised given, so that there is no characterising of it to be challenged, how can it, thus devoid of significance, serve as a basis upon which any edifice of beliefs can be raised?

These questions have led many to hold that while any body of justified beliefs will do justice to experience taken all together, this doing of justice must involve the accurate, critically thoughtful apprehending of the given, and is not merely a reckoning with the brute, uncompromisable, unnegotiable given nature and fact of some experiences. According to this picture, the body of responsibly held human beliefs will take account of, do justice to, many experiences at once, together. Hume's own treatment of miracle reports accords better with this second picture. It has also been the claim of earlier portions of this book that an apologetic argument may most effectively be advanced as an argument which seeks to offer the best overall account of, to do justice to, a range of factors, taken together. There is thus some agreement between Hume and an en-

[2] E.g. H. H. Price, *Perception*, London, 1932; A. J. Ayer, *The Foundations of Empirical Knowledge*, London, 1940.

lightened apologist (more enlightened, that is, than the apologist whom he portrays as presenting us with an uninterpretable, ineluctable, adamantine given, as a foundation) about the structure of responsible believings. An explanatory account, of something in particular, will be a portion, a sector of the integrated mass or body of well-founded beliefs, the portion which shows how particular (perhaps problematic) *data* are to be accomodated, how they fit in, as organically related to the whole body.

It will be helpful, in order to clarify our view of the present state of the book's argument to think further about the proper structure of our body of beliefs. It will also help us, as we go on, to gain a better perspective on issues which we have yet to consider. In view of the wide-ranging, ingenious, sophisticated and continuing character of this debate in the philosophical literature what follows is (at best) an introductory sketch or indication of a possible standpoint. While it lacks the depth necessary to be a contribution to epistemology, it aims to provide an epistemological orientation relevant to our concerns about miracle reports.

So firstly, explanatory accounts require to do justice to the *prima facie* character of *data*, not necessarily or simply to a single perhaps particularly prominent *datum* on its own, though it may appear to be that, but possibly (and more usually) to the characters of all of a number of *data*. In being grasped, any *datum* is subject to careful judgement so that it may be grasped in its true character; the present point is that conclusions about what it truly is that is given are constrained (though not wholly and uniquely determined, as we shall see further) by what is immediately apparently presented to us. We must, that is, do justice to the *prima facie* nature of the given, perhaps by (carefully) accepting it as it presents itself, perhaps explaining it, or explaining it away. However, in its apparent given character, it must be reckoned with.

Such accounts will, secondly, require to be self-consistent, strictly self-consistent in respect of strict logicality, and at least somewhat inductively self-consistent in that no part of the account renders any other part unacceptably improbable on inductive grounds; the more inductive inconsistency there is in some overall account, the less satisfactory the overall account will be in this respect.

Thirdly, antecedently held and supposedly well-founded beliefs are, of course, points of relevance (sometimes suggestive points of departure, sometimes constraints) for the emergence of any such account, in that consistency of both sorts, with the existing body of beliefs, directs and constrains the new explanatory construction; logical consistency dictates some deductions, and rules out other incompatible statements; while inductive consistency renders propositions proposed as components of an account very probable, very improbable, or somewhat probable between these extremes. In this way the newly found and most likely explanation of the range of immediately problematic *data* will be grafted onto, or will grow from, the established body of beliefs, and will come to form a part of it. Thus, while for convenience we may roughly divide off a part of our body of belief and understanding and think of it as our account, of the life of Augustine, of the Copernican Revolution, or of the Russian Revolution, as the case might be, these parts must be related in consistency to the single organic whole structure of our knowledge.

These requirements for an acceptable account need to be interpreted by each other; each needs to be informed by the other.

So, the first of the *desiderata* in a satisfactory account stresses the proper respect which must be accorded to the not-to-be-explained-away, intractable firmness of the given, the *data*. Yet what 'proper respect' consists in will involve an appeal to inductive consistency; how far in the light of experience of such things it is probable that the *prima facie* character of *this* experience, or report of experience, or piece of documentation, or whatever the *datum* may be, can reasonably be accounted for in this way or that. Thus rough limits are set to what can decently, justifiably, be made of *data*, without saying that the *data* for an enquiry are such stark unyielding brute givens that there can be no question about how they are to be accounted for. These are rough limits only because inductive consistency is a matter of degree.

For example, a *datum* for an enquiry might be the report's

reaching us that an art gallery attendant saw a large brown patch where no brown patch should be, on the gallery's most celebrated English landscape painting. Has the painting been damaged, or may this *datum* be interpreted as deriving from a misheard remark that he saw round thatch in the painting, or could he have been suffering an after-image consequent on looking at a strong light? Further information will help us to judge the probabilities of these and other proposed explanations. If some wider version of events tries to adopt the after-image thesis when there apparently was no strong light, and the gallery attendant on all available, evidence was not such a fool as to confuse an after-image with an actual mark on the surface of the painting, this may well be judged an unsatisfactory lack of respect for the *prima facie* nature of a *datum* because the improbability of the after-image thesis is judged to be too great. The view of the gallery attendant himself about whether the *prima facie* character of what he remembers seeing fits in with, is inductively consistent with, one or other alternative explanation will carry weight insofar as he has special access to that experience of his.

What will *be* too great an inductive inconsistency to be borne here is not capable of being exactly specified; and nor therefore can it be determined by any exact and rigorous decision-procedure whether the limits of toleration have been exceeded. This truth, just now set out in relation to the acceptable appropriation of *data*, is equally relevant to all judgements respectively about what is required or what will be unacceptable degrees of inductive consistency or inconsistency. Thus the demand for inductive consistency – in some account, in the proper interpretation of *data* or in the relating of a developing explanation to antecedently held beliefs – may be more or less well satisfied; the best available overall account may still present problems by containing components which, on the rest of the account and in the light of antecedent beliefs, are rather unlikely. If the account deals effectively with other, otherwise problematic, points, people may well and reasonably adopt the account while for example trying to uncover operant factors which would render the seemingly unlikely component less unlikely. In that way they will hope that the account can be improved in respect of inductive consistency. None of this means that any account will be deemed unsatisfactory just in that it tells us something unusual occurred. The fuller clarification of this point must await further discussion (below pp. 191 ff.) but it turns on the conceptual fact that an event is unlikely under a particular description, and given particular circumstances. A good explanation can show that while an event may have been unlikely under some true description of it and in some circumstances, there have been circumstances and a proper description of it which do not render it at all unlikely to have occurred.

Again it may prove persistently difficult to devise an account which squares well with the initial problematic *data* and is at the same time tolerably consistent with the body of antecedent beliefs; one avenue of exploration will then be to see whether some pertinent items out of the body of previous beliefs are suspect, less well founded than had been supposed. Thereupon, scrutiny of some components of the conventional wisdom may strengthen suspicion of *them* so that their status shifts. They move from the accepted background, and join the class of the presently problematic. The aim in debating and constructing explanatory accounts is to accommodate all that we are aware of within our self-consistent picture of the world, and the distinction between matter for a problem and background beliefs is relative to the occasion and circumstances, and the stage of an enquiry. What comprises matter for a problematic and what comprise antecedent assumptions depends not only on the present novelty of the *data* but also on the emergence of difficulties in meeting the consistency requirement. Some items of the body of accepted beliefs will be so well established and will underpin so many other confidently accepted beliefs that the contemplation of their revision or overthrow will be undertaken if at all, only after less drastic explorations have failed. Yet the emergence of some new hard *data may* lead to revolution in the established order of believing which will be the more proper and (one hopes) likely, the more fully and soundly what was previously responsibly believed can be consistently accounted for by the new theory. (The reasonable person will also recognise that, often, the reliable judging about how some *datum* is best accounted for will take time, and care.)

Strongly attested putative-miracle reports might emerge, which cannot adequately be accommodated into a body of antecedently held secular (that is, having no theistic, deistic or atheistic commitments) belief, nor by any secularly permitted revisions within that body. If a satisfactory corpus of belief which does justice to *data* and respects consistency requirements is then to emerge, and these pressures and strains within the structure of beliefs are to be relieved, the possibility, which has been explored in this book, of invoking the intelligent, intelligibly purposeful agency of a god who rules over nature and history, may be explored. Inductive consistency may then be maintained if some discernible intelligible purpose would be served when the god who is postulated is supposed to act, or to have acted, in a miraculous way which squares with the *data*.

On some occasion when what is claimed to be a putative miracle is reported, it will be possible to accommodate the fact of this report's having been made into our body of knowledge, doing justice to the *datum* (maybe documented testimony, a report of eye-witnesses, or even possibly (acknowledging Mackie) the 'testimony' of one's own experience) while maintaining inductive consistency in the ways already touched on, *without* invoking any miracle-working agent. If the *datum* can be explained, given its circumstances and attributes, as a likely hallucination, deception, misunderstanding or, generally, error, or if revision of existing beliefs about nature can readily be effected to allow for the new phenomenon (a new sort of psychosomatic healing, perhaps) while still doing justice to previously reported experience, there is little pressure to postulate a miracle-working agent. However (as it has been the main point of this book to argue), in the face of some *data* it may, in other sorts of cases, be the best way of satisfying the *desiderata* for explanatory accounts to propose the extraordinary activity of a miracle-working god.

Leaving aside for the moment the specific concern about reported miracles, explanatory interpretative accounts are, we have said, (1) constructed out of given material, whose character as given is not, as it presents itself to us, quite determinately established but comes to be more firmly and exactly fixed in ways which respect its *prima facie* nature, as given, within limits of acceptability; (2) integrated by both deductive and inductive requirements of consistency (which still allows for a particular new given to require and give rise to accounts which are not merely derivative from the rest of the body of belief in that they could not, without this given, already have been derived from the body of belief by deduction or induction); and (3) comprehensive in scope: even accounts which have the limited aim of making sense of some particular, focussed-on *data* do nevertheless belong by integration, as at (2) above, to a network of belief which seeks to do justice to, make sense of, everything.

People of an empiricist tendency, or people who favour a view of the structure of belief whereby there are fixed unproblematic given foundations, may wonder whether in this picture of the organisation of our beliefs, the authority of the particular experience is too easily negotiated away in order to meet the claims of consistency. In response to which, we may remind ourselves that the 'claims of consistency' here are made (on the assumption that events occur in accordance with regularities of sequence) in order to give due weight to all experiences. So, while the whole system of our beliefs is formed, revised, confirmed or enlarged, in response to experience, particular experiences are, out of respect for other experiences, subject to interpretation, and to be accounted for in whatever way forms the best overall account of it and of other experiences.

There are enquiries which take their rise from some given whose nature as given is obvious, in itself uncontroversial and agreed; enquiry is necessary to explain how this given, with its evident nature, comes to be as it evidently is. The example of the waterspout (in Chapter 9) was given to illustrate just such a case. Yet the seeming unmalleability of the given, and its non-negotiable nature in such cases, flows from its being manifest to all concerned; the character of the given stares us in the face. It should not be imagined that there is therefore nothing interpretative in the confident recognition (as it is believed to be) of the qualities of the given.

In fact, where the foundational given is thought of as someone's experience as of seeing a coloured patch, a given which is as bare and uninterpreted as can be, such as would be reported by 'I am aware of what seems to me to be red, as I recall the meaning of "red"', even there interpretation is involved in the tentative application of the description 'red'. It may nevertheless still be contended by the foundationalist that interpretations so cautiously qualified as to be proof against error may enable experiences to act as unamendable givens with which, as unamended, nothing given or taken away, any body of knowledge must reckon, and on which, because of their unmovability a body of knowledge may rest securely, as it can rest on few other bases.

Since the ability to use a language correctly is something which must be learned inter-subjectively, in relation to shared experience, our ability to *speak* of experiences that seem to us to be of red is derived from our possession of ordinary public language, and we do not as a matter of psychological priority or order of origination generate our larger body of beliefs about the world by ourselves deriving them from priorly received private experience. However, if the aim is to set out a rational reconstruction of the wider belief system which we have, showing how our beliefs are justified, rather than how histori-cally, causally, they came into being, appeals to private experiences are possible and are surely to the point. Experiences which can be described in the qualified cautious way which runs minimal risk of error do serve to shape, constrain or support any body of rational beliefs about the physical world.

However, this is not to concede that anything very like our ordinary body of beliefs can be deduced or otherwise rigorously derived simply from private experiences thus made public by being described. Notoriously, attempts to deduce such systems of beliefs about our world as we actually have, from experienced givens which are as barely and cautiously interpreted as can be, fail, because no belief about an aggregation of such qualified experiences, actual or possible, is equivalent to a belief about these common, nodal, principal constituents of our believed-in world, namely physical objects. A belief about a physical object involves belief in a degree of permanence and public availability which belongs to the object, and involves thinking something more and other than of some stuff, such as some sand or some water would be. None of this is entailed by anyone's having the qualifiedly described experiences. Moreover, a belief that a physical object is of some particular kind, say, that it is an orange, involves beliefs about some properties of that object which are not actually being experienced. Our belief systems require, are constrained by and do reckon with, minimally interpreted experienced givens; but belief systems of the kind we have are not able to be deduced from such bare sense-data. Perhaps we appropriate so much of our experience and frame our beliefs as being about physical objects because it helps us to cope better, make better sense of our experience, that way. This view, being approximately the view of Quine[3] seems preferable to the Kantian doctrine that it is by the necessary constitution of our mind that we make sense of our raw, bare, experience in physical object terms; preferable because for one thing psychologists such as Piaget have shown that young children go through a stage in which their experiences are not organised into, grouped in terms of, physical objects.

Completely uninterpreted experiences cannot function as foundational, or as constraining, in relation to belief systems. Yet as soon as interpretation takes place, the given ceases to be incorrigible, indubitable. Suppose that someone reported an experience of hers as follows: 'I am aware of what seems to me to be gamboge, as I recall what gamboge is.' Doubts about the value of this evidence might arise because the experiencer has descended, through years of frivolous careless malice and habitual use of speech to manipulate people and amuse the speaker, to a condition where she hardly knows herself what is genuinely believable in what she thinks or what is seriously meant in what she says. Such a person might come to fear her own easy-going, insouciant self-deception, and to doubt her own reliability; and the rest of us might well, also, doubt the evidential value of what she says. Doubts may, more obviously,

[3] W. V. O. Quine, 'Speaking of Objects' in *Ontological Relativity and Other Essays*, New York, 1969, pp. 1–25.

arise over whether she has a proper grasp of what gamboge is. Doubts may arise even over calling something 'red', not because (as in the case of gamboge) it is relatively rarely that the description is employed, so that its meaning may have become confused and not corrected, but perhaps because what she takes to be red most people would think of as pink, or maybe what she conceives of as red includes what most people would regard as being purple.

However a person conceives of, and couches a report of, an experience, whether in maximally cautious terms or in terms of physical objects, or of things whose thing-hood is more puzzling, like the sky or the climate of Nepal, what they themselves and everyone else has to go on, in order to accommodate what is reported into their beliefs, is what is conceived, and is in terms of what is said, and only by derivation from that does anyone except the experiencer have access of any sort to what experience was experienced. Raw experiences cannot as they stand, uninterpreted, their significance unrecognised, contribute anything to our body of beliefs; but of course the body of our beliefs, which is affected (enlarged, constrained, revised as the case may be) by the interpretive accounts given of claimed experiences, will be ill-founded indeed if there are no individuals' experiences, which the interpretive accounts actually are of, about. If our belief system is to avoid a free-floating detachment from the world which we experience, it must be answerable to, must seek to do justice to, experience. Notoriously, belief systems whose advocates will accord respect only to requirements of consistency (and upholders of the coherence theory of truth are examples of this[4]) have difficulty in countering the claims of alternative but equally self-consistent belief systems. Indeed, why should anyone think that any of these self-consistent systems accurately or even approximately describes the world, unless some attempt is made to reckon with our experience? So our experience is, constitutes, an essential given, for a body of belief which is properly believed, that is which is reasonably

[4] E.g. F. H. Bradley, *Appearance and Reality*, London, 1893, Chs. 15 and 16; B. Blanshard, *The Nature of Thought*, London, 1939, vol. II, Chs. 15–17; K. Lehrer *Knowledge*, Oxford, 1974.

taken to describe the world which exists outside of the belief system and which the beliefs are about. Yet only in description or report do we have a given which can constitute a *datum*, a problematic or a question, and which can contribute to the formation of beliefs as a significance-bearing factor.

What significance it has, how it should best be assimilated into the rest of the belief system, will often, as with reports of putative miracles, be a matter for reflection or debate which in principle may seek consistency with and draw implications from any part of the existing body of belief and/or come to call in question any part of the existing network of related beliefs.

Within the whole edifice of justified human belief, of course, there are constituent parts, and there are (formal) structures. People can become specialists in dealing with issues which arise only in one part of the edifice (as it may be, physics, plant physiology, Roman history or Hispanic lexicography) requiring to give scarcely a thought to the relevancies between their areas of competence on the one hand, and on the other, spheres of different competence or that body of non-specialist belief called common sense; but relevancies there are. Generalisations whether developed and arrived at within a particular specialist field, or as pieces of common sense, will if true apply everywhere and be vulnerable to refutation anywhere. Logic and mathematics, which, so pervasive is their relevance, *might* rather be seen as prescribing and describing frequently and generally repeated structure than as sectors or components or members of the body of belief, constrain, enable and, generally, direct acceptable beliefs in all fields and spheres.

Some issues will have resolutions which reverberate only locally, and could call for little or no reappraisal of the rest of our body of belief. Very many historians' questions, as for example why Gladstone's Irish policy was not adopted, or who killed J. F. Kennedy, will likely have answers whose implications will not go much beyond our views on politics and society in Britain and Ireland in the last three centuries, and in America in the present one, respectively. To many people, these are important. Yet our answers in these areas are unlikely to lead to radical reconsideration of our view of other periods and places, let alone of the nature of historical enquiry, or of the value of testimony, or of the very possibility of knowledge of the past.

The birth date of Anselm of Canterbury is not quite certain, though it is probably 1033. Yet the emergence of a confident justified answer, whether it is 1032, 1033 or 1034 will require few adjustments in our belief-edifice. By contrast if, somehow, it turned out that he was not born at all, and that he never existed, our understanding of the Middle Ages and of the assessment of much historical evidence, and with that, much else which rests on similar historical evidence might well require revision. In that case we require to explain how the evidence be understood and why it has been so persistently misunderstood. We require, also, to ensure that by understanding evidence consistently in the new way we shall be able to deal satisfactorily with those other issues which are touched by the revised attitude to such evidence. The far-reachingness into the belief system of the effects of some incongruities, or dislocations to the network of belief as it has previously stood, brings out how systematically integrated the body of belief is. The fact that other questions may be settled without a wide-ranging inquiry, other discoveries domesticated without disturbance, does not show that these matters are not likewise tied in to the single (interwoven) texture of credenda. Rather it indicates that they fit the existing set-up rather comfortably, which will lead to their ready acceptance and give no cause to reconsider what has seemed to serve well. Only if the textile's pattern must be changed to fit in a new shape at a particular place, or alter the recurring motif is there any call for a re-weave; but that does not mean that where the cloth can be added to without altering or re-doing what has already been done we are not dealing with a single interwoven fabric, the make-up of all of whose parts mutually inter-relate.

This web of belief (the telling title of a book[5] in which Quine and Ullian present a view of the network of belief rather like the account given here) aspires to be constrained by *data*, comprehensive, and coherent in that within the system of beliefs which are required to enable us best to cope with our experience, every

---

[5] W. V. O. Quine and J. S. Ullian, *The Web of Belief*, second edition, New York, 1978.

datum is accommodated in tolerable inductive comfort and without contradiction. Economy is also valued, though what more exactly this means is hard to specify. Occam said that we should not multiply entities beyond necessity. Yet how pressing does a necessity have to be to justify entity-postulation? Indeed, relatedly, since beliefs about physical things are not entailed by beliefs about minimally interpreted experiences, do we ever need to postulate entities at all, and if we do should we be happier with fewer entities but of more kinds? (Whether we can distinguish kinds, and whether kinds are themselves entities will be contributory issues, here.) What exactly is it to postulate an entity anyhow? Of the necessity, we may ask 'necessity for what?'. Sophisticated discussion of these issues continues. For our purpose we can simply note that, on any view, there may be a trade-off between explanatory deficiency and entity-postulation.

Quite apart from considerations of simplicity, the (inter-) connectedness of the parts of the belief system also involves there being trade-offs, where some beliefs will, as compared with other beliefs, be interpretatively and explanatorily advantageous on some points, but on other points ill-founded, unhelpful, obscuring, raising puzzles and problems. Given what now appears the best attested belief about the earth's primeval chemical soup and the conditions surrounding it, it now seems unlikely that the building blocks of life could, as had been thought, have come about by chance; yet alternative theories, for example about the arrival here of bacteria from other planets in other planetary systems (on meteorites, or seeded by an intelligent race, dying-out elsewhere?) have scant evidential support. These theories gain believers, and maybe credibility, from the weaknesses of the alternatives.

On one suggested identification of the dark lady of the sonnets (that is, of Shakespeare) many of the lines and figures of speech will be able to be given particular meanings and a point rather more convincingly than on another proposal, while that other proposal may render obvious and forceful the meanings of lines or whole poems which the former suggestion leaves obscure, banal or incoherent, but yet lose some substantial interpretative gains of the former. In these circumstances, a further identification can be sought which would illuminate all the *data*, or it may be possible to show that what has seemed problematic for one of the existing hypotheses can be accounted for, maybe as not actually written by Shakespeare and so not properly belonging to the corpus, maybe as having a point which new Elizabethan language study makes plausible.

Of course, not every view which seeks to do justice, attaching neither too little nor too much importance to any of the *data*, needs to leave some factors dealt with unsatisfactorily. Perhaps Germany's condition in the 1920s and Hitler's influence on events were jointly necessary and together sufficient to bring about the Second World War. Yet there are those who say that without Hitler the war would still have happened because of the capacities and the appetites of the German economy, and the intolerable constrictions, deprivations and humiliations imposed on Germany following World War One. By contrast, the view of it as particularly Hitler's war affirms the decisive role played by Hitler's expansionist determination, his vigorous opportunism and military bluff-calling in the period which led to the war, which, given Hitler, would have occurred anyway even though Germany had not been straitened and aggrieved. Maybe each of these two factors on its own was a sufficient condition for the occurrence of the war. These views aspire actually to do justice, without awkward remainder, to the *data*. Which, if either of them succeeds in that aspiration is a matter for argument, but each may properly aspire to deal justly with all factors.

The prevailing hypothesis that Lee Harvey Oswald, unaided, not in association with others, maybe mildly deranged, killed Kennedy, squares with a good deal of the evidence. There is further evidence whose hardness is contested, for example, that shots were seen and heard to come from 'the grassy knoll', that is, from a direction quite other than Oswald's supposed firing-point and the reported direction of entry wounds, and yet other evidence whose relevance is questioned, for instance, that people were seen running away from the area from where the alleged non-Oswald shots seemed to come, and that most of the people who were close to the incident in such ways as might have given them access to an understanding of, or suspicion about, the episode, alternative to that which prevails, were dead soon after it, many of them in apparently accidental and violent and somewhat obscure circumstances. All of this may cast doubt on the prevailing theory, and prompt other conjectures besides the Oswald-as-lone-maverick view. The lack of any hard evidence of a conspiracy would make it unreasonable to explain the deaths of those close to the incident as the results of (what would have to have been) a wide-ranging conspiracy, even though these deaths are remarkable if they were merely coincidental. Still, coincidences which are as remarkable do happen. If, however, some rather hard evidence of a conspiracy is available (for instance, an amateur film showing shots from the 'grassy knoll'), the deaths – though not in themselves giving a sufficient reason for belief in a conspiracy – would strengthen, that is, make it more reasonable to believe, that conjecture. The prevailing belief has the advantages of relative simplicity, and completeness in raising no (or few) further problems; but it may not explain as much as an alternative, if it were called for, would explain, some of which may not, on its own, stand in evident, uncontroversial need of explanation.[6] On their own, the facts about the deaths may surely contribute some credibility or probability to the conspiracy theory which that theory would otherwise lack; how this is so, is a question which it is desirable to address, but given its difficulties, and in the interests of the order and intelligibility of exposition, not, perhaps, here, yet.

To each of these issues which have been given as examples, a great many subsidiary issues feed in, contributing essential background and assumptions which can come to be in themselves contentious, and to be reconsidered, particularly if what had been the prior, primary focus of inquiry proves hard to

---

[6] The qualification 'if it were called for' properly reminds us that we are talking about a system of those beliefs which are required; without that 'being required' all manner of fantastic beliefs which would be consistent with one another and be put under no constraint by our experiences, might be adopted. Quine's thesis that theories which are intended to be believed are underdetermined by *data* may be taken to call in question the requiredness of beliefs and systems of belief; but Quine's thesis is controversial, in part because it undercuts the requirement requirement.

make sense of. These fed-in factors (including beliefs about natural laws, or generally accepted history, or economic tendencies, or . . .) connect the primary focal matter to the wider overall web of belief; and into these fed-in factors there will again in time be further feedings-in, and to these feedings-in yet further. Lest the philosophically conditioned seem to themselves to scent an infinite regress here, it can be stressed that what is envisaged is rather a complex network or web of beliefs, involving many and varied connexions set out sometimes in circular configurations, which as a whole and economically seeks best to square with our experiences. The circularity here is not vicious circularity in argument but rather the interconnexions of a consistent rather wide-ranging account which can come to touch variously on the same claim in its differing relevancies.

It is easy to see an appearance of circularity in arguments, cases, which have or claim what can be called integrative force. For example, when the exegesis of a passage or a poem is being undertaken, line 6 may, out of several rather more than less possible meanings, be interpreted as having meaning m_a, while a puzzling phrase in the last sentence of the passage is held to mean m_b; in this way the force of the whole piece is readily intelligible as being that the ancient author is expressing his attitude to an aspect (known to us) of his historical context. The genuine attractiveness and strength of this account, let us suppose, lies not much in the illuminating, the explaining, of the particular expressions, from line 6 and from the last sentence, if each is considered with little weight being given to its context in the passage; and in particular each being considered without reference to the other. The proposed meanings of these expressions, where each is treated in detachment from the other, considering semantics, syntactics and comparisons with other uses of the same word at the relevant period, may even be rather less probable than some known alternatives. What gives the theory its persuasive force is, rather, its rendering the passage as a whole coherent and pointful; taking its proposed readings together yields an interpretation-of-the-whole which is better than any alternative interpretation-of-the-whole. The proposal intelligibly integrates, that is, reveals the integrity of the entity entire, as no other theory does. This interpretative proposal does not stand only, or so much, on an accumulation of independent probabilities as on superior integrative power. It enables us to see intelligible relationships between parts of a whole whose parts complement one another in the intelligible whole.

For another example of a case where integrative power together with *prima facie* circularity are exhibited, consider the circumstances in which geologists or physical-geographers have attempted to measure the distances and detect movements in the relations between great land-masses; for example, to determine whether America is easing away from, or getting closer to, Europe and Africa, or neither. Suppose that the instrumentation and the ability to measure accurately is at a stage of development at which considerable margins for error have to be allowed, and as yet only a small number of measurements have been made, so that while it appears rather likely that the continents are slowly separating, it cannot yet be said categorically that this is so; the evidence tends to favour it. At the same time, the respective large-scale shapes of these land-masses, as seen by the cursory inspection of globe or atlas, suggest that at one time they were pulled apart. They look as if they might fit together, like pieces of a long-broken plate where some smaller fragments, as is the way, have gone astray, leaving gaps or unevenness of fit. This appearance of fit could be accidental, coincidental. Fine reckoning of the probability here will be far less possible even than over the measurement of continental movement. Yet, given that the measurements tend to favour the separating-movement hypothesis and that that hypothesis would explain (though not necessitate, since other factors could have been at work since the great fracture) the appearance of fit, we have the makings of an account whose two principal pieces of contributory evidence each gives the overall account more claim on our assent if they are taken in context with each other than when they are each treated as making their weight felt in detachment from each other: each reinforces the probability of the other in affirming the one overall account (that the continents are drifting apart), and in so doing each confirms the congruent interpretation of the other. It may even be that, while it would be rash to believe the continental-drift-apart thesis on the evidence of one or other of these factors on its own, or (whether or not this be psychologically possible) on the basis of the sum of the respective tendencies or probabilities of each taken on its own (that is, when in the assessment of the weight of the tendency of each, prior to their being added, no cognisance of the other's relevance is allowed to be taken), it may be that it would be reasonable to accept the drift thesis if both are taken together; this, notwithstanding the circular appearance in saying that the drift thesis is only effectively supported by either of these evidential factors if it is taken to be supported by the other.

Finally, circularity might with some show of warrant be alleged in many historical accounts, such as this, where Churchill's defeat at the British General Election of 1945 is being explained. Simplified to give the broad gist, the explanation runs thus: a concern among British people that the economic and social experiences of the 1930s should and could (most likely by a mix of collectivist and Keynesian policies) be improved upon was deeply and widely felt; yet Churchill was regarded as having little enthusiasm about such matters, and as being opposed to collectivist and uninterested in Keynesian proposals. The circularity can be thought to arise because, of these two factors, the former, being the British people's deep and wide concern to improve on the 1930s, will have been a factor of causal significance in Churchill's defeat only if the latter, being Churchill's supposed weakness in these areas, was also a causal factor in his defeat. Similarly, the latter can only contribute to the explanation of the defeat if the former also does.

In the question about continental drift, the probability contributed by each principal factor in part depends on the probability contributed by the other. Where the textual interpretation is being undertaken, the acceptability of each of the two proposals about problematic expressions depends on the acceptability of the other.

The contemplation thus far of these three examples may already make it clear enough that vicious circularity is not involved. The sophistry of suggesting that it is may be helpful in prompting a better understanding when the sophistry is unmasked. Here, part of what must be recognised is that where the acceptability of our beliefs depends both (roughly) on their squaring with evidence and on their inductive coherence with other beliefs, inductive coherence can bring together the components of an account which together will be more belief-worthy than each component would be when it is (artificially) considered to have no relation to the other components. The whole account taken together seeks to give the best account, in accordance with criteria previously described in this chapter (for example, doing justice to experiences, logical coherence and seeking optimal inductive coherence, coherence with accepted background beliefs) and it is this total account which is to be assessed as a whole. The components which are supposed to give one another credentials but allegedly circularly so that neither is credit-worthy, are not separately, each on its own, up for assessment. If it is the account as a whole which is to be evaluated, the question of the credibility of each component-apart-from-others may not be necessary.

Someone pressing the vicious-circularity charge might press the analogous claim in relation to a proposal for the correct placement of a piece in some sector of a 1000-piece jigsaw puzzle where the picture is made up of rather diffuse colours, rather indeterminately formed, portraying, say, the surface of the sea on a misty day. The pictorial attributes of the pieces from this sector of the picture therefore give some, but rather little, guidance to those struggling with the puzzle. Suppose that about a dozen pieces are fitted snugly together so that they compose what could well be a coherent picture of sea-surface; this arrangement is proposed as a complete sub-sector of the puzzle. The objector would say that, of each piece, we cannot believe that it is correctly placed unless we have grounds to hold that its interlocking neighbours are correctly placed; and we cannot know that they are correctly placed unless we know that it is. Thus any such proposal must fail by reason of its circularity. Since it is the integrity of the whole portion, in its representation of a given picture-part, which is critical here, the dilemma of the vicious-circularity accuser is a false dilemma. (Proposing solutions for crossword puzzles can raise relevantly analogous points, for example, where 7 Down and 4 Across intersect.)

The impression of circularity may perhaps arise also from the way in which a comprehensive interpretative account can be specified, so as to make plain what the account says by setting out just the same points, insights, descriptions, etc., as will be set out to justify or vindicate the account. Contrast with this the practice in logico-deductive reasoning where the proposition to be proved is set out and the supporting reasoning which gives grounds for the proposition can emphatically not be the re-statement of the proposition itself. If it were, the reasoning would be question-begging, which may be regarded as a species of vicious circularity, with the smallest possible circle. Again the analogy between a comprehensive explanatory account and a proposed jigsaw solution may help; a proposed jigsaw solution is best specified by exhibiting the pieces in the proposed arrangement and the grounds for advancing the proposal are best set out by once again, showing the pieces in the proposed arrangement.

Where an account, as often in historiography or textual interpretation, and as in our whole belief-network, claims integrative power,[7] it will be able to be stated *and* defended in the same way, by laying out the same considerations. Plainly, there is no question-begging or debilitating circularity involved.

In order to complete this brief sketch of that epistemological doctrine by means of which light can be shed on what is involved epistemologically speaking when miracles are reported, and at the same time to begin the aimed-at illumination, some more

---

[7] Both B. G. Mitchell and R. G. Swinburne have advanced the understanding of types of cumulative case, and have variously advocated their employment particularly in the assessment of world-views. Yet neither has clearly distinguished integrative force (in which Mitchell seems the more interested) from the accumulation of mutually unrelated independent probabilities. See Mitchell, *The Justification of Religious Belief*, Ch. 3, where note 15 is of special interest; R. G. Swinburne, 'Arguments for the Existence of God', in J. Houston (ed.), *It is Reasonable to Believe in God?*, Edinburgh, 1984; this was the first of Swinburne's Wilde lectures the rest of which were later published as *The Existence of God*. Some further attention to cumulative cases has been given by W. J. Abraham in Abraham and Holtzer, *The Rationality of Religious Belief*, Ch. 2.

needs to be said about how inductive consistency is properly to be understood, assessed and maximised. Hume's attitude to a putative-miracle report is, in effect, that the requirements of inductive consistency compel us to account for the occurrence of any such report without conceding that any putative miracle actually took place. A putative miracle is an event which, *inter alia*, occurs contrary to natural law, and a natural law summarises uniform human experience, so far as that is known in circumstances of the sort which it covers. Inductive consistency has seemed to call for our believing only in the occurrence of events of a kind which the relevant natural law, the law covering these sorts of circumstances, specifies as happening. The analogy requirement which is so insisted upon by those who have offered a philosophical exposition like that of Bradley or (more derivatively) Troeltsch of the historical critical method, is the demand for inductive consistency in a variant idiom. Satisfying the analogy requirement is taken to necessitate being in accordance with the relevant laws of nature, so that, once again, reports of putative miracles have to be accounted for in such a way as avoids accepting that the putative miracle happened.

Perhaps it is understandable that inductive consistency, or analogy, should be thought to demand conformity to natural law with no exceptions, because almost always conformity to natural law will be required by them. As we saw (in Chapter 9) it is usually a fair presumption, prior to rational enquiry, that natural law will obtain. However, inductive consistency, or analogy, should not be understood as being just equivalent to conformity to natural law. Rather, they consist in there being some true description of the reported events, under which these events conform to (a) previously experienced pattern(s). This formulation is wider than the simple 'conformity to natural law', even as it secures the point of the demand for inductive consistency: that for an event to be intelligible it must conform to some pattern of previously experienced occurrences. Yet this wider formulation does allow for the possibility that a being which has power over the processes of nature might cause events to occur anomalously, for purposes of his which are nevertheless intelligible, perhaps on the basis of other experience of purposive activity in somewhat analogous circumstances, perhaps because some of the (likely) outcomes of this action could well be intended, given whatever other beliefs, proposals or suppositions about the suggested possible agent will hold promise of explanatory efficacy, probably as part of some integrative case.

Of course there will be respects in which each course of events is unique; and so no course of events will be, in all respects, like any other. Yet it does not follow that because there are disanalogies between one set of circumstances (or one event, or one thing) and another, there are no analogies between them. That is just as well because argument by analogy, inductive reasoning generally, would be altogether impossible if any disanalogy, disanalogy in any respect, rendered these respective sets of circumstances (events, things) quite incomparable. People have confusedly talked and written as if the uniqueness or the historical particularity, of some thing, state of affairs, or person, places them outside the scope of any reasoning on the basis of experienced shared properties (so that descriptive natural laws and prescriptive moral laws will be equally irrelevant to them). Certainly, on the basis of those properties in respect of which they are unique, there can be no argument of an inductive or analogical kind. Yet insofar as there are, as there will be, (other) features which are shared or analogous, such as between circumstances, events, persons or states of affairs, then inductive or analogical reasonings are possible. Something's uniqueness, it is salutary to register, is in respect of some particular property possessed, which might be the peculiar combining of other properties; to say only that something is unique tells little, and properly invites the question 'unique in what respect(s)?'. Something which was supposed to be unique in all respects, or simply unique, could not be appropriately described, because no general descriptive expression whatever would apply to it; and so it would be altogether incomprehensible. These homely conceptual points require to be brought out, for many reasons. Their illumination exposes much lofty 'existentialist' deployment of the notion of uniqueness, applied to persons and situations so that no general laws (descriptive or prescriptive) apply, and exposes as ineffectual those appeals to something's historical particularity which are made with a view to evading all judgements about it which would be appropriate in virtue of its being something of a general kind. Though the need to bring down these dismal, jerry-built structures is great indeed, the conceptual clarification of uniqueness requires also, and more to our purpose, to be addressed to those who invoke uniqueness in relation to arguments from analogy to the origins or governance of the (admittedly, in *some* respects, unique) universe. Thus, many people have argued that because there is only one universe (and maybe there can only be one universe), we cannot have experience of the origins or government of other universes which might be somewhat analogous to ours, so as to found an argument from analogy to conclusions about the origin or control of this universe. In this Hume led the way.[8] Many others have followed.[9]

It has not so often been specifically contended that, since appeals from the putatively miraculous to the existence/activity of God also depend on analogical argument, and then, since we have no experience of our own of how a god, or other agent who has power to order the course of events, will act to carry out known purposes such as revelation or salvation, we cannot get the requisite analogical argument going. Yet the conceptual issues raised in this latter sort of case, which more immediately concerns us now, are the same as those which arise in the case which has been extensively debated, namely the argument from (or for) design. It is important to clear away misconceptions, accumulated muddled prejudice or venerated error, so that neither of these analogical arguments is misguidedly rejected, ruled out by often endorsed but mistaken reasoning.

---

[8] See Pike, *Hume: Dialogues Concerning Natural Religion*, p. 30. The following appears towards the end of Part II:

When two *species* of objects have always been observed to be conjoined together I can infer, by custom, the existence of one wherever I *see* the existence of the other; and this I call an argument from experience. But how this argument can have place where objects as in the present case, are single, individual, without parallel or specific resemblance, may be difficult to explain.

[9] For example, Flew in *God and Philosophy*, pp. 71–4, in the course of which he quotes C. S. Peirce as remarking 'Universes are not as plentiful as blackberries'.

Suppose that we have experience of someone's acting in such a way as to reveal the fact that it *is* they who is acting. A spy sending radio messages from enemy territory might identify herself by some stylistic foible which listening natives of the spied-on country would be unlikely to catch; an irregularity of syntax or idiom might serve either as a pre-planned means of identification, or as an *ad hoc* expedient adopted by the spy because she has confidence that the specific irregularity will be noted by the people at home and recognised as peculiarly appropriate to her (maybe because the irregularity is commonest in the region or city from which she comes). Again, suppose a medieval prince disguises himself and mixes with his people, as one of them, meeting, talking, visiting, eating and drinking, encountering them in their sorrows and joys. Out of sympathy for the wretched poverty of some man's dwelling place, he may promise that this man will soon be visited by people who will take him to a better dwelling in the neighbourhood; or hearing that a widow is being oppressed by a bullying relative, he says that he will see to it that the problem is ended. In due course, what he has undertaken comes to pass; his power thereby begins to be revealed.

These, and other, sequences of events can be invoked as analogies (in that like all analogies they are *somewhat* analogous) to enable our understanding of otherwise incomprehensible, unassimilable reported putative miracles; if the report is strong, and hard to explain away as some species of error, then inductive coherence may be most satisfactorily retained if, on analogy with some such purposive activities as were instanced in the previous paragraph, the putative miracle can be accounted for as (a) god's revealing or beneficent action. For this to be likely there would have to be an appropriate wider context, such as for instance the career of a prophet of striking insight and power in his teaching, whose activity is associated with other reported putative miracles. In such a way an integrative account may be developed, accommodating the report and the reported putative miracle into an inductively coherent whole. Inductive coherence *is* retained in that the previous experiences

which furnish or enable an explanatory analogy[10] constitute
that background of happenings in relation to which (whether by
being an instance or an intelligibly imagined analogy) the
occurrence of the putative miracle makes sense. If, in such a
fashion, a reported putative miracle can be made sense of,
inductive consistency will have been satisfied; and if inductive
consistency is best satisfied, optimally satisfied, that way, the
putative miracle (with its report) can be incorporated into the
complex but integrated structure of what it is reasonable to
believe. In that case, any alternative ways of accounting for the
putative-miracle report will put greater strains on inductive
consistency, will be less satisfactory in respect of inductive
consistency, than that which says that the miracle actually took
place, as it gives its account of a god's purposes worked out in the
wider overall circumstances in which he has thus acted miraculously. The gains, in one direction, from upholding the natural-
law-inviolate will result in greater strains in another, as attempts
are made to explain how the report came to be made; so, if an
account of these matters, and of some others besides, presents
itself in which the occurrence of the miracle fits in, as do other
concomitant factors, with the postulated purpose of a postulated
god, then the least strained, the most inductively coherent, most
overall satisfactory explanation may well require us to say that a
god has brought about a miracle.

Refusal to contemplate postulating a god, even in view of the
costs incurred by the refusal, is to elevate ontological economy to
a supremacy which not even Occam accords it when he says
'*Frustra fit per plura quod potest fieri per pauciora*'.[11] Depending on

---

[10] In fact previous actual personal experiences (or vicarious, reported actual experiences) of rather closely analogous cases, such as those of the spy or the king, will not be
necessary for the acceptance of a reported putative miracle; what will be necessary is a
proper understanding of what will help to fulfil the possible, identifiable and
understood postulated purposes of an intelligent (divine) agent, and how it will help.
Whether this understanding comes by closely analogous previous actual experience,
or otherwise, the sound grasp of what could be purposed by such a miracle as is
reported, in the circumstances, is what is necessary if a miracle is to be found a place in
the network of our belief.

[11] 'What can be done by fewer is erroneously done by more.' William Occam, *Summa
Totius Logicae*, ed. P. Boehner, St Bonaventure, New York, 1951, line 12.

what counts as a *necessitas* and on what a necessitas is necessary
for, another of his *dicta* might be taken to be more restrictive:
'*Numquam ponenda est pluralitas sine necessitate*'.[12] Of course if the
'necessity' is what is necessary for our arriving at the account of a
matter which least strains inductive consistency then a postulating of God, in the circumstances just sketched, will be licensed
by what Occam said. The more commonly given version of
Occam's razor: '*Entia non sunt multiplicanda praeter necessitatem*'[13]
seems to be a rendition of his gist rather than his *ipsissima verba*.
In any case no one is bound to regard Occam, or the razor which
bears his name, with a respect due to authority even if we could
be confident about how the razor, *or* what he actually said,
should apply to the issues which concern us. Actually, Occam's
exhortations to ontological economy were not urged in relation
to experience-based reasoning, about the (empirical) world,
inductive argument, but rather with respect to reasoning in
philosophy of logic, such as reasoning about whether there are
natures as well as the things whose natures they are, or about
whether there are propositions – the proper bearers of truth or
falsehood which sentences express – as well as the sentences
which express them.

Certainly it would be hard to defend a refusal, urged simply in
the interests of theoretical economy, to postulate the existence of
an as yet unobserved planet, such as Pluto was, in face of
responsibly acquired experimental readings which would be
explained as being the effects of such a planet, and to insist that
the readings *must* have been in error or have been deceitfully
reported by scientists who perhaps crave the limelight. (Let us
suppose, so as to approach more closely the assessment of
historical evidence, that the experimental conditions and
readings are, in practice, hard to recreate and repeat.)

If the ontological economiser says that what must be
minimised is the postulating of unobservable entities, or of
supra-human agents, such that *any* other sort of explanation, or
even suspension of judgement, is *always* to be preferred to an

---

[12] 'A plurality is never to be proposed without necessity.' William Occam, *Super Quattuor
Libros Sententiarium*, 1495–6, 1. dist. 27, qu.2, **K**.
[13] 'Entities are not to be multiplied beyond necessity.'

account which invokes such things, the following case should give him pause: an aeroplane is flying high over the ocean and through cloudless sky. Among the passengers are several mathematicians making their way to a congress of their kind, and one of them cries out, intrigued, that he sees a meaningful pattern forming, apparently out of foam or froth, on the surface of the deep. As they watch there is generated a spread of symbolism on the sea which one of the number-theorists excitedly recognises as a proof of Fermat's Last Theorem. For a third of a millennium mathematicians have sought, and failed, to devise either a proof or a disproof of this proposition. Reflection on the theorem of Pythagoras makes many of us familiar with the fact that satisfying the equation $x^2 + y^2 = z^2$ are several well-known sets of natural number substitutes for x, y and z. Thus 3, 4 and 5, or 15, 8 and 17 will do. Fermat invites us to consider $x^3 + y^3 = z^3$ and more generally $x^n + y^n = z^n$ where $n > 2$, and his theorem states that there is no set of whole numbers which will satisfy the equation where $n > 2$. Now, on the water, sits the long-desired reasoning which, with some obvious gaps easily to be filled in, proves the theorem. Subsequent enquiry establishes that in this closely monitored part of the ocean, neither submarine detector apparatus nor submarine communication systems nor dolphin-researchers nor normal radars, nor other comprehensive survey of the area immediately set in train, nor analysis of many samples of the water, can offer even the beginning of an explanation of the phenomenon. If, in addition, some of the number-theorists on board the plane were devout people, who had prayed for some years for the issue of this theorem to be resolved and if practical, as well as theoretical, benefits flow abundantly from this intellectual advance, would an ontological economiser (perhaps a non-devout, non-praying number-theorist on the plane) be justified in ruling out any/all possibility of the involvement of an unseen benevolent intelligent being, so that explanation of this naturally unexplained event by invoking such a being is quite excluded in advance of any further reflection? Of course, before entertaining the possibility of such a being, a cautious person might perhaps reasonably enough wish to be satisfied both that every avenue of possible natural explanation has been explored, and that enough is known about the sorts of natural circumstances which might (however remotely) possibly create the puzzling phenomena to justify our confidence that a natural explanation will not be found.[14] Yet, if a person has good grounds to be satisfied on these counts, a ruling-out of any consideration of possible theistic explanations must merely be arbitrary – unless some hitherto unconsidered reason for it can be advanced. There are, no doubt especially among the late twentieth-century western educated classes, people who are psychologically so entrenched in the conviction that there will be a natural explanation for everything, a conviction which has been very useful as the scientist's heuristic assumption, that they balk ungovernably and are not open to possible persuasion at the suggestion of a theistic account. However, if there is no good reason to exclude the action of a god as a possible explanation, the entrenchment and the balking are psychological problems, obscurantism to be dealt with by kind persistence and persuasion, or by therapy, rather than treated as a rational constraint on our belief.

If a theistic proposal is adopted partly, as it may be, in order to account for well-attested events which run counter to natural law, the entire system of our beliefs, which in its content will not be very different, will acquire a pervasive new aspect. To explain some anomalous event as part of, according to, the divine purpose is to posit a god who has power over natural processes. Insofar as he has such powers[15] (and maybe we should not yet assume that he has similar powers in relation to all natural laws), natural processes occur with unaltered regularity, or irregularly, either way according to his will and intention. We have no reason either, to actually confine his powers, and it may be that he who can act anomalously in some respect *can* so act in any or all. In our cognitive dealings with this world in which a

---

[14] For a closely analogous example, and argument, see R. G. Swinburne's paper 'Miracles', *Philosophical Quarterly*, vol. 18 (1968), pp. 320–8.

[15] Those who concur, with R. G. Swinburne's (and Bishop Berkeley's?) version of the Argument from Design in *Philosophy*, which concludes that the temporal order, pattern in the succession of events is best explained theistically, will of course have an additional basis for treating the order, which natural laws describe, as dependent on God.

god is supposed to have worked miraculously, we shall not take it simply as a brute structural given for our system of belief that natural laws are inviolate and inviolable; the faithfulness of God who will not cause the world's processes to depart from their almost universal regularities except for good reason – good for us, in particular – undergirds the way the world goes, and hence our confidence in our beliefs about its consistency. So, although belief in a miracle-working god should make no difference to the working procedures of most practising scientists or historians, most of the time, affecting them only on the exceedingly rare occasions on which some miracle-hypothesis seems to have some point and some promise, the underlying conception of the world which is being studied, will be significantly different, as compared with that of those scientists or historians who rule out (for whatever reason) any possibility that a god may act miraculously.

If there are many different cases where strongly supported reports arise of what appear compellingly to be infractions of natural law, and if there is an interpretation or relatable group of interpretations of these events which would account for their occurring as reported, in terms of a god's discernible purpose or consistent mutually assisting purposes, then the likelihood that any one of these reports is properly to be explained by a god's having acted is greater than if there were the reports only of that single anomalous event. Shortly we shall look at the argument which Hume urges against any such interpretation of any one reported putative miracle, namely that there are well-based reports of other putative miracles whose promising-looking interpretations are incompatible with the proposed theistic interpretation of the particular reported putative miracle under examination: each religion has its own alleged miracles, but the religions are in competition and are incompatible, so the respective alleged miracles cancel out each other's credibility.

However, it is best first to draw out an important implication of the picture of a systematically integrated structure or network of our acceptable beliefs and of the integrative and cumulative character of much of the argumentation which supports these beliefs. This implication is that a very commonly expressed dilemma is to be rejected because the alternatives with which it presents us should not properly be presented as exclusive or exhaustive. The alternatives supposedly arise where a putative miracle has been reported and there is justification for its being believed in. It is then said that there will be a body of related interpretative theological theory or doctrine such that either the alleged miracle (if it is well attested) supports the doctrine, or the doctrine (if it is well founded) lends weight to the claim that the miracle happened: either miracles carry doctrine or doctrine carries miracles. Let it be granted that there *are* both kinds of situation which, in differing epistemic circumstances, do obtain. B. B. Warfield notices and employs the distinction and contrast between miracles carrying doctrine and doctrine carrying miracles in a number of places,[16] such as pages 36–7 where Sir James Fitzjames Stephen is quoted as saying that nobody is converted in the nineteenth century as Gibbon was in the eighteenth by a belief that 'as a fact, miracles were worked in the early church, and that, as a consequence, the doctrines professed at the time must be true. As a rule, the doctrines have carried the miracles . . . ' Later (page 58) Warfield points out that a Catholic believing in a church which has been given power to work miracles will properly be predisposed, as a Protestant will not, to believe in miracles which are alleged to have been worked to attest to Catholic truth. Warfield can go further than the mere identifying of this sort of case. Reflecting on the Lourdes pilgrimages and their outcomes, he says, 'of course, as R. H. Benson puts it, "those who believe in God and His Son and the Mother of God on quite other grounds", may declare that "Lourdes is enough" [that is, to require belief that reported miracles have happened at Lourdes as reported]. But this is not to make the miracles carry the doctrine, but the doctrine the miracles, in accordance with J. H. Newman's proposition that it is all a matter of point of view, of presuppositions.'[17]

No doubt Warfield is correct that the Lourdes case as described by Benson is an instance consistent with Newman's claim; but it should be noticed, first that Newman's proposition,

[16] B. B. Warfield, *Counterfeit Miracles*, Edinburgh and Carlisle, PA, 1972.
[17] Ibid. p. 123.

if it is taken to mean that the presuppositions cannot be affected, made questionable or supported, by strong reports of putative miracles, does not *follow* from the Lourdes example so described. Even more to the point, Newman's proposition, so understood, should not be accepted, even though many have accepted it. A corollary to the invulnerability of presuppositions to strong miracle reports would be that reports of miracles can have no apologetic value because the sceptic's assumptions are invulnerable. As a believer's assumptions will effectively carry the miracle, so a sceptic's will sink it. Among those many who have espoused this view are Diamond,[18] Hick,[19] Mackie[20] and Penelhum;[21] many names could be added to the list.

Already in this book there has been brought out the falseness of the claim to completeness and exclusiveness of the following alternative: *either* one is a religious sceptic, a Stratonician atheist, a naturalist, or something of the sort and so one discounts the truth of miracle-stories because of one's premises, *or* one is a supernaturalist, a religious believer, a theist or the like, and one is then prepared to accept at least some well-attested miracle-stories where the miracle fits well with one's other beliefs. There is, as in effect was pointed out, a *tertium quid*, the position of being an undecided enquirer. Now, further, that we better understand the structure and aim of our belief systems, by which we seek overall to maximise the justice which is done to experience, rightly relying on their cumulative and integrative power to commend themselves to us, we can see yet more clearly that those who affirm Newman's proposition, those who present these alternatives as necessarily exhaustive and exclusive, are indeed mistaken. If a person does have very strong good reason to hold that accounts of violations of natural law are never credible, then, in that epistemic circumstance, a report of a putative miracle will have to be dealt with by that person in the light of his strong reason to discount it, and to explain its existence as some species of error or deceit. Equally, if someone has a well-established reason to expect that God may give a sign which runs

---

[18] M. Diamond, *Contemporary Philosophy and Religious Thought*, New York, 1974, p. 69.
[19] Hick, *Philosophy of Religion*, p. 40. [20] Mackie, *The Miracle of Theism*, p. 40.
[21] Penelhum, *Religion and Rationality*, pp. 275–80.

counter to the usual course of nature, then the justification of that prior attitude will make it more likely that a report of a miracle is to be interpreted by that person as true. In contemplating these possibilities we are treating the miracle report as *the* problematic uncertain matter about which a verdict must be reached on the basis of other things we (think we) know; and we are invited to identify and recognise those sub-sections of our whole systems of belief which constitute arguments to lead to one verdict or another.

Some issues connect very widely through the whole network of our beliefs, tentacles of implication reaching to and from these issues to many parts of the system; in a matter like this a narrowly bracketed treatment will not suffice. An issue which has implications for the structural skeleton of our whole corpus of beliefs has the potential to force re-assessments (and maybe cause havoc) throughout the whole body. Take Rupert Sheldrake's contention that the regularities in nature which we have regarded as universal and describable by formulated scientific laws are actually habits, which are formed as similarly structured entities, atoms or animals, have influenced each other in a way akin to resonance (he calls this influencing 'isomorphic resonance'); but habits which are changeable as and when some members of the isomorphic group acquire new traits. So new regularities can come to be (albeit non-consciously) 'learnt', and new laws obtain.[22] A view like this connects in mutual implication with vast areas of our believings, with the ways of acquiring beliefs, with our conceptions of the past and of scientific method. The pervasiveness of its relevance, conferring a new aspect and altered fresh perspective on very many things means that the range of factors which may be pertinent to the assessment of the thesis cannot be narrowly restricted. Perhaps a view like this is not yet *quite* so far-reaching and difference-making in its implications as to constitute an alternative 'world-view'; still, one thing which is at stake is how well the several implications of the claim fit the wide range of disparate *data* (maybe otherwise non-related) which it touches.

[22] Rupert Sheldrake, *A New Science of Life*, London, 1983, and *The Presence of the Past*, London, 1988.

For the undecided enquirer, and for those who are open-minded in their agnosticism or atheism, strongly founded reports of putative miracles likewise invite critical consideration of a far-reaching, thorough-going re-interpretation of everything that happens, has happened and will happen. Since the interpretation affirms the power of a purposive god over and in every event, this does count as the proposal of a world-view.

This chapter's ground plan for an epistemology enables Hume's treatment of the reported miracles of the many religions to be better evaluated. Hume regards a miracle reported and affirmed within one religious tradition as giving support to that system of religion so as to weaken the claim and the credentials of any alternative competing system of religion. Among those weakened credentials will be reports of putative miracles which are adduced as grounds of the alternative religious system. Reports of putative miracles which abound in the several arguments of the respective apologists for the numerous systems of religion serve to offset each other by reducing the evidential weight of each report, so as to make it fall yet further short of the great weight needed to outweigh the evidence for the relevant law of nature, and so as to cancel each other out. The evidence for a putative miracle in one religious system is, Hume thinks, as directly destructive of the credit of the report of a putative miracle which supports an opposing religious system as the evidence of witnesses giving mutually unreconcilable evidence in a court case. His reasoning is, he says 'that of a judge, who supposes that the credit of two witnesses, maintaining a crime against any one, is destroyed by the testimony of two others, who affirm him to have been two hundred leagues distant, at the same instant when the crime is said to have been committed'.[23]

Before we turn to the most philosophically substantial matter, two other significant weaknesses in Hume's case must be brought out. First, Hume assumes that alternative, different religious systems are incompatible; for him they are mutually inconsistent, nor can they be made consistent by amendments or adjustments which will leave them (reasonably to be thought of

---

[23] Hume, *Enquiries*, p. 122.

as) substantially the same systems. Syncretistic accommodations
are not entertained, and the possibility of them not explored. Yet
if the opposition and competition between systems is reduced or
eliminated, Hume's point will be at least affected, possibly
destroyed.

Nor is it clear that every miracle needs to support those
components of religious systems which genuinely are mutually
excluding; healing miracles reported within many religious
traditions whose systems are significantly incompatible might be
taken as expressing and supporting the benevolent goodwill of
whatever are the universe's ruling powers without necessarily
endorsing whichever other, erroneous, beliefs are accidentally
historically associated with the healings. Indeed, if there were
many strongly attested putative miracles which *seemed* to give a
basis for mutually incompatible religious systems, rather than
our appealing to the incompatibility of the systems to weaken the
credibility of these apparently strong reports, we might use the
strength of the reports to call in question those features of the
respective systems which generate the incompatibility. Hence,
revising our interpretation so as to give proper respect to the
strength of all the reports of putative miracles hitherto adduced
in the interests of their respective incompatible systems, we
might correct and reconcile the religious systems. Hume simply
ignores these possibilities. He assumes monotheism, and while
that is no doubt justified insofar as his readers would wish that
assumption to be made, it makes syncretism or the reconciling of
miracle-founded systems harder. Even so, it does not of itself rule
out, without the need for exploration and reflection, all such
possibilities.

Second, the extent to which reports of putative miracles are in
fact found in, and interpreted as a basis for, distinct religious
systems is a factual matter which calls for more careful attention
than Hume takes time to give. The incidence of claimed miracles
in Islam is low; and little if any burden of vouching for, or
warranting, Islam rests on them.

Even if all religious systems did invoke miraculous events,
some attention would need to be given to the strength or weight
or evidential value of these respective reports in themselves, and

to how far other factors in their religious systems add to or subtract from the credibility of the miracle reports. Among these other factors will be questions about how seriously and literally reports of putative miracles were intended; were they meant and understood to be colourful stories only half-believed by anyone? Or were they reported and taken with historical seriousness? Hume gives the impression of assuming that the weight and the seriousness are in every case similar enough for differences to be ignored in practice. Yet it may be that one religion can fairly claim in support vastly more and better-attested miracles than all others, even though all others *claim* some miraculous support, albeit meagre and feebly attested. If that be so, it will be of importance, and will greatly affect the force of what Hume does say. That issue is in the province of the descriptive scholar of religion and of religious history, as much as of the philosopher or theologian.

The matter of most philosophical pertinence concerns Hume's conception of the way in which testimonies to putative miracles which are offered in support of different religions count against each other, and should be reckoned as weakening each other. His use of the courtroom analogy helps us to see the weakness, or at best the limitation, of his conception, and suggests the sort of development needed to move to a better understanding.

Only in a fatuously inept criminal court is it possible that the case for the prosecution should consist simply in the fact that two witnesses say they saw the accused commit a crime at time t, and the case for the defence consist simply in the fact that two witnesses say they saw the accused at t, but so far from the location of the offence that he could not have acted as he is accused of acting. In an effective court of justice, the defence would try to discredit the testimony of the prosecution witnesses and reinforce that of their own, while the prosecution would try to undermine the credibility of the defence witnesses and strengthen that of their own. Questions would be asked on both sides about the respective circumstances in which the witnesses claim to have seen and heard what they say they saw and heard, and about what *exactly* it was that they did see and hear.

Implausibilities in, or inconsistencies between the parts of, the versions of events given by the witnesses will be made much of or played down or explained away. Any permissible claims about character strengths and weaknesses in witnesses, or about witnesses' interests being served by their giving evidence, will be advanced. Attempts will be made to have witnesses seem shifty or straightforward. In such ways will the weight or strength of each testimony be debated. At the same time, unless the information before the court is very scanty, perhaps due to failures of memory or just lack of evidence of any sort, alternative accounts of a range of *data*, no doubt each account leaving gaps which it would be desirable to fill, or containing poorly supported points, will be constructed and commended; and the evidence given by a witness will be judged in part by other merits of the account with which it coheres, which it supports and which supports it.

Let us assume now, with Hume, that no accommodations are possible between these accounts. If, as the cases unfold, one of the accounts which is developed becomes increasingly unlikely in itself and even without reference to the strength of the alternative account, the credibility of the witnesses for the unlikely account may well go down because of the weakening of the overall account. When an account is weakened to the point of its being rejected, the testimony of the witnesses who supported it may often (as surely in the case of Hume's court case) quite probably be put aside, discounted as mere error or deceit; their evidence need then be considered no more. The same will hold if an account is rejected not only because of its own weaknesses, but when it is compared with the much greater strengths of some alternative incompatible account; the testimony of witnesses which formed part of the rejected case may often properly be discarded, set aside and ignored. Having been considered, dealt with, and disposed of so as to be altogether discounted, the witnesses' evidence for the rejected case need not be counted at all against the evidence of the witnesses in the better, to-be-accepted account. Indeed, the best account, where there are several competitors, may see off its rivals one by one without having its evidence of testimony countered and weakened cumulatively by each piece of testimonial evidence which is offered in favour of some other inferior case.

When we come to Hume's procedure for determining the probabilities of reported miracles which have been alleged in support of different religions, his conception of our weighing the reports of alleged miracles against one another treats the reports as though our attempts to appropriate and assess them do not properly or at all involve our appraisal of the whole systems of belief, religious or otherwise, within which it is proposed that the reports be fitted, with which the reports best cohere. It is ironic that he should be at fault in this way because when he begins talking about the alternative religious systems, each of which invokes reports of miracles in its support, he shows awareness of the reports' having a credibility which rises or falls together with (though not necessarily in direct proportion to) the credibility of their respective systems. He appears, there, to manifest epistemological awareness. Yet his setting reports of putative miracles off simply against each other, as if the reports of alleged miracles apparently in favour of any one religion should be opposed and weakened and overcome by the accumulated reports of alleged miracles seeming to favour other religions, is a deterioration into crudity. Still cruder is the notion that the witnesses of putative miracles belonging to these other religions should be treated as if they were eye-witnesses of the allegedly miraculous events which were reported in the interests of the first religion but who deny the account given by the witness for the first religion.

Much more could, perhaps should, be said about the different kinds of cases where there is evidence of testimony in favour of a discredited account. Sometimes, we have just seen, the testimonial evidence may be quite discounted; but sometimes it will still require to be reckoned with, and should be re-interpreted or at least treated as remaining problematical. Still, enough has now been said to reveal as, at best, inconclusive, Hume's simplistic attempt to cancel putative-miracle reports in the interest of any one world-view just by appeal to the supposedly countervailing weight of reports of miracles brought in aid of other world-views.

CHAPTER 12

Reported miracles in theology

There has been wide acceptance by modern theologians both that the claims of the historical-critical method must be accepted and that they require reports of miracles to be dealt with as not veridical, either interpreted so as not to be claiming to tell *wie eigentlich gewesen ist* ('how it really happened'), or rejected as falsely making that claim. These theologians, like Bultmann, MacQuarrie and others whose arguments about the concept of the miraculous were reviewed earlier in the book, and in practice many exegetes who understand the historical-critical method in that way, affirming its soundness and submitting to its prescriptions, have already been directly confronted and controverted.

However there are others, whose attitudes call for particular attention. Some (few) affirm the authoritative competence of historical science and the essential, decisive, not-to-be-circum-vented task of historical research as basic to theological construction, but apparently maintain that, nevertheless, accounts of miracles are at least sometimes credible (notably, for example, Pannenberg). Some are ambivalent about the claims of the historical-critical method, claiming in some places that it has value, in others that it embodies unacceptable assumptions, but that in any case miracles are to be believed in on the basis of Revelation rather than by the exercise of normal historical judgement (notably, for example, Barth). Some maintain that to treat allegedly miraculous alleged events, like the resurrection of Jesus Christ, as if they were public occurrences in our common, shared, space and time, as the preceding arguments of this book have encouraged us to do, is to misunderstand their character, and that when a better view is taken much of that argument is seen to be beside the point (for example, Cupitt or Mackey). Relatedly, some have offered other, particular, reasons, quite apart from the contentions of Hume, Troeltsch or the historical-critical method, for concluding that particular alleged miracles as traditionally conceived of cannot have happened as traditionally supposed (for example, Cupitt). It is with the claims of such theologians and their theologies that this chapter is concerned.

Pannenberg[1] rejects attempts to by-pass historical reasoning, both because he wishes to affirm the historicity, the occurrence in the past of our time and space, of the events which are the subject of christian proclamation, and because he wishes to establish and defend it on the basis of reasoning. So he criticises, for example, Althaus, for relying on a capacity of intuitive perception, allegedly giving certainty about past events, which can be trusted as an alternative to the exercise of scientific historical judgement. Although some such intuition may function alongside or instead of proper historical enquiry, the accuracy of its perceptions cannot properly be trusted so long as they are untested; and the testing, to establish whether what is intuited is or was actually as intuition would have it, must be by the instruments of historical criticism. Whatever may be the psychological priority or simultaneity as between this intuition and the exercise of historical scientific judgements, epistemic trustworthiness lies with historical science; if the deliverances of intuition are to be accepted, historical research must confirm them. Otherwise we shall be prey to subjectivism, which is not accountable to any norms which command respect, which is arbitrary, against which Pannenberg quite generally sets his face.

Accordingly, appeals to a Revelation equally require rational confirmation if they are not to be mere arbitrary commitments, for all anyone knows corresponding to nothing which is truly the case. A theology, like that of Barth, which is devoted to what is

---

[1] See especially W. Pannenberg, *Jesus – God and Man*, translator D. Priebe, London, 1968.

apprehended as Revelation must offer reasons, some confirmatory grounds as judged by critical standards which obtain somewhat generally, for treating the proclaimed revelation as anything of the kind; otherwise theology rests on 'a subjective act of the will or an irrational venture of faith',[2] and its discourse, unintegrated with other fields of rational discourse by rational constraints and licences, analogous to those which obtain elsewhere, suffers the 'self-inflicted isolation of a higher glossolalia'.[3]

For Pannenberg, the kinds of reasoning which best serve as the basis for the christian gospel are anthropological, and historical. The gist of the anthropological contention is that the fact of human questioning about man in the world presupposes and invites answers; as offering answers to such questioning, religious discourse has meaning. Ongoing human experience, insofar as it touches on these questions, is predominantly of a personal reality correlative to our experienced personhood. So says the history of religions. Moreover, we experience the world as a history of novel events whose full nature comes to light in a future which has yet to be completed; and a reality like this can be grounded only on such a God as is disclosed through the Judaeo-Christian scriptures, in the history of which they speak. Even as Pannenberg has expounded these theses, they raise many questions both as to their meaning and as to their cogency; this sketchiest of outlines does no more than indicate principal themes with their connexions. It also indicates how the anthropological leads into the historical. Pannenberg gives no place to a distinction between on the one hand a salvation history whose course or constituent events, although they supposedly existed in our time and space, are inaccessible to the methods of the scientific historian, and on the other that ordinary history which is in practice or in principle open to the investigation of historical study. The only history which he recognises, which he identifies with revelation, is that which can be researched and

[2] W. Pannenberg, *Theology and the Philosophy of Science*, translator F. McDonagh, London, 1976, p. 273.
[3] W. Pannenberg, *Basic Questions in Theology II*, translator G. H. Kehm, London, 1971, 'Types of Atheism and their Theological Significance', p. 189.

reconstructed by critical historians. So Pannenberg aims to escape from that subjective arbitrariness which disqualifies reliance on what claims to be a non-defensible revelation.

As is well known, the Resurrection of Jesus Christ is for Pannenberg one historical event, perhaps *the* one such event more than any other, which confirms both the Jewish apocalyptic hope of resurrection which is the (highly significant) context of the Resurrection of Jesus, and the oneness of Jesus with God; awareness of this historical resurrection of Jesus is therefore central to the recognition that history is revelation. Yet Pannenberg insists we gain our knowledge of this resurrection event as responsible users of the methods of critical history. In view of the standard understanding about what historical-critical method consists of, how can all these Pannenbergian things be? How can the criteria for rational credibility, proper to that method, allow, permit, (let alone prescribe) acceptance of Jesus' resurrection?

Pannenberg is aware that people will balk at this purportedly scientific history of the resurrection, and he attempts to deal with their likely misgivings. Taking Troeltsch's version of the historical-critical method as widely approved, authoritative, even canonical or magisterial, Pannenberg considers the leading principles, as they figure in Troeltsch's account, of correlation and analogy.[4]

If the principle of correlation requires the complete (causal) determination of all events such that the whole course of history is rigidly set, settled and established by the events comprising some long-past primal state of affairs, and there remains no room for contingency among events, Pannenberg rejects the principle. However he thinks that none of these undesirable implications need follow from the correlation principle better understood as making a weaker, or more modest, claim: that all historical events have causal relations with other events. He seems to intend by this that all historical events have consequences; and that while some events are not altogether causally determined by antecedent circumstances, they will be given

---

[4] See, notably, Pannenberg's paper 'Redemptive Event and History' in the book *Basic Questions in Theology I*, translator G. H. Kehm, London, 1970, pp. 15ff.

some measure of increased probability by some of the conditions which surround them. Many people have believed in that sort of free will[5] which makes it possible for rewarding or punishing, praising or blaming a person in respect of their actions to be not merely or even at all manipulative in intent or effect but also deserved by that person's own meritorious or iniquitous contribution which, as their own, was not simply determined by prior conditions; many have believed in human creativity whereby a creative person contributes something new, not merely re-arranging received material according to some predetermined process. People holding any such belief will concur with Pannenberg here in rejecting a quite deterministic interpretation of the correlation principle, if it is to be affirmed. Also, Christians who wish to insist that Jesus Christ was fully human, belonging to our history, will wish as a consequence to insist that the events of his history have a causally significant, if not wholly-determining, context, and that they have consequences in and for our history. So he was cradled in Israel; and he called disciples, some of whom were peculiarly, though not of themselves sufficiently, causally efficacious, in the emergence of the church. Thus Pannenberg's endorsement of an acceptably qualified or perceived principle of correlation will be widely supported. It is with the principle of analogy that wrestling is necessary.

The individuality and particularity of events and people will it may seem, *prima facie*, elude the grasp of historians who employ analogy as their intelligibility-extending instrument or technique. Because analogy assimilates the newly appropriated to the already known by recognising a respect, or respects, in which they are somewhat alike, so analogy apparently serves to specify, correlate and illuminate precisely those attributes or aspects of the newly captured historical portion or entity in which is it *not* exceptional, idiosyncratic, individual. If analogy is understood as working only in this way the historian will, it may seem, fail to do justice to particularity, to uniqueness, and may even seem to impose blinkers which will prevent particular-

---

[5] Often called incompatibilist free will which is, allegedly, incompatible with complete causal determinism.

ities or uniquenesses from ever being recognised. If this be so, then so much the worse for analogy.

Pannenberg insists[6] that satisfactory historical method will, and does in fact, employ analogy in such ways as yet to secure the recognition and portrayal of the individual, the eccentric, and not only of the typical. So he says,

If the historian keeps his eye on the non-exchangeable individuality and contingency of an event, then he will see that he is dealing with nonhomogeneous things, which cannot be contained without remainder in any analogy. Provided that historical science is occupied above all with the particularity and uniqueness of phenomena, its interests must therefore be focused more upon the ever peculiar, non-homogeneous features, rather than the common ones first obtruded by analogies.[7]

Especially within Christian theology it is important 'that analogies between historical events should not be one-sidedly employed as expressions of homogeneity, but rather used to determine in each case the degree and limits of an analogy. In this way, precisely by uncovering analogies, it will be possible to trace the individual and characteristic features'[8] of events and testimonies. Here Pannenberg is both reflecting upon historians' method in general, and applying these general reflections specifically to theologians' practice. He goes on to censure the levelling out, or elimination, of the distinctivenesses in the history to which the Bible bears witness, and in the witness itself, by the history of religions school in its use of analogising procedures, as it lays too exclusive an emphasis on parallels between religious phenomena.

Since Troeltsch was the leading member of the history of religions school it is appropriate to bring out the misuse of analogy in that school's practice, not only by way of helpful illustration, but also so that the endorsement of the principle of analogy, which Troeltsch authoritatively described, is not taken to endorse its abuses. Pannenberg is correct to insist that each event or entity has its own individuality, is distinctive in some way, and cannot be similar to anything else in all respects. A

[6] Pannenberg, 'Redemptive Event and History' in *Basic Questions in Theology I* especially pp. 39–50. [7] Ibid. p. 46. [8] Ibid. p. 48.

converse of the philosophers' principle of the Indentity of Indiscernibles is the discernibility or distinguishability of non-identicals: if there is/are more than one thing or event they must have some differing attributes. Again he is right not to take Troeltsch's practice as unimpeachable commentary on the analogy principle; many others, as our earlier expositions show, have written more fully and subtly than Troeltsch, in effect on this matter. The use of analogy *is* essential for historical understanding; yet, as Pannenberg says, it must be compatible with discerning individuality. He says that the cognitive power of analogy 'is greater the more sharply the limitation of the analogy is recognised in each case',[9] but he does not tell us how the limitations are to be recognised. Since the only intelligibility-extending method spoken of here is the analogical, how does the limiting of analogical inference happen?[10]

The first step towards an answer is to recognise what is too seldom noted, that analogy, similarity, parallels are in respect of a particular attribute, or of particular attributes. So, while two situations, events, people may well be analogous in some respects, they will also be disanalogous in others; and, as noted already, they cannot be exactly alike in all respects and still be numerically distinct situations, events or people. Thus, to take one example, the uncontroversial exercise of historical judgement, involving analogical extension from known correlations, to gather new material into the sphere of the understood, leads to the following well-founded attributions to Abraham Lincoln: that he became President of the United States having had almost no experience of exercising large-scale, widely significant government administration; that his country confronted and lived through a crisis whose resolution entailed unprecedented bloodshed, requiring the maintenance both of unstable alliances

---

[9] Ibid. p. 47.

[10] That the satisfactory dealing with this problem is of great importance is underlined by Van Harvey: ' . . . Christianity is confronted by a dilemma: without the principle of analogy, it seems impossible to understand the past; if, however, one employs the principle of analogy, it seems impossible to do justice to the alleged uniqueness of Jesus Christ. A great deal of the discussion in contemporary Protestant theology over the nature of hermeneutics is . . . an attempt to deal with this dilemma', *The Historian and the Believer*, London, 1967, p. 32.

and of the will of a volatile public; that issues of quite basic political and moral principle, as well as sectional interest, underlay the emergency with which he dealt.

His distinctiveness lies in this combination: the steady reliable vision, the consistency of purpose through fundamentally altering circumstances, the sound judgements about people and opportunities, and the effectiveness of tellingly expressed appeals to principle, all in the context of a terrible war about which he was receiving strident inconsistent advice from many people of long experience, and (at the least) all this in someone with experience neither of high administrative office nor of fearful and fateful national struggle. While each of these attributes of Lincoln can be established by routine historical enquiry benefiting from abundant evidence, utilising other knowledge, often implicitly, to draw conclusions which depend on analogies between the already-known and the newly-arrived-at, the distinctive combination is (obviously) not as whole known by an analogy from a person or persons who possessed that combination of qualities, and was otherwise like Lincoln. Rather, it is the addition or aggregation of results (which do severally depend on analogical reasonings) which yields perception of the particular, the individual. This further step, of adding, conjoining attributes which have been derived by analogical reasonings, can enable the historian to grasp what there is in people or situations, or other entities in history, to which in respect of some cumulation or totality of their qualities there is no known analogy. Here, then is one way of understanding and supporting Pannenberg's contention that, while analogy is an essential technique for the historian, he is not required so to employ it that he excludes or passes over distinctiveness, as Troeltsch tended to do. By the simple expedient of conjoining the attributes in a subject of our interest, we can reveal distinctiveness, or uniqueness, even though each of these attributes is established by analogical reasoning.

Moreover the limitations of one analogical argument, inference in respect of one attribute or one recurring constellation of attributes, emerge when the contrary force of another piece of analogical reasoning, in respect of another attribute or constellation of attributes is brought out. People who have not experienced high administrative office would not, on the basis of our knowledge of that attribute, inexperience, on its own, be expected to master complex administration and command statesmanship so as to show immense practical wisdom in man-management, make effective rallying appeals to high principle, and maintain a sound sense of proportion, in a deep crisis. That line of reasoning, resting on that analogy, gives us reason to expect Lincoln to have been a somewhat unsuccessful president. Yet, of course, other pieces of reasoning, appealing to masses of other evidence but arguing equally analogically lead us to reckon that Lincoln was in fact great in all these ways, and more. In such a manner, the inconclusive strength of analogical reasoning in respect of, on the basis of, one attribute can be revealed by analogical reasonings on the basis of another or others.

So far, then, what Pannenberg says is defensible; and if there is to be a credible case presented by the critical historian for a resurrection it is helpful (even though this is not the kind of objection to a historian's case for the resurrection which is usually most strenuously pressed) to recognise that (1) the fact of the resurrection's uniqueness, or singular or unusual character, does not of itself render the resurrection inaccessible to historical, analogical reasonings, and (2) the outcome of one line of analogical reasoning may be qualified, or countered or perhaps set aside by another analogical inference based on another analogy from another attribute. For example, not just what may be rendered probable analogically from his having been dead may be of interest or relevance to the issue of the alleged resurrection of Jesus; but also, if it is an open question whether there is a god, it will matter what may be rendered probable by strong attestation of Jesus' resurrection together with his costly faithfulness to his unusual divine vocation, as he understood it to be, the fact that (other) miracles are attributed to him and the contemporary understanding of resurrection which derived from Jewish eschatology. There may be a description of the resurrection, (for example, as the extraordinary action of a god whose recognisable purpose in acting is aided by the extraordinariness of the event) in virtue of which the resurrection should not be ruled out simply because it is the rising of a dead person.

Establishing (1) and (2) is to confirm a necessary condition for there being an historical case for the resurrection. If the crudely defective, derivatively Troeltschian, way of understanding the application of the principle of analogy is allowed to stand, there *will* be no known way of countering the experience-based claim that dead people stay dead.[11]

However, (1) and (2) do not constitute a sufficient condition for there being a historian's case for the resurrection. The superficial, even crass, deployment of the analogy principle fails to recognise that, in various ways, different analogical reasonings can interrelate (for example combining, or countervailing). At least as great a threat to a historically argued-for resurrection, in most people's eyes, is the great *strength* of the analogical argument against it. A resurrection has seemed to be not merely rather distinctive (the singularity problem), but altogether ruled out, because it would be contrary to natural law. Pannenberg recognises and addresses this central question in the following paragraph:

The possibility of the historicity of Jesus' resurrection has been opposed on the grounds that the resurrection of a dead person even in the sense of the resurrection to imperishable life would be an event that violates the laws of nature. Therefore, resurrection as a historical event is impossible. Yet it appears that from the perspective of the presuppositions of modern physics judgements must be made much more carefully. First, only a part of the laws of nature are ever known. Further, in a world that as a whole represents a singular, irreversible process, an individual event is never completely determined by natural laws. Conformity to law embraces only one aspect of what happens. From another perspective, everything that happens is contingent, and the validity of the laws of nature is itself contingent. Therefore, natural science expresses the general validity of the laws of nature but must at the same time declare its own inability to make definitive judgements about the possibility or impossibility of an individual event, regardless of how certainly it is able, at least in principle, to measure the

---

[11] For a helpful and critical account of Pannenberg's views, see D. Holwerda's paper 'Faith, Reason and the Resurrection' in *Faith and Rationality*, eds. A. Plantinga and N. Wolterstorff, Notre Dame, Indiana, 1983, pp. 265ff.

probability of an event's occurrence. The judgement about whether an event, however, unfamiliar, has happened or not is in the final analysis a matter for the historian and cannot be prejudged by the knowledge of natural science.[12]

The first of his two arguments is not clearly expressed. If he means that at any time only some out of all the laws of nature are known, questions must follow, for example about whether we *ever* know laws of nature to be laws of nature rather than as-yet-unrefuted, even long-standing, conjectures, or, if we can know some laws of nature to be laws of nature why might we not in fact know or come to know all the laws of nature there are, even if, perhaps, we could not know that we knew them all? Whatever Pannenberg's views on these points might be, the immediately critical crux is that even if we do not know all the laws of nature there are, where we do know a law of nature, then the possibility of an event which would be contrary to that law, remains as problematic as it would be if we knew more laws, or all laws, of nature.

Pannenberg's language can, however, be taken to say that somehow, we know only part of each law of nature, by which he might mean that there are circumstances, actual or possible, but as yet unenvisaged, to which the applicability of the law will be in doubt.

In advance of encountering, or at least envisaging them, we do not know how the law applies. Take Boyle's Law, to the effect that the pressure of a given mass of gas is inversely proportional to its volume at constant temperature. As it turns out, Boyle's Law holds good generally only when qualified by a correction, attributed to Van der Waal. For all we can say, laws of nature which we have uncovered will turn out to apply generally only when subject to qualification; so that as matters now stand we have an incomplete grasp of how they are accurately applicable (subject or not subject to qualification, as the case may be); or we have confidence about how they apply only in respect of the sorts of cases in relation to which we know them to have been applicable, whereas about other sorts of possible or actual cases

[12] Pannenberg, *Jesus – God and Man*, p. 98.

we have as yet no such firm confidence. If this does represent Pannenberg's thought, he might wish to recommend a likely qualification for laws of nature such as ' . . . provided that God does not act extraordinarily, for some recognisable purpose'. The recognisable purpose apparent in Pannenberg's mind would be the anticipating or preliminary fulfilment of resurrection promise.

That these developments move in a worthwhile direction has already been advocated in this book. However, whether they really are Pannenberg's own proposals is a matter of guesswork; it is better to advocate or evaluate them for their own sakes without further risking fathering them on him, even though his own cryptic unclarity invites the charitably motivated fathering. In fact it seems unlikely that he *can* have intended all that is now speculatively attributed to him, because people disinclined to allow a 'scientific' history of the resurrection will, as a matter of fact or general tendency (whether justified or not) be at least as unwilling to admit reference to a god, in either historiography or science. This is not the best place at which to pursue yet further the assessment of ideas which are more probably being read into rather than read off Pannenberg's text; evaluation has already taken place in exposition and advocacy of them earlier in the book. If these are not what Pannenberg did intend, they are what he could usefully have said in aid of his proposals.

What now of Pannenberg's second and much more lengthily given reason for admitting the possibility of a resurrection, notwithstanding its being contrary to natural law? He says that an individual event is never completely determined by natural laws, that conforming to law embraces only one aspect of what happens, that from another perspective everything that happens is contingent, and that the validity of the laws of nature is itself contingent.

If by this he means that the acceptability of the relevant laws of nature is not alone a sufficient determinant of what actually takes place because very many differing circumstances could conform to the laws, then he is correct. Newton's Laws of motion might apply equally to universes containing ten objects of equal mass, ten objects of varying mass, ten million objects, objects all of which are at rest relative to each other or objects all of which are in motion relative to each other; indeed, an infinity of universes whose objects differ as to the speeds and directions of motion is possible, each of them conforming to Newton's Laws. What actually happens at any time depends, we might say, on the laws; but also on (prior) conditions, on which particular contingent circumstances (out of the vast range of possibilities which would equally accord with the laws) actually obtain. What the world contingently contains may be supposed to depend on what was contingently the case at whatever past time we choose to regard, or are required to regard, as, for our purposes, the initial given condition.

Additionally, those who believe in contra-causal free agency will see free actions as contingent, and as the causes of newly begun sequences of contingencies.

Hume has taught or re-affirmed a lesson, now well-taken, that it is also a contingent matter what the laws of nature are. Our universe could have been governed by other natural laws than those which do apply; that is why it is a matter for empirical discovery which do (or perhaps better do not) apply. Pannenberg may also mean that it is a contingent matter that the universe conforms to laws at all, is a cosmos rather than a chaos. So even if events were altogether and sufficiently determined by whichever laws hold good, it would still be a contingent matter what actually happens, because it is a contingent matter whether any natural laws hold good, and if so, which laws.

It is hard to see what Pannenberg means by what he says if he does not mean these things, all of which are entirely defensible. The trouble is that they do not lead to the conclusions which he tries to draw.

Firstly, from the fact that prevailing laws of nature do not on their own constitute the sufficient, complete determination that this or that particular event occurs, it does not follow that they do not constrain at all. It is consistent with saying that operant laws of nature do not alone resolve, fix what actually takes place, to hold that they may nevertheless serve on their own to exclude or rule out the occurrence of some (kinds of) things. That is what *would* be supposed by most of the objectors to the historicity of

Jesus' resurrection, whom Pannenberg is (unsuccessfully) trying to counter here.

Moreover, the necessity which these objectors attach to all events' conforming to natural laws – any natural laws at all, or the particular laws of nature which are actually believed to prevail – need not be the sort of necessity which Pannenberg sets aside. If the objectors are clear-headed and well informed, indeed it will *not* be that sort of necessity, logical or metaphysical necessity. Rather their point will most powerfully be that if (whether contingently or not) some formulation does express a law of nature, does describe how nature generally works in the relevant specified circumstances, then necessarily any event which would be an infraction of that law will have a probability of zero, and will be in that respect impossible. Nothing which Pannenberg says about natural law's contingency, or merely joint determinativity, effectively touches that point.

Nor does Pannenberg acknowledge or attempt to deal with the objection (that is, to a scientific history of the resurrection) deriving from historical methodology and the ethics of belief. This objection makes claims not about what can or cannot happen but about what the historian may or may not properly affirm, and what may or may not properly be believed; this is, of course, the import of Hume's and Troeltsch's attacks on the possibility of intellectually respectable belief in any miracle, and in particular the resurrection of Jesus Christ.

Since Pannenberg's theological proposals give a central place to the resurrection of Jesus Christ, understood as belonging to the past which historical enquiry can grasp, it is necessary to the continued life of these proposals that the objections specified in the previous two paragraphs should be effectively dealt with. Pannenberg, it now seems, fails to deal with them for himself;[13] but on the basis of the argumentation of this book, an effective defence can be made out.

The respective defences against the distinct objections run in

---

[13] Though Pannenberg does offer rather detailed particular historical arguments (in *Jesus – God and Man*, Ch. 3) for his historical conclusion that the resurrection of Jesus Christ did take place, he did not deal effectively with the question of general principle as to whether any such arguments for a miracle could succeed.

parallel. An event which would be a violation of a natural law will have a probability of zero on the basis of one particular description of it; in that the event is described in such a way that it is contrary to the law, and so long as the supposition is excluded that the normal course of nature may have been departed from, the event will have no empirical probability; that is, it will have zero probability; it will be empirically impossible. However, other descriptions of the event may be possible. Thus it may be describable as having been strongly attested to; and it may be describable in such a way that its occurrence conforms to, and adds point to, a promising historical hypothesis about the purposes of a being who was at work fulfilling these purposes in a particular stretch of history and could have acted irregularly in nature in order to effectively accomplish these purposes. The well-attestedness of the putative miracle may contribute force to what might already be a promising hypothesis, promising in part because it would explain some other *data*. Moreover, the contrary-to-law character of the alleged event may well be especially significant in enabling it better to fulfil the god's supposed purpose. Described, and seen, in these ways, the alleged event both gains intelligibility from and (because there is no other available explanation of an anomalous event), adds explanatory force to the promising hypothesis.

Since there is no reason to exclude the possibility that a god may act anomalously to further his purposes, the occurrence of such an anomalous event cannot be ruled out either; and, as a well-attested event which contributes to a promising explanation in terms of a god's purposes, a putative miracle cannot simply be ruled out by appeal to what usually, in the ordinary course of nature, takes place.

Since the impossibility here alleged to belong to the transgression of the law is not absolute (as logical or, presumably, metaphysical impossibility *would* be), but relative to available information or to other judgements of probability, the impossibility here can in principle and maybe in practice be eroded or dissolved or undercut, so as even to make possible the responsible judgement that Jesus Christ's resurrection happened.

In parallel fashion, while forming their historical beliefs about the past, *responsible* people should be ready to consider whether there may be some justification for thinking that the regular patterns of natural occurrence, on the basis of which we should naturally arrive at our beliefs, may have been intelligibly departed from, perhaps in order to achieve a god's purpose. In order to arrive at a conclusion that this is what has happened analogical reasoning will still require to be employed, for example, about what intelligent agents having consistent purposes of a specified kind may be expected to do. Thus responsible historical belief-formation, directed by appropriate reasoning and norms, (that is, scientific history), may arrive at belief in the miraculous, even in the resurrection of Jesus Christ, if there is good evidence for it and an important theological point in it.

Pannenberg's theology, therefore, needs to invoke the arguments of these latter two paragraphs. Obviously these are the arguments which are more fully made out in the rest of this book. If the most cogent objections to Pannenberg's view are to be met, and if his central claims are to be well founded and well defended, he urgently needs to call in aid these very arguments.

Karl Barth advocates the rigorous employment of the historical critical method in our appropriating of the biblical documents and literature; because the scriptures are a human word it is proper to apply scientific historical method to them. Barth is clear that scientific historical enquiry will not issue in knowledge of the miraculous; such knowledge, for example knowledge of the resurrection of Jesus Christ, is due not to the exercise of historical scholarship but to revelation received by faith.[14] According to Barth the miraculous events, especially the resurrection, which we come to know in this fashion, did nonetheless occur in time in the same time-series as events which the scientific historians can properly comprehend.[15]

One question which Barth's contention readily and rightly raises is whether a claim to revelation may not be unreliably subjective. Pannenberg's reasons for refusing, in historical

---

[14] K. Barth, *Church Dogmatics*, Edinburgh, English translation of successive volumes published from 1956, vol. iv/1, p. 446.
[15] Ibid. iii/2, p. 624, and iv/1, p. 333, also iii/2, p. 446.

enquiry, to trust appeals to intuitive certainty (such as those in which Althaus apparently had confidence) can properly be paralleled by reasons for withholding assent from unsupported claims to revelation. In a world where conflicting claims to revelation are well known, the general need of grounds for accepting any alleged revelations is particularly obvious.

Further difficulties emerge for Barth when we try to work out how, if at all, the human world which is subject to the historical critical method is supposed to *relate* to the divinely given revelation about a miracle which takes place in time. No human word is particularly fitted, on Barth's view, to convey God's revelation; no human word, such as the word of scripture or of the preacher, can by its normal semantic force capture God, who remains free in relation to any human discourse. So much is well known to be Barth's teaching.[16] In accordance with it we do not come to know, for example, that the resurrection has happened because the resurrection narratives, by their normal meaning, inform us of it; in fact the sense of the human word of the narratives is not worthy, or fit, or apt, to convey the revelation.

Accordingly, the revelation of the resurrection to us will be quite unrelated to the normal sense or force of resurrection reports or narratives and is no more appropriately to be occasioned by them in particular than by any casual word or event, whatever its semantic content, if any indeed, may be. The bizarreness of this, to take one point, involves our saying that the recounting of the Good Samaritan parable, or of a nursery rhyme, is as relevant to the revelation of the resurrection as are the (so-called) resurrection narratives and therefore might as fittingly be read on Easter Day.

Barth does not always say effectively the same thing when he is talking about the relation between the biblical text and God's self-revelation. The foregoing critical remarks take the grand statement of general theory about the matter in *Church Dogmatics* I/1 to be the view that must be taken seriously. Yet when he comes to write about the scholar's handling of the texts which

---

[16] See ibid. 1/1 (on the three-fold form of the Word of God).

deal with the resurrection,[17] and we have left behind such large theological categories as the Word of God, the christological analogy for the coming together of the divine and human, or inspiration, and left behind also the ambitious schematism of the threefold form of the Word of God, he envisages the text as pointing to the resurrection in ways which can be interpreted well or badly. So (having discussed the propriety of 'saga', 'legend', or 'myth' to speak of the resurrection accounts) he writes:

But whatever terms we select to describe the New Testament records of the resurrection and their content, it is quite certain that we do not interpret them, i.e., we do not let them say what they are trying to say, if we explain away the history which they recount, a history which did take place in time and space, and that not merely in the development of a conception of the disciples, but in the objective event which underlay that development.

Taken on its own, this passage conveys a less bizarre, more readily accepted, doctrine of scripture than Barth's large principal treatment. However, the passage is not on its own. For one thing it seems incompatible with the earlier teaching that the human word has no capacity or competence by its own qualities to convey the reality of what is revealed, being entirely helpless, like the sinner, wholly dependent on divine grace to carry out God's purpose – in the case of the Word, God's self-disclosure.

For another thing, a lack of cohesion emerges when we think more carefully about how, as Barth sees it, the historical critical method is to be applied, for instance to resurrection, or resurrection-appearance, reports or narratives. The outcome of applying that scientific method would have to be that the existence of these texts is accounted for otherwise than as somewhat accurate reports of events which they purport to describe: they will perhaps emerge as not intending, properly understood, to claim descriptive truth, or they will turn out to be pious exaggeration, or explainable error. The reader or hearer who is aware of this kind of appropriation of the texts according

[17] For example, ibid. IV/I, p. 336.

to the historical critical method will treat them as the scientific historian's conclusions dictate, adopting some such view of them as accounts for them without involving a resurrection. *This* accounting for them will surely be very different from the view which should be taken of the texts, how they should be read, what they intend, how they came into existence, how descriptively accurate they are, if we held that a resurrection did in fact happen, even though the texts when treated according to the methods of the scientific historian, did not of themselves lead to that conclusion. So if we come to know the resurrection by revelation, our view of these texts (how they should be read, what they intend, etc.,) ought, surely, to be changed thereby. What view is the person who is both a critical textual scholar and a believer in the resurrection to take of the meaning, the force, of the text? Is his critical historical standpoint to be persisted in, leading to one view of the text; or does the knowledge which revelation gives legitimately come into the reckoning so as to lead to a modified or even radically different view about the text?

Barth does not advise the believing recipient of revelation to abandon the historical critical method in biblical study. It does not so much solve the problem as bring it out more starkly to pronounce that it is as scientific historians and critics that we must take the one view, and as believers we must take the other view of the text. What are we to hold merely as truth-seekers? Regarding the import of the text it is proper, maybe, to take one view as critical scholars and another as, by faith, beneficiaries of revelation. Yet what are we to believe, not *as* anything? Simply, what are we to conclude about the import of the text?

So long as the unity of truth and the unity of the enquiring person (theologian, believer, bible student) are maintained, as they surely have to be, it is left unacceptably obscure by Barth how the text should be handled, how these questions should be addressed, let alone answered.

Finally, though relatedly, it is at least questionable whether Barth needs to be so insistent that the resurrection, while objectively occurring in our time, is not accessible to historical enquiry. As the quotation from Barth shows, and as he makes clear elsewhere,[18] he envisages the resurrection as having consequences, in particular in overcoming the disciples' unfaith so that they come to faith and their conception of the resurrection develops; also, the New Testament records derive from the resurrection event. The primitive church, its emergence and early character, can be counted as results of the resurrection. Certainly that event has causal contact with history which *is* accessible to the critical historian. How, then, can the critical historian ignore or bracket off the resurrection, when he comes to speak, as he *is* allowed to do, of those events which the resurrection conditions causally?

Whatever Barth's answer would be to that specific query, presumably the reason for putting the resurrection event itself out of range of scientific historians will be that it is itself not caused by that which is accessible to historians, namely: it is an act of God. As a consequence, firstly, while the resurrection does have causal connexions with that which figures in critical history, these connexions are one way – from the resurrection to its consequences. By contrast, events which are available to the scientific scholar both affect *and* are themselves causally affected by other events which are open to the critical historian. Secondly, Barth would hold that there is no analogy from experienced history to an act of God such as to render an act of God historically intelligible.

Those who believe that human beings are endowed with (non-causally-determined) freedom will be unimpressed by the first of these points: at least many free actions of human beings will have consequences which lie within the domain of the historical investigator, and these free actions themselves will often likewise be subjects for historians' attention,[19] even though, being non-determined, free actions, *ex hypothesi* they will lack causes, and *a fortiori* they will lack causes which can be the subjects of scientific historians' attention. In the respect of having causal consequences but not having causal antecedents which determine them, free actions are therefore analogous to

---

[18] Notably ibid. IV/I, p. 341.

[19] This is notwithstanding the awkwardness for Bradley's theorizing about critical history which he himself sought to deal with, as described earlier.

miracles which are conceived of as having only one-way causal connexions with the investigably historical; yet free actions can be treated by the historical scholar, so why not the miraculous?

If, as seems to be the case, the onus of answering falls on the by now familiar contention about the analogy principle, which was cited as Barth's second reason for excluding the resurrection from the sphere of the critical historian, the significance of this by now familiar line of response is underscored. As an action of an intelligent agent, whose intelligible purposes we (think we may) have recognised, an act of God can be analogous to the actions of persons known in our mundane experience. So events which would otherwise be difficult to explain may *be* made intelligible, incorporated in our system of beliefs, by utilising that analogy. 'Scientific' historians have (mis)understood themselves or been encouraged by philosophers and theologians to (mis)perceive themselves as having no analogies to draw upon, in terms of which to account for a transgression of natural law. Certainly *qua* transgression of natural law, or *qua* act of God, it will be difficult to find incorporative analogies for reported miracles whereby they may be part of our body, or network, of beliefs; the mistaken supposition is that something which lacks analogy under some one description can find no analogy in our experience in any respect whatsoever.

Barth has, or appears to have, plentiful company in advancing these claims. The hesitation is due to the brevity with which the view is often put as if it were a widely familiar thesis known to all theological schoolboys; so that it is hard to be quite certain whether perhaps some variant is what is in the writer's mind. James Barr is one such,[20] and he suggests (rather against other evidence, one would have thought[21]) that Bultmann might have been another. Barr writes:

We might take this opportunity to return to a remark of Bultmann's which was quoted earlier. When he says that 'an historical fact which involves a resurrection from the dead is utterly inconceivable', this is understood by fundamentalists as 'denying the resurrection'. But surely

---

[20] James Barr, *Fundamentalism*, London, 1977, pp. 257f.
[21] Cf. the earlier treatment of Bultmann in Ch. 6 above.

the statement may deserve to be understood in a sense relevant to the matter of evidence which we have just been discussing. Bultmann is saying, or we can say whether he says it or not, that, if there is such a thing as a resurrection, it belongs to a category of events which do not take a normal place in the sequence of historical explanation and cannot be accounted for in its terms. There may be difficulties in this, but it is a far more Christian, and also a far more 'supernaturalist', approach than the one through historical evidence just discussed.

In view of the difficulties for this view which have been set out, Barr's inadequate reckoning with them is reminiscent of those preachers who are supposed to have said 'Having acknowledged these deep difficulties we will now pass on'.

The difficulties should matter to Barr more than they seem to do because the life of the central consensus of the views of critical scholars which he seeks to represent, over against Fundamentalism, depends on the resolution of the difficulties. Barr indignantly repudiates the Fundamentalists' accusation that critical scholars, in advance of looking at texts, exclude the possibility of miracles and of supernatural factors. So he says that Bultmann, whose remarks to this effect are widely quoted by conservative scholars, does not speak for the generality of mainstream biblical critics. Yet he himself wishes, as we have seen, to invoke a conception of historical enquiry on which miracles cannot be appropriated, comprehended, into our historical understanding. So if, as he says, 'We believe in the resurrection and in some degree other miracles also', how is this belief based, and what if anything is its content? This kind of attempt to combine belief in miracles with historical critical method is either hollow, or unstable, certainly ill-thought-through. Indeed, when he writes ' . . . we believe that "supernatural" events, like the more important miracles and the resurrection of Jesus from the dead, can occur and have occurred; this is a part of our Christian faith which we do not deny or diminish, though we have no universally agreed understanding of how such events can take place or what we should make of them',[22] it is made explicitly unclear what this confession of faith amounts to. In view of the

[22] Barr, *Fundamentalism*, p. 236.

problems facing Barth, it is not perhaps surprising that Barr's left hand takes away what the right hand seemed to give, because Barth's position is similarly unsatisfactory.[23]

Writers such as Don Cupitt and James P. Mackey argue that the resurrection narratives and affirmations of the New Testament are not in fact, as they have problematically seemed, reports about an event in our space and time (whether or not it is specifically locatable by the scientific historian). Rather they are theological interpretation, which express conclusions of the first christians' inferences about Jesus Christ (Cupitt), or they are affirmations of Jesus Christ's divine power, immanent in history, as it was known in their experience by the first christians (Mackey). These writers develop their respective cases, spilling at least as much ink in trying to bring out the profound defects in the principal rejected alternative view as in giving sustained support to their own. This principal, and allegedly problematic, alternative, the Event conception of the resurrection (Cupitt's terminology), or the proof-miracle conception (Mackey's) at least closely resembles the view which is being sympathetically explored in this book.

Cupitt distinguishes what might be called straightforward Event theories, in which the risen Jesus Christ is a man like other men who having been dead now lives again, and meeting him is like the ordinary meeting of another person, from what he calls psi-theories. These latter depart from straightforward Event theories to take account of the New Testament indications that the risen Christ was not altogether like other people, for example in that his body could pass through walls, could appear suddenly, maybe travelled unusually, was not recognised and then, strikingly, was recognised. Psi-theories postulate a para-normal seeing and/or a para-normal object of the seeing into which (and here is the important common factor between straightforward Event theories and psi-theories) historical research may yet properly seek to enquire. This classification itself becomes problematic as Cupitt employs it, because he applies

---

[23] If viewpoints gain credibility out of the difficulties for the alternatives, and if the Barth/Barr view is seen as the only alternative to Fundamentalism, it is not surprising that Fundamentalism continues to have adherents.

what is essentially Hume's reasoning about the credibility of miracle-reports, albeit with some Cupitt emphases, only to reports of the resurrection understood as a psi-phenomenon; but if Hume's argument has force at all, it will apply also to reports of the resurrection understood as the raising up of a person whose body is perceived in the ordinary way and which has the attributes of a normal body. Simply because the resurrection would be a raising from the dead, it would still have the sort of extraordinariness which makes either for its incredibility to the rational person who accepts Hume's norms or, if some additional explanatory extraordinary factor is postulated or suspected, for the problem of estimating the probability of these events at all. Yet Cupitt employs the Humean argument only against belief in the resurrection on the psi-theory of the resurrection, offers no other arguments against the resurrection's credibility on a psi-theory, and employs other arguments, which are of special interest here, about the resurrection understood according to an Event theory. It seems doubtful whether there is a point in distinguishing psi-theories from the Event theories.

Apart from the eccentric limitation to psi-phenomena, Cupitt's employment of the Humean argument is along standard Humean lines, inviting responses of sorts which have already been developed in this book and, for their re-employment now, need only to be sketched.

Cupitt depicts the apologetic argument as having two distinct stages, of which the first is the contention, supported by the ordinary standards of evidence, that an extraordinary event has occurred; this accomplished, the apologist then moves on, in the second stage, to advocate an explanation for this extraordinary event.

However, this misrepresents what is the apologist's optimum legitimate strategy, and makes the apologetic bound to fail. As has been argued in earlier chapters of this book, the question should be whether the apologist's system of advocated beliefs better accounts for all the *data*, including importantly, if not critically, the evidence for the extraordinary event, than an alternative system. The way in which the Humean, analysing the allegedly two-stage argument, requires what he takes to be the ordinary standards of evidence to be employed in a separate first stage unfairly presumes the correctness, rights of tenure or prior claim of a system of beliefs alternative to the apologist's, and improperly excludes consideration of, and the necessary comparison with, the apologist's favoured belief system.

When Cupitt considers the apologist's allegation that the ordinary rules of evidence are or may be incompetent where a miracle is supposed to have happened, he presents us with the common alternatives: either our experience *is* a reliable guide to what happens in all cases of whatever kind (in which case the reported miracles will, *qua* transgression of natural law, be maximally improbable), or our experience is altogether untrustworthy, so that if it cannot be taken to rule out the reported miracle, neither can it give grounds for trusting the evidence for the miracle (in which case the reason for accepting it is undercut). The possibility that the presumption of the trustworthiness of experience, as a guide to what happens, might be generally maintained while yet being subject to intelligible exceptions is not entertained by Cupitt; yet, as has been seen, that is, for the present question, an all-important possibility. Relatedly, neither is the further possibility explored that an intelligibility-giving analogy with known intelligent agency might both uphold and apply the analogy principle and thereby make sense of the problematic event, which under some description is a violation of natural law, so that the irregular mode by which, in this unusual case, past experience is a guide to what happens, may be understood.

Yet Cupitt not only provides gainful employment for the principal previously argued contentions of this book; he also advances further reasons, which are specially to be examined now, for rejecting Event theories of the resurrection.

1. Admittedly Event theories may secure the identity of Jesus Christ resurrected with the one who previously lived and preached and was crucified, and be advocated importantly for this reason by Event theorists.

1.1 However, such theories cannot secure the identity of the Jesus Christ who lived among us, pre- or post-resurrection, with anyone who dwells, has his being, in the other world, the world of God's promise, the heavenly world. That other world is spatio-temporally discontinuous from this so that physical continuity between them is impossible. Yet Event theorists also wish to assert the crucified Galilean preacher, the resurrected Jesus Christ *and* the now exalted Saviour to be the identical person and they believe that an Event theory is required if this identity is to be maintained. If bodily continuity is even necessary for personal identity (Cupitt repeatedly represents Event theorists as advocating the stronger thesis that it is constitutive of personal identity), the beliefs of the typical Event theorists generate serious problems; but if bodily continuity is not a necessary condition of personal identity a major reason for advancing Event theories disappears.[24]

2.1 Quite apart from that issue, a straightforward Event theory would be in practice indistinguishable from the thesis of Paulus: that Jesus did not die, but (was) revived in the tomb and managed to make his way out. The more strictly and straightforwardly the risen Jesus Christ is assimilated to the pre-mortem Jesus Christ, the more firmly is this the implication.[25]

2.2 If, however, some 'glorification' (roughly, the possession of advantageous properties said in the Gospel narratives to have belonged to the resurrected Jesus yet not normally found in humans' bodies) is attributed to the body of the resurrected one, bodily continuity is abandoned and a loss or evacuation of determinate meaning is suffered by the resurrection claim, so that the remoter the reported resurrection experience becomes from any other experiences, the harder it becomes to judge of its truth.[26]

3. Still, if it can be concluded that the risen Jesus Christ, possessing a glorified body, appeared to the apostles, perhaps this Event, albeit not quite 'straightforward', will provide the origin and ground of Christian faith for the apostles, substantiating their christian beliefs? Cupitt thinks that Event theorists attach the greatest weight to this double reason for their kind of theory: it both accounts for the outburst of dynamic faith and the explosion of its expression, especially in beaten men, and it

[24] Don Cupitt, *Christ and the Hiddenness of God*, London, 1971, pp. 154–5.
[25] Ibid. pp. 156–7. [26] Ibid. pp. 155, 157, 162.

verifies the content of that faith, most immediately constituting an anticipatory earnest and pledge of God's new resurrection-world into which Jesus Christ leads the way. It is this double significance which is above all the point of Event theories.[27]

3.1 However, if we require to postulate a resurrection world to come in order to understand the resurrection-Event, and we required the resurrection-Event to confirm the resurrection world to come, we have an unacceptably circular argument.[28]

3.2 Further, if the resurrection-Event verifies an existing belief or expectation, it cannot be and does not need to be such a bolt from the blue as Event theorists suggest: it will already be somewhat expected; and faith in a raising of Jesus will be explainable without the bolt from the blue. If, on the other hand, the resurrection were an altogether unexpected new thing there will, *ex hypothesi*, be no belief which it confirms, and, being of obscure significance, it cannot give rise to a new dynamic, determinate faith and preaching.[29]

3.3 Insofar as some Event theory rests on a supposed need to find a cause for the transformation of Beaten Men into confident men of faith and heralds of the resurrection, the theory is ill founded because experience teaches that inspiriting heartening beliefs about their resurrected heroes commonly do emerge among the powerless, dispirited, disheartened or marginal.[30]

Taking these points in turn, it should be contended in response to 1, that bodily continuity may be neither constitutive of personal identity, nor a necessary condition for it, but rather one, perhaps even the most weighty possible, of a group of multiple criteria for personal identity. In that case Cupitt presents false alternatives: either bodily continuity is a necessary condition for personal identity, in which case the identity of the risen Christ with the exalted Christ becomes problematic, or bodily continuity is not a necessary condition of personal identity in which case a major reason for advancing an Event-theory of the resurrection altogether disappears. These are not all the possibilities: bodily continuity may be an important but not essential criterion for personal identity.

Indeed, a good case can be made for saying that this is so, that

---

[27] Ibid. p. 159.   [28] Ibid. pp. 161ff.   [29] Ibid. pp. 159–62.   [30] Ibid. pp. 141–2.

the multiple criteria view is true. Suppose[31] that MacKay is a mathematician, a topologist, internationally known in his field. One day in the course of a seminar in Cambridge he disappears; by this is meant not that he gets up and leaves the room, but that one moment, during a discussion of the Poincare conjecture, MacKay is seated there at the table, and the next moment he is gone, his chair empty. Suppose, further, that at a seminar of topologists in Canberra taking place contemporaneously, suddenly, and as it turns out on subsequent reflection (on clock chimes which were sounding in both places) at exactly the same time, there is present equally abruptly and mysteriously a person who looks, talks, thinks and reacts like MacKay. He is briefly discomposed by the new surroundings and people and especially by the change of topic: he mutters 'I thought we were supposed to be discussing the Poincare conjecture.' He has the same physical and psychological qualities, the same smell, the same capacities, the same virtues and vices, likes and dislikes, the same information and expertise and the same memories as MacKay; he knows some things which only MacKay knew or knows. The surprised Canberran topologists who know MacKay immediately take this man to be MacKay.

Even though we rule out any thought that somehow his body has been transported at speeds which are scarcely physically admissible, and there is therefore not bodily continuity between the person who disappeared and the person who appeared, the conclusion, on the information given, that this is MacKay is not arbitrary. For one thing, if the same putative MacKay appeared in a session of the Canberra seminar two years after the original MacKay had been assassinated by a deranged Ph.D. student, and buried, his remains still being in the grave, there would be less readiness to identify the two; and if the new arrival in Canberra topology appeared while the proto-MacKay continued present and participating in the Cambridge group, there would be much less inclination to identify them.

Suppose a different case: that a person wakens up one

This argument owes much, in respect of its substantial points and in respect of its entertainment value, both to John Hick and to P. G. Wodehouse. See Hick's contribution to *Body, Mind and Death*, edited by A. Flew, New York, 1964, pp. 270–3, and Wodehouse's *Laughing Gas*, London, 1957.

morning puzzled first that he seems not to be in a bed in St
Mary's Hospital but in a bed in a suburban bedroom; then he is
startled that he is accompanied by a woman who is (a)
unrecognised by him, (b) seems a decent woman, yet (c) is
unperturbed and not even interested that he is there; further, he
is astonished to discover that he is taller and more bulky than he
was, that he has red hair and, on getting up and looking in the
mirror, that he is, as he put it, quite unlike himself. It emerges in
due course that this man believes himself to be O'Day, that
O'Day was certified dead in St Mary's Hospital, and that all his
memories complete, all his physical and psychological dispositions, all the other possessions and attributes but those essentially tied to his body, now lying in the hospital morgue, now belong
to the person embodied in a large red-haired body which Mrs
Fitzhugh takes to be obviously that of her husband. If we assume
the bodily continuity of this large red-haired body and exclude
any thought, say, of the replacement of the body with which Mrs
Fitzhugh went to bed, is the bodily continuity sufficient to
constitute the wakened one Fitzhugh, all of whose memories,
knowledge, dispositions, traits, accent even, have disappeared?
Perhaps most people would say, albeit with puzzlement, that,
somehow, O'Day had taken over Fitzhugh's body.

Attention to these cases prompts the following: that the
philosophers' widespread enthusiasm for bodily continuity as
being necessary for, or constitutive of, personal identity, expressed by Cupitt echoing Geach,[32] derives from the widespread
awareness of Bishop Butler's objection to the use of exclusively
psychological factors, especially memory which is the likeliest
candidate, to secure personal identity. Butler points out that not
any memory (such as, let us say, Smith's memory simply of there
having been German air raids on Britain) will serve. Unless a
particular true memory or instance of a middle-aged man is
specifically a memory *of himself* as having been present at, or
involved in, the remembered event (say being a child in a shelter
during a bombing raid), the memory could not serve to secure
the personal identity of the middle-aged man and the child.

---

[32] Cupitt, *Christ and the Hiddenness of God*, p. 156.

That is, the required sort of memory actually requires, *presupposes*, the concept and the fact of the personal identity of the person whose memory it is. Butler's reasoning is supposed to be generalisable, to apply to all memories, so that memories, the likeliest-seeming of our psychological assets to constitute our identity through time, turn out not to do so.

Yet even if the identity of adult and child cannot be made good by some single memory because that memory, to be of the required kind, involves or presupposes the personal identity it is supposed to capture, it will not follow that it is impossible to compose personal identity by psychological ingredients. While a single memory of the required kind may not do the job on its own, a group or cluster or set of memories, involving associated knowledge, belief, perhaps also attitudes, and dispositions or capacities, might secure a person's identity; the individual memory will then be the memory of that person in that it belongs in that larger dispositional and psychological bundle. Thus, while no lone, unassociated memory can secure a person's identity, it does not follow that personal identity requires, let alone is, bodily continuity.

It is worth returning to the case of MacKay, of Cambridge and Canberra, in order to notice that different sorts of bodily discontinuity will weigh differently in considering these examples, where issues about personal identity arise. Three different kinds of cases involving bodily continuity were hypothesized; the different attitudes which it would be reasonable to take about the identity of the Canberra *arriviste* in these respective circumstances bring out both that bodily continuity is not alone necessary for, nor constitutive of, personal identity (the latter point is made also by the O'Day/Fitzhugh example) and also that treating all cases of bodily discontinuity as alike, and of like significance for questions of personal identity, is simplistic.

Since Cupitt wrote, well-argued-for doubts have been expressed[33] to the effect that those qualms about the meaning and possibility of personal identity's being maintained from this life

---

[33] By George Mavrodes in *Nous*, vol. 11 (1977), pp. 27ff: 'The Life Everlasting and the Bodily Criterion of Identity'.

to the postulated next life, qualms which led to insistence on bodily continuity as criterial for personal identity, are or may with equal justification be paralleled by qualms about the conception of the identity of space-time points (or, one might add, of minimal portions of matter); yet space-time points (or minimal portions of matter which maintain their identity through time) must be invoked if we are called upon to give an account of the nature of any bodily continuity. If this is right, whatever is problematic about a person's identity from this life into the life everlasting, the criteria for personal identity which are supposed to bring out that problematicity turn out to be as problematic themselves if the troubling question is asked about them. Maybe the reasonable person can best apply her un-studied concept of (personal) identity, and with fair confidence, without fear of criteria which themselves require it to be further explained (which could only be done, if at all, with difficulty) how they ever would or could be satisfied. The alternative is that all judgements of personal identity are arbitrary, whether they concern this life only, or a life-to-come.

If Cupitt associates himself with those, sceptics and believers, who have insisted on applying bodily identity or continuity criteria for personal identity, because they hold that judgements of personal identity which are made without applying such criteria will be improperly arbitrary, the hitherto unrecognised cost for him (that *all* judgements of personal identity are to be eschewed because they are inevitably improperly arbitrary) is likely to prove unacceptably high. It seems that he will be unwilling to pay it; but even if he is willing to do so, he can hardly blame others who are not willing. Indeed, unless it is made out that Mavrodes's arguments are not sound, Cupitt's thesis 1 cannot confidently be urged upon us all.

Finally on 1, developments in cosmology in recent times make questionable Cupitt's insistent worry that for an Event theory to be maintained a continuous space-time track is needed for the body of Jesus if he, the identical Jesus of Nazareth, is to enter the heavenly world. Thus Hawking can write of the possibility that an imaginary astronaut might be able to see a 'naked singularity', such as the collapse of a massive

star into a black hole: 'he may be able to avoid hitting the
singularity and instead fall through a "wormhole" and come
out in another region of the universe. This would offer great
possibilities for travel in space and time'.[34] He goes on: 'close to
naked singularities it may be possible to travel into the past'. If
the physicist can hypothesize such space-time transposition
without there being pressing questions about the continuous
identity of the astronaut, Cupitt's difficulties are less worrying
for Event theorists because it is now far from clear that
spatio-temporal continuity is to be understood in such a way as
to exclude Event theorising. In the world of the modern
cosmologist, the Cupitt-proposed condition for a resurrection
body which even in the heavenly world maintains continuity
with the this-wordly body, that it be 'in principle open to
astronomical observation',[35] is now also, and relatedly, of
doubtful force because it is not sufficiently clear what, if
anything, it may usefully mean. There is much in the modern
cosmologist's universe which is not observable.

Reference to these cosmological matters leads on to the point
that, as the cosmos is now conceived of, the assumption behind
most of the discussion of this issue 1 out of Cupitt's case, that the
heavenly world must be in another space-time from ours and
must be spatio-temporally discontinuous from this world, can be
questioned both as to what it means and as to whether it is true.
Whence comes the brisk confidence that the heavenly world
cannot be (in) a region of our space-time? Speculation further
will, here, be inadequately informed and ill-advised. Yet, once
the assumption is questioned, it does appear questionable.

Throughout his discussions under 2, it is assumed by Cupitt
that if the resurrected person is described on the one hand as
altogether like the (normal) pre-mortem carpenter of Nazareth,
or on the other hand simply as glorified in some way(s), it is only
or mainly as falling under *that* limited description, whichever of
these he is, that he is to be appropriated: his factuality assessed
and his meaning grasped.

Accordingly, the report of an appearance of a (somewhat)

---

[34] Stephen W. Hawking, *A Brief History of Time*, London, 1988, p. 89.
[35] Cupitt, *Christ and the Hiddenness of God*, p. 155.

abnormal, 'glorified', body is especially hard to assess for truth, because described simply in some abnormal glorified aspect, and with nothing noted about its effects on alleged witnesses, or about what else they said about it, or about such concomitant circumstances as the non-production of a body dead or alive by Jewish enemies, or about whose body this was, his claims and history and the likely significance of these, (let alone about the possible purposes of God), there is little basis for judging what, guided by experience, to make of it.

If, alternatively, the only description under which we are allowed to consider it is that of being altogether like the normal Jesus who was taken and crucified, and if it is simply as someone who falls under that description that we must account for it by reference to the guidance of past experience, the likeliest explanation may well be found by adopting Paulus's suggestion. Yet, in forcing us to discuss the post-crucifixion Jesus either simply *qua* 'glorified', or simply *qua* normal, the attribution of these qualities having been detached, isolated from all contextualisation, all concomitant or antecedent or consequent circumstances, all grounds, and taken out of their networks of variously related beliefs, Cupitt imposes a distortingly abstract perspective, and discusses false alternatives. There is a network of beliefs. There will also be other descriptions which witnesses or believers will be ready to apply to the resurrected one, besides his being 'glorified' or being normal; and these will affect our appropriation, our understanding of the resurrected one.

If we can add, for instance, that the rather quick onset of Jesus' death would lead the executioners to check his condition rather carefully, that subsequently none of the authorities claimed to have captured him or produced his body, that the weakness and difficulty in walking of a recently crucified and grievously harmed person would make the seemingly good physical condition of the body itself peculiar, the assessment could well change. Still more it may change if a resurrection would, in that context provided by the pre-mortem life and career of the resurrected one and the context of current Jewish expectations and understanding, accord with the intelligible purposes of a powerful intelligent divine agent, as these may be understood by analogy with the purposes of known intelligent agents. Yet Cupitt insists on dealing with the resurrection as falling under some one description, and that considered in detachment from, and exclusive of, all other descriptions, as if that was the only description under which it falls; and the main thrusts of 2.1 and 2.2 depend on that assumption and that disorientated perspective.

He sees the way open, then, to present, albeit from an unusual particular angle, the false alternative: either an event is treatable by critical history, in which case it will have no theological implications, or else it has theological implications in which case it is indigestible by the critical historian. Notwithstanding the novelty of the route, the conclusion, which is that of Hume and Troeltsch also, is no more justifiably arrived at here than by the other arguments dealt with earlier.

Additionally however, Cupitt's claims are seriously flawed because he presents and then discusses these alternatives, in 2.1 and 2.2, as if he is thereby capturing the essential issues at stake. Yet few there be who maintain an Event theory with the straightforwardness and purity, bordering on perversity, outlined in 2.1; rather the glorification which (more or less following the New Testament narratives) people have most usually attributed to the risen Christ necessitates neither bodily discontinuity in him, nor extraordinary cognitive powers or occurrences, of the sorts proper to typical psi-phenomena, in the witnesses, nor any loss of objectivity in the post-resurrection Christ. Nor does it require that the extraordinariness of the risen Christ, whatever problems there be in assimilating it to past experiences, should be indescribable: the witnesses are usually thought to point intelligibly and even strikingly to the glorification precisely by their accounts of the experiences, the peculiar (in both senses) nature and circumstances of the post-resurrection encounters, so that these resurrection claims do not lack, nor are they evacuated of, determinate descriptive meaning. Rather the descriptive content which they do possess is what confronts readers and hearers and challenges them to account for, to see the further significance of, what is reported.

All of these supposed, but falsely supposed, implications of the

'glorification'-alternative which are error-promptingly pro-
pounded by Cupitt should properly be set aside. When that has
been done, what he presents at 3 as the point of the Event theory
is *not* merely a proposal which can be entertained and discussed
only by first setting aside a whole raft of probably insurmountable difficulties, merely pretending for the sake of argument that
they may be soluble. The proposal at 3 should be considered not
as an already doomed notion which may be further examined,
for interest, or to establish yet another count for the indictment,
but as the principal and so far unfaulted contention of Event
theorists.

Although Event theorists are presented at 3 with some
admixture of the factitious starting of doubts contrived by
Cupitt, most Event theorists would still see Cupitt as correctly
claiming at 3 to have captured their main import, and would
accept that Cupitt's remaining (three) objections have become
the properly determinative issues.

At 3.1, Cupitt sometimes depends on the conception already
exposed as a half-truth, trading on ambiguity, that insofar as an
Event-account of the resurrection goes beyond pure – or mere –
Eventness, to involve some extraordinary 'glorious' component,
it becomes indeterminate in meaning and inaccessible to
historical enquiry. The ambiguity traded-on is over the lack of
meaning allegedly suffered by (reports of) the glorious resurrected Jesus. What must be grasped first is that there are two
respects in which meaning may be present or lacking: over
whether the brutish *datum* to be interpreted has in itself
determinate properties enough for us to apprehend it firmly at
all, and then over whether there is an interpretation, a
significance for it. Granted that under a description which deals
only narrowly with the glorifying features of the resurrected one,
the significance which yields an explanation may well require to
be sought out with particular strenuousness and ready analogies
from previous experience may be hard to find. Nevertheless,
since for example putative witnesses' somewhat determinate
reports, and circumstances apparently intertwined with the
consequence or outcomes of the resurrection are accessible to
historical enquiry, historical enquiry may in the course of its

labours present us, as indeed it does, with a given which *has* determinate describable features and is an account not empty of determinate meaning. Indeed that meaning-content makes it a determinate *datum*, and a problem which requires to be reckoned with but which is not to be readily resolved on the assumptions of the scientific historian as these assumptions are normally employed. To meet the challenge, these assumptions *can* be employed in an extended or atypical way while retaining analogical explanation, so that analogy from the activity of purposing agents is applied to account (still by analogy) for this anomalous behaviour of the natural world and so give it its wider significance and explanation. Thus, notwithstanding Cupitt's misleading ambiguities the apologists' case *can* be launched.

Cupitt's argument is, next, that an Event-account of the resurrection involving a glorified body requires to be *given* determinate content, which it will otherwise lack, by being placed in the context of a wider explanatory theory; but that if its meaning-content has to be conferred in this way, the account of the resurrection, thus drawing its substance from the wider theory, cannot then without circularity provide evidential support for the explanatory theory.[36] Cupitt's objection trades on the ambiguity in saying that there is a lack of meaning in resurrection-claims which speak of a glorified body. As an otherwise surprising reading on a research scientist's instrument needs to have its significance brought out by placing the phenomenon in its newly understood theoretical explanatory context, so there is in glorified-resurrection claims a lack of the explained significance which can come only when this extra-ordinary claim is placed in the context of some overarching account.

However, like the scientist's reading, there is in a resurrection report enough determinacy, enough distinct meaning, for it to constitute a *datum*, a problem. Cupitt seems so enthralled by the respect in which there is a significance-lack that he fails to see that resurrection reports do also have a meaning whereby they

---

[36] Ibid. p. 162.

constitute, or purport to witness to, a somewhat determinate and problematic given. Even if we do arrive at a measure of confidence about how to understand the problematic given, the reported miracle, only after we have set it in a wider context, explaining it in terms of the action of a divine agent, there need be nothing circular about claiming then that the *datum* lends support to the divine-agent hypothesis. The provision of a comprehensive explanatory account, which will explain a range of somewhat determinate *data* can *both* give intelligibility and significance to the *data*, and secure evidential support from them. Cupitt is prevented from seeing this, and his contention has some *prima facie* plausibility, by his supposing that the Event theory's *given* report of a putative resurrection miracle as reported by a witness has no determinate character whatever until the theoretical framework is supplied in terms of which it is to be given significance, and understood. Granted that we may not yet know what, more fully, to make of it, until the explanation is given, there is nevertheless a determinate it (in particular, the report of a putative resurrection miracle) of which something (further) requires to be made even before the something more actually is made of it.

It is a compelling surmise that Cupitt comes to write as he does because he supposes the alleged experience of the first putative witnesses of the resurrected Jesus to have been indeterminate in quality, like the more indeterminate sense-data lovingly discussed by philosophers of perception. The content of this kind of experience is in itself so indefinite that any interest it has for us is not available to be read off its observed, but all-too-vague, appearance, but has to be read on to the indeterminate *datum* in accordance with the prescription of a wider-ranging theory held by the perceiver. (Here a theory includes and, most typically is, a set of beliefs, assumptions usually, which seems to make sense of experience, generating in us expectations about how the world will or will not be.) Thus an experience of a rather brownish blob or patch may usefully be described at all only when it has been interpreted in terms of some theory- (or quasi-theory-) prompted attitude of the perceiver. How far the indeterminacy of some experience requires that a prevailing belief or theory must introduce the interpretive specificity necessary to make the experience relevant to our interests will depend on what our interests are and on the degree of determinacy of the experience in itself. Cupitt conceives of the resurrection appearances, when they are spoken of by Event theorists, as being in themselves indeterminate to such an extent that they require interpretative shaping by the employment of a theory. If this is a correct diagnosis and aetiology of Cupitt's outlook, his mind is so captured by a resurrection-appearance-as-indeterminate-sense-*datum* model that he does not raise the question as to whether the resurrection appearances are not in themselves actually complex and determinate so that they can contribute something substantially definite *to* an explanatory theory; yet Event theorists would surely argue, and with justification, that this latter is the alternative which is advanced by them.

What was described by those who claimed to have seen the Lord admittedly sometimes had meaning contributed for them by their thinking theoretical thoughts, for example about the hope of Israel as depicted in the scriptures and expounded *en route* to Emmaus; but it was not, as presented in the New Testament, generally so lacking in determinacy in itself that only the overlay of the theoretical grid gave it definiteness. The voice of the resurrected Christ together with his appearance (to Mary), and what he said (to Saul/Paul) are presented as determinately recognisable factors, no doubt prompting further reflection, but first compelling responses of, predominantly, more conative and affective kinds. At other times the sight of Jesus, perhaps unexpectedly and surprisingly among them, is enough for the witnesses' recognition and response, which implies a determinate being-recognisable-as-Jesus; and there are the concomitant empty tomb and non-production of the body. All of this (and more could be cited) gives the Event theorist the determinate input from the resurrection experiences, and associated circumstances, which he appeals to as supporting and shaping, and not only being shaped by, resurrection doctrine.

To see how inappropriate to most cases is Cupitt's view of the relation between experience and theory of doctrine, consider the following. You are on a visit to up-country South Africa, with a friend who is a distinguished zoologist. On your first day after arrival you are out walking, getting a sense of the place, when two terrified men come running towards you round a bend in the road. They shout as they pass 'There's a huge alligator coming this way.' Your zoologist friend is sceptical. 'There aren't any alligators here', he says. Yet you think you recall seeing some reference, in a guide book or in your hotel lobby, to an alligator park, a sort of zoo devoted to alligators. Alarmed testimony, and the experience of the terrified men, taken together with a knowledge of alligator habitats tends to favour the theory, hunch, suspicion or mere possibility, that there is such a park in the vicinity, and the suspicion, hunch or theory gives strength to the obvious interpretation of the experience and the witness of the terrified men, namely that they saw an escaped alligator. If you were Cupitt, you would, apparently, treat the panic-stricken report of the men *not* as evidence that there is an alligator on its way, because that would, you should say, if you were Cupitt, involve a circular procedure: it involves interpreting the men's supposed experience, a quickly moving patch of grey-brown in the undergrowth, beady eyes, or a full alligator-view, as the case might be, as being a glimpse of an alligator on the basis of the existence of a nearby alligator park and yet at the same time treating the experience so interpreted as confirming the (otherwise less than firm) notion or theory about the presence of the alligator park. Such errors are dangerous.

This example can stand for those many in which an experience (a) has some determinate features (about some of which there may be uncertainty); (b) can have one view of it confirmed by its fitting a surmise or theory for which there may or may not be other grounds, but which offers what seems to be the only available explanation of the experience; (c) can contribute to the confirmation of that theory or surmise. The sorts of commonplace integrative cases in which this book has dealt yield further instances. The Event theorists' view of the resurrection may also be a perfectly respectable example, for all Cupitt says in 3.1.[37]

---

[37] Essentially the same points are also made by Cupitt more starkly, and maybe a little patronisingly, in Cupitt's correspondence with C. F. D. Moule. See D. Cupitt, *Explorations in Theology 6*, London, 1979, p. 30.

In 3.2 the Cupitt-presented alternatives are falsely presented as exclusive. It is not true that there must *either*: (a) have been a belief or expectation to which the resurrection of Jesus so precisely conformed, or which it so exactly fulfilled, that his resurrection would have been the looked-for outcome of his career, and that resurrection faith could or would thus have arisen without the bolt from the blue of the alleged brute Event, or (b) have been no belief or expectation of that kind, with the consequence that if the resurrection, or the reported resurrection experiences, were to occur, their significance would be unknown, or at best obscure.

Common or garden examples will reveal the falseness of these types of alternatives: what of the news of a large legacy from Aunt Millie in Australia, unexpected because we did not know that she was even ill, nor that she was rich, but which confirms our belief or suspicion that she was interested in us and fond of us? Here is an event (the coming of this news) which is not, as it occurs, expected yet which confirms some of our expectations; Cupitt's dichotomy does not accommodate such cases. Brief reflection on Pannenberg's traditionalist teaching brings out another significant possibility, and Cupitt's weakness. In the time of Jesus Christ the expectation existed, and was shared by many, of a general resurrection at the end of the age, usually associated with the establishing of his new order by the Messiah. For a crucified individual person to be designated Messiah by his single resurrection, which is given as the anticipation and pledge of the new age to come, was clearly not the exact content of what had been looked for in the commonly held belief. It was not a straightforward instance of what had been believed, nor a precise fulfilment of the expectation. At the same time it is not altogether unrelated to that expectation; while in some respects it contrasted with the expectation, in others it fulfils the expectation. Sometimes it manages both of these by fulfilling the expectation's broader, more general, content or gist, but in specific ways which were not, specifically, expected. It is a modification of the expectation so as to bring the expectation, now modified, together with striking determinate yet extraordinary experience. In this most significant of events in the career of Jesus Christ we see, what is often to be seen at other points in his life, that he fulfils Jewish expectation but only in such a fashion as calls for modification in the received form or specificity of the expectation. It *is* recognisably (that is, under some obviously apt description) or at least arguably, the expectation in question; but it is fulfilled in a fashion which is in some respects unexpected. This is what the Event theorist affirms, but Cupitt fails to acknowledge.

Where an existing expectation is thus fulfilled in an unexpected way, the belief that there has been (in its unforseen mode) a fulfilment of the expectation, albeit a fulfilment of an unanticipated specific sort, cannot be explained as having arisen out of the expectation, as some sort of deduction from it about what must, in accordance with the expectation, have happened. Nor, on the other hand, can it be said that no hope or expectation whatever existed to guide, to contextualise, people's understanding of the new and striking occurrence. So Cupitt's supposedly exclusive alternatives fail to consider the actual claim of the Event theorist; Event theories find space between the crude polarities of the horns of Cupitt's factitious dilemma. Thus, the Event theorist has nothing to fear from 3.2.

The Beaten-Men argument is the target in 3.3, as Cupitt points out how commonly just such beliefs as that their dead hero has been resurrected have arisen among the dispirited, powerless and marginalised. Since beliefs of that kind, Cupitt contends, have psycho-social, or sociological, causal explanations rather than rational credentials and a basis in fact, the Beaten-Men argument undermines rather than supports Event theories of the resurrection of Jesus Christ: to the extent that the apostles were Beaten-Men then transformed, an explanation for their resurrection faith alternative to the Event theorist's explanation is indicated.

As it stands, Cupitt's attack on Beaten-Men-ism cannot be conclusive: it does, admittedly, seem to be true that demoralised people have often been known to find purpose and confidence on the basis of remarkable beliefs which appear, under scrutiny, to have been generated by something like these people's self-affirming wishful thinking or by the fiducial, pertaining-to-belief, analogue of the disposition by which Hope springs eternal in the human breast. This fact should prevent us from at once simply inferring some objective cause for the raised morale and the new belief. However, it will not follow from these tendencies amongst the demoralised that their new-found conviction and their invigorated spirit were not brought about by objective events such as form the content of this belief. The impact of objective fact upon the dejected *is* also a possible explanation of their bold resolution, as is the psychological self-induction hypothesis. What is required, if in a case in question the issue is to be decided, is further and more determinate evidence about the particular case than merely that it is a case of cowards-turned-heroes or wimps-made-staunch. So how far are boat-owning independent fishermen, a collaborative (that is, with the occupying force) tax official, and the others of the disciples who forsook him and fled, of the psycho-social types which properly fit into the psychological self-induction explanation of their transforming belief? How likely would the profession, even proclamation, of the trans-forming belief by such people be, on psychological grounds, if they had in fact stolen the body of Jesus? If they did not remove it from the tomb, how likely is it that someone else did? How significant is it that the body was not produced? How strong is the so-called Empty Tomb tradition, if indeed there is such a tradition, made distinct by reference to factors within the ancient texts and the life of the early church, rather than by reason of and with reference to modern attitudes or preoccupa-tions? Would the content of the belief which changed Beaten Men into men of assurance have been so puzzlingly enigmatic in some of its significance, and would it have diverged in problem-atical ways from the common eschatological expectations, if it was generated out of the apostles' *psyches*, to restore their life's meaning and give them a sense of worth, as the followers of a Messiah rather than of a failure? Why could it not have been believed, for example, that without any extraordinary trail-blazing anticipatory resurrection of this individual, on his own, Jesus would soon be vindicated in glory at the general resurrection when he would, as Lord, inaugurate the new age in which they would have a leading role? Why this individual's resurrection, now, given that a belief much closer to the more conventional hope would serve the (presumed) psychological needs at least as well? Why these features, of recondite or veiled significance, and those features whose peculiarity seems to serve no purpose, of a psychological sort, which could not be served more conventionally? These questions are only some of the many more which flow into, or from, the assessment of the Beaten Men argument. Yet even to bring these forward is to demonstrate how very short a way Cupitt takes or how very little a way he goes with the question and how far from decisive his point remains, as he leaves it. Indeed, his contribution in making it is to prevent the apologists' use of the Beaten Men appeal from being as superficial as it might be. Both sides are required to go beyond ungrounded speculation as to whether the new-found confidence-giving beliefs of formerly Beaten Men derived from some striking event, which with its clear import revivified them, or from their possibly illusion-generating psychic dispositions, whose function would be to sustain the believer's self-image.

The social-psychological account of the transformation of the Beaten Men, which Cupitt identifies as a competitor to the apologists' appeal to their restoration of morale, will, if it is accepted, present a challenge to Cupitt also. For if it should offer a broadly correct view about the origin of Easter faith, it will render otiose the theological type of theory which he favours. Only if the social-psychological account, in terms of the beliefs which downtrodden people generate to boost themselves, or give themselves meaning, – only if this account fails, or if the theological account is better supported, can the theological account stand. Cupitt shows no awareness that he has issued a challenge to himself as well as to the standard apologist, by his treatment of Beaten-Men-ism. Indeed if, as he seems to do, he actually endorses a version of the social-psychological thesis, he needs to explain how his views are consistent.

The grounds which he offers for his theological theory, apart from the alleged inadequacies of all the alternatives, are that there is much theological argument in the New Testament in which affirmation of the resurrection of Jesus goes along with people's recognition and proclamation of him as Messiah and Lord. In Cupitt's view, the former is a form or implication of the latter: to proclaim his resurrection is to proclaim Jesus as Messiah and Lord; and it was by reflecting on his being Messiah that the apostles were led to conclude his aliveness, his resurrection.[38] In the order of realisation Messiahship and Lordship come before, and (this appears to be Cupitt's meaning) constitute, the substantial content of resurrection faith.

Difficulties in this are: by what course of argument might the apostles be supposed to have moved from thinking of Jesus as Messiah and Lord to thinking of him as alive, as resurrected? Why aliveness, why resurrection as an implicate of Messiahship or Lordship? If it was not an argument that led them to their resurrection affirmation so much as the application of some conventional understanding of the specific significance of aliveness or resurrection, what was that convention? Is there any evidence of the existence of any such convention? Is there any evidence in the pages of the New Testament that people really did argue in this way, as distinct from suggestions proposed by us, which are no more, and if anything less, indicated by the text itself than the traditional Event theory reading, to the effect that they might have done? Cupitt seeks to illustrate and confirm his theological theory by instantiation, and, perhaps to answer some of these points, as follows:

For example, St. Paul, explaining the gospel in some hellenistic synagogue, might reason like this: he would argue from the Old Testament about the true character of the expected Messiah and the manner in which God would bring in his kingdom at the end of time. He would try to show that the Messiah must suffer, and he would speak of Jesus, the crucified Messiah, and argue that this man is now made Lord and Christ, the first fruits of a universal harvest. That is, I can imagine him preaching and proving Jesus as crucified and risen Messiah without its being necessary for him to invoke a Resurrection-Event or eyewitness testimony to it. They are, I think, logically superfluous, and were perhaps developed rather in the way the legend of Mary's virginal conception of Jesus was developed, as a picturesque reinforcement.[39]

[38] See Cupitt, *Christ and the Hiddenness of God*, pp. 164ff.
[39] Ibid. p. 167.

It is a telling refutation of this to compare it with the way in which Paul does actually speak of the resurrection, not as an implication of other noetically prior facts, but as fact to be set beside other given facts (such as that he died for our sins according to the scriptures (1 Cor. 15.3)), a given from which, if any argumentation is involved, we argue *to* his sonship rather than the other way round (Romans 1.5, and see below on Acts 17). The thrust of the apostolic preaching, as, for example, in Acts 2, would be feeble indeed if the resurrection were understood as the implication of messianic expectations and prophecies together with the facts of Jesus' career and death. Why should Jews now accept that Jesus was the Messiah, so that these prophecies and expectations should apply to him and so his resurrection be deducible? They have no reason that Peter gives. Is it reasonable to think they were cut to the heart now, by reason of Peter's unconventional and (as it would be without a resurrection event) rather eccentric, strained exegesis? The sermon only has force if the reason for recognising his Messiahship is a new thing to be reckoned with, whose extraordinary occurrence is to be explained *by* Jesus' Messiahship and Lordship.

Again, what sense would Paul's preaching of the resurrection to the Greeks at the Areopagus have, and what could he have supposed it to have, if the resurrection affirmation is a derivation in some (obscure) way from the application to Jesus of the Jewish conception of Messiahship? The only sense which can be made of Acts 17.31 is that the extraordinary event of the resurrection may be expected to catch the attention of anyone, Greek or Jew, as calling for an explanation which Paul then proposes for his hearers' further interest. The order of recognition here, the direction of assurance-giving, is the opposite of that which Cupitt claims. Cupitt's standpoint would have to be that, by the time Paul is in Athens, the mutual implications between Messiahship and Lordship, on the one hand, and resurrection on the other, have been well established in the church's mind, and to interest his audience he chooses to begin with the concept which would be more accessible, less foreign. Yet since, on Cupitt's Theological theory, resurrection will only be less foreign-*seeming*, and it will require to be explained to the

Greeks that it is an implication of Messiahship and that its meaning is (part of) the meaning of Messiahship, any interest generated in his audience will be short-lived. They are likely to have been as puzzled as many modern enquirers have been by the claims of theologians like Cupitt, puzzled about why and how the allied implication is supposed to hold good, or concerned to know by what convention Messiahship and resurrection are related, puzzled over how the implication follows, and what the distinct content of resurrection teaching actually is. Again, the cognitive order, the order of assurance-giving clearly set out in Acts 17.31 will be in the wrong direction. If the resurrection is to give assurance that Jesus is the Messiah, then it must be possible to know what the resurrection is, and that it has occurred, without knowing that Jesus is the Messiah. An Event theory makes this possible as the Theological theory cannot.

James P. Mackey's category of what he calls 'the proof miracle' view of the resurrection at least closely resembles Cupitt's Event-theory type. To it Mackey opposes his view which takes the apostles' experiences after the crucifixion of Jesus to be basically significant (being the essential warrant for resurrection doctrine, what prompts and justifies it) as theological theories will not.[40] Mackey speaks of these appearances as experiences of divine power in which God is known as 'truly active and releasing a transforming benevolent spirit into the world' (p. 72); and he affirms that the experiences should be treated not as evidence for a quite distinct resurrection of Jesus which would be a necessary condition for the appearances; rather, these experiences/appearances themselves constitute the resurrection of Jesus. We might reasonably classify this as an anti-realist conception of the resurrection.[41]

Yet what was it about these experiences, indeterminately characterised as they are by Mackey, which justified their being described in any way rather than any other? Why are they not the good feelings of people born under Earth signs, as they commune with their roots? More pointedly, even if we do accept

---

[40] See James P. Mackey, *Modern Theology*, Oxford, 1987, pp. 66ff.
[41] For an account of realism and anti-realism see Michael Dummett, *Truth and Other Enigmas*, London, 1978, e.g. pp. 145ff.

that they were experiences of the divine power, as he releases a transforming benevolent spirit into the world, why should the experiences/appearances be talked of as the resurrection of Jesus? Why not say, for example, that it is his post-mortem spirit abroad, rather than it is he, himself? Why should there be a clear distinction made in christian teaching and observance between the resurrection and the coming of the Spirit, between Easter and Pentecost? Why should the appearances supposedly be experiences of Jesus himself *redivivus* (page 77) rather than of, say, the same spirit who dwelt in him? Answers to the effect that it is the Church, living as Church, which is the living Jesus and which is the paradigm locus of resurrection experience appear to draw upon a highly selective minority of New Testament narratives for their paradigm (since many of the narratives of appearances, which are not selected as paradigmatic, are not of communal experience or experience in the community). Here the question has only been pushed back: why describe the experience of divine power within the Church as experience of Jesus-raised-up, rather than simply pneumatologically?

Furthermore any anti-realist view must apparently discount the Empty Tomb tradition. Perhaps that *is* justified, but argument is needed for it. Again, an anti-realist conception of the resurrection, on which the experiences of the apostles were not merely evidence for the resurrection but actually were, actually constituted, the resurrection, will have difficulty in making conceptual room for the unbelief, or sluggish belief, of some of the first witnesses of the resurrection (for example, Luke 24.36ff). They knew for sure that they were having these experiences, so what was it they were withholding their belief *about*?[42]

Mackey's particular version of resurrection anti-realism, whereby experience of God's beneficent spirit in the world is (identical with) experience of the resurrection, is particularly hard to square with the gospel accounts of early witnesses' having experiences of the risen Jesus, yet not believing, or only

---

[42] Just as it has been one of their philosophical attractions that anti-realisms generally exclude scepticisms, so, by corollary, at least some sorts of unbelief cannot be accommodated in any anti-realism.

slowly thereafter coming to believe. No doubt, interpretation rules could be proposed whereby the gospel accounts really mean that these apostles had an experience of God's beneficent spirit but did not (or not straightaway) recognise it as such, provided that some content could be given for this idea of experiencing God's beneficent spirit yet not (readily) recognising it as such. Yet this last is not obviously a straightforward task; and the interpretation rules must be shown to be not merely capricious or factitious, but expressing historically understood conventions, or they will be merely arbitrary, and make no claim on us. In view of these weaknesses and unresolved questions, Mackey's anti-realist conception of the resurrection cannot reasonably be embraced as if it, any more than Cupitt's theological conception, presented an obviously attractive alternative to Event theories.

These problems and questions for Cupitt, Mackey and others like them, do not amount to a definitive and final refutation since further argumentative moves can be attempted. Still, the *prima* (and *secunda*, and *tertia*) *facie* difficulties for Cupitt, Mackey and others are daunting.[43]

For reasons such as those presented, it may be judged that Cupitt and Mackey, and other theologians of similar views, have advanced and persisted in very unpromising courses of argument. Some readers may indict such theologians for (non-deliberate) fantastication, a theorising not so much imaginative as perverse. If so, this question is obvious: why should intelligent people find themselves advocating such indefensibly improbable things? The answer is inviting: that they feel driven, pressured, to put forward what would be insupportable were it not for the Hume/Troeltsch view of what is reasonably to be believed. Acceptance of Hume/Troeltsch rules out those interpretations of the evidence which could, and would otherwise, commend themselves. If that is indeed the explanation for theologians' supporting or feeling that they must propose grossly flawed theses, the removal of the pressure imposed by the Hume/Troeltsch orthodoxy may well be experienced as a

---

[43] Other authors, such as C. F. D. Moule, in his dialogue with Cupitt, (see note 37 above), have of course advanced several of them in some form.

liberation, and as opening the way to more rationally satisfying accounts of the *data*.

The orthodoxy, about what it can be reasonable to believe, of those who follow Hume and Troeltsch gives support to another very widely held conviction among theologians: that the interpretations or conclusions of the critical historian are of necessity irrelevant to the faith of believers. The principal argument in support of this, advanced notably by M. Kähler[44] has been that because of the greatness, the eternal or cosmic significance, of what is at stake, or because of the wholehearted character of authentic faith, certainty must belong to christian belief; but a faith which derived its confidence from the qualified, revisable, incompletable enquiries of the historian, could not have this required certainty. An apologetic appeal to reported putative miracles would run counter to this dichotomy between history and faith; but Hume and Troeltsch have seemed to dispose of any serious pressure to review the dichotomy from that quarter.

Revisability also attaches to theses about the relations between faith and history, however. Must certainty characterise all faith? Is not resolution in holding on to that of which we were once sure, but are not now so sure, a feature of faith as distinct from sight? Even if certainty is essential to faith, may certainty not after all be had on the basis of an accumulation of probabilities, as Newman argued in the *Grammar of Assent*?[45] Thus we are certain that the British mainland is an island, and that the New Testament was all written before AD 600. Maybe a religious commitment, while not simply a rational inference, should be in accordance with the best available reasoning, and have the stability born of a proper reluctance or refusal to change course at once for any new *prima facie* relevant factor without being altogether unrevisable? These are at least arguable positions. And so the overthrow of the Hume/Troeltsch standard for believing in reported putative miracles may serve

[44] See Martin Kähler, *The So-Called Historical Jesus and the Historic Biblical Christ*, English translation and edition by C. E. Braaten, Philadelphia, 1964, which is helpfully discussed by Harvey in his *The Historian and the Believer*, Ch. IV.
[45] J. H. Newman, *Grammar of Assent*, Indiana, 1979.

to open a way towards an integration of history and faith, towards a theological reunion whereby theological reasonings and conclusions belong in our one interconnected web of belief (though not, obviously, independent of revelation), and towards a rethought relation between faith and reason.

Bibliography

Abraham, W. J. and Holtzer, S. W. (eds.) *The Rationality of Religious Belief*, Oxford, 1987.
Adams, R. M. *The Virtue of Faith*, Oxford, 1987.
Ahern, Dennis M. 'Hume on the Evidential Impossibility of Miracles' in *Studies in Epistemology*, ed. Nicholas Rescher, Oxford, 1975, pp. 1–31.
Alexander, H. G. (ed.) *The Leibniz-Clarke Correspondence*, Manchester, 1956.
Alston, W. P. 'God's Action in the World', Essay 10 in *Divine Nature and Human Language*, Ithaca, 1989.
Altaner, B. and Stuiber, A. *Patrologie*, Freiburg, 1978.
Anselm, *De Conceptu Virginali* in *Anselm of Canterbury*, eds. J. Hopkins and H. Richardson, Toronto and New York, 1976.
Aquinas, *Summa Theologiae*, Blackfriars edition, London and New York, from 1964.
Summa Contra Gentiles, translated by Anton C. Pegis, New York, 1955.
Augustine, *De Trinitate* in *Patriologiae Latinae*, ed. J. P. Migne, Paris, 1861–1900.
De Cura pro Mortuis Gerenda in *Patriologiae Latinae*.
De Civitate Dei, in *Patriologiae Latinae*.
Epistle cxxvii, in *Patriologiae Latinae*.
De Peccatorum Meritis, in *Patriologiae Latinae*.
De Genesi ad Litteram, in *Patriologiae Latinae*.
De Utilitate Credendi, in *Patriologiae Latinae*.
Ayer, A. J. *The Foundations of Empirical Knowledge*, London, 1940.
Barr, J. *Fundamentalism*, London, 1977.
Barth, K. *Church Dogmatics*, succession of volumes, Edinburgh, from 1956.
Blanshard, B. *The Nature of Thought*, London, 1939.
Bradley, F. H. *Appearance and Reality*, London, 1893.
Collected Essays, Oxford, 1935.

Broad, C. D. 'Hume's Theory of the Credibility of Miracles', *Proceedings of the Aristotelian Society*, vol. 17 (1916–17), pp. 77–94.

Bultmann, R. *Jesus Christ and Mythology*, New York, 1958.

Existence and Faith, ed. S. M. Ogden, London, 1961.

Craig, E. J. *The Mind of God and the Works of Man*, Oxford, 1987.

Cupitt, D. *Explorations in Theology 6*, London, 1979.

Christ and the Hiddenness of God, London, 1971.

Davies, B. *An Introduction to the Philosophy of Religion*, Oxford, 1993.

Davies, P. *God and the New Physics*, London, 1983.

Diamond, M. *Contemporary Philosophy and Religious Thought*, New York, 1974.

Dummett, M. *Truth and Other Enigmas*, London, 1978.

Edwards, P. 'Heidegger's Quest for Being', *Philosophy*, vol. 64, 1989, pp. 437–70.

Flew, A. *Hume's Philosophy of Belief*, London, 1961.

God and Philosophy, London, 1966.

Flew, A. (ed.) *Body Mind and Death*, New York, 1964.

Hume *Of Miracles*, La Salle, Illinois, 1985.

Fuller, R. H. *Interpreting the Miracles*, London, 1963.

Geyl, P. *Debates with Historians*, London, 1955.

Grant, Robert M. *Miracle and Natural Law in Graeco-Roman and Early Christian Thought*, Amsterdam, 1952.

Hacking, I. (ed.) *Scientific Revolutions*, Oxford, 1981.

Hansen, J. 'Can Science Allow Miracles?', *New Scientist*, vol. 94, no. 1300 (April 1982), pp. 73–6.

Harvey, A. E. *Jesus and the Constraints of History*, London, 1982.

Harvey, V. A. *The Historian and the Believer*, London, 1967.

Hastings, J. (ed.) *Encyclopaedia of Religion and Ethics*, New York, 1913.

Hawking, S. W. *A Brief History of Time*, London, 1988.

Helm, P. (ed.) *Objective Knowledge*, Leicester, 1987.

Hick, J. *Philosophy of Religion*, Englewood Cliffs, NJ, 1963.

Holwerda, D. 'Faith, Reason and the Resurrection', in *Faith and Rationality*, eds. A. Plantinga and N. Wolterstorff, Notre Dame, Indiana, 1983, pp. 265ff.

Hume, D. *An Enquiry Concerning Human Understanding*, ed. L. A. Selby-Bigge, Oxford, 1902.

A Treatise of Human Nature, ed. L. A. Selby-Bigge, second edition with textual revision, by P. H. Nidditch, Oxford, 1978.

Kähler, M. *The So-Called Historical Jesus and the Historic Biblical Christ*, translation and edition by C. E. Braaten, Philadelphia, 1964.

Lakatos, I. 'Methodology of Scientific Research Programmes', in *Criticism and the Growth of Knowledge*, eds. I. Lakatos and A. Musgrave, Cambridge, 1970, pp. 91–196.

Lehrer, K. *Knowledge*, Oxford, 1974.

Lewis, C. S. *Miracles*, London, 1947.

Lewis, H. D. (ed.) *Contemporary British Philosophy*, London and New York, 1956.

Locke, J. *Essay Concerning Human Understanding*, ed. P. H. Nidditch, Oxford, 1975.
The Reasonableness of Christianity in *The Works of John Locke in Ten Volumes*, London, 1823.
A Discourse of Miracles in *The Works of John Locke in Ten Volumes*.
A Third Letter concerning Toleration in *The Works of John Locke in Ten Volumes*.

Mackey, J. P. *Modern Theology*, Oxford, 1987.

Mackie, J. L. *The Miracle of Theism*, Oxford, 1982.

McKinnon, A. '"Miracle" and "Paradox"', *American Philosophical Quarterly*, vol. 4, 1967, pp. 308–14.

MacKinnon, D. M. *The Problem of Metaphysics*, Cambridge, 1974.
Themes in Theology, Edinburgh, 1987.

MacQuarrie, J. (ed.) *Contemporary Religious Thinkers*, London, 1968.
Principles of Christian Theology, London, 1966.

Mavrodes, G. 'The Life Everlasting and the Bodily Criterion of Identity', *Nous*, vol. 11 (1977), pp. 27ff.

Mill, J. S. *A System of Logic*, London, 1843.

Mitchell, B. G. *The Justification of Religious Belief*, London, 1973.

Newman, J. H. *Essays on Miracles*, London, 1890.

Nineham, D. *The Use and Abuse of the Bible*, London, 1976.

Nowell-Smith, P. H. 'Miracles', in *New Essays in Philosophical Theology*, eds. A. Flew and A. MacIntyre, London, 1955.

Occam, W. *Super Quattuor Libros Sententiarum*, 1495–6.
Summa Totius Logicae, ed. P. Boehner, St Bonaventure, New York, 1951.

Paley, W. *A View of the Evidences of Christianity* in *The Works of William Paley*, Edinburgh, 1830.

Pannenberg, W. *Jesus – God and Man*, translated by D. Priebe, London, 1968.
Basic Questions in Theology, vols. I and II, translated by G. H. Kehm, London, 1970 and 1971.
Theology and the Philosophy of Science, translated by F. McDonagh, London, 1976.

Peirce, C. S. *Values in a Universe of Chance*, ed. P. P. Wiener, New York, 1958.

Penelhum, T. *Religion and Rationality*, New York, 1971.

Peterson, M. et al., *Reason and Religious Belief*, New York, 1991, Ch. 9.

Pike, N. (ed.) *Hume: Dialogues Concerning Natural Religion*, Indianapolis, 1970.

Price, H. H. *Perception*, London, 1932.

Quine, W. V. O. *Ontological Relativity and Other Essays*, New York, 1969.

Quine, W. V. O. and Ullian J. S. *The Web of Belief*, second edition, New York, 1978.

Sanders, E. P. *Jesus and Judaism*, London, 1985.

Schleiermacher, F. D. E. *The Christian Faith*, translated by H. R. Mackintosh and J. S. Stewart, Edinburgh, 1928.

Schmitals, W. *An Introduction to the Theology of Rudolf Bultmann*, London, 1967.

Sheldrake, R. *A New Science of Life*, London, 1983.
The Presence of the Past, London, 1988.

Smart, N. *Philosophers and Religious Truth*, London, 1964, Ch. 2.

Swinburne, R. G. 'Miracles', *Philosophical Quarterly*, vol. 18, (1968), pp. 320–8.
'The Argument from Design', *Philosophy*, vol. 43, (1968), pp. 199–212.
The Concept of Miracle, London, 1970.
The Existence of God, Oxford, 1979.

Troeltsch, E. 'Historiography' in *Encyclopaedia of Religion and Ethics*, ed. J. Hastings, New York, 1913, vol. VI, pp. 716–23.

Ward, B. *Miracles and the Mediaeval Mind*, London, 1982.

Ward, K. *Divine Action*, London, 1990.

Warfield, B. B. *Counterfeit Miracles*, Edinburgh, 1972.

Whybray, R. N. *The Making of the Pentateuch*, Sheffield, 1987.

Williams, B. 'Deciding to Believe' in *Problems of the Self*, Cambridge, 1972, pp. 136–51.

Wodehouse, P. G. *Laughing Gas*, London, 1957.

Wollheim, R. *F. H. Bradley*, London, 1959.

Wollheim, R. (ed.) *Hume on Religion*, London, 1963.

Young, R. 'Miracles and Epistemology', *Religious Studies*, vol. 8 (1972), pp. 115–26.

Index

Abraham, William J., 190n
Adams, Robert M., 3, 98n
Alston, William P., 3
Altaner, Berthold, 15
analogy, 47–8, 64–5, 74, 76–82, 191–5, 212–16
Anselm of Canterbury, Saint, 20
apologetics, 9–12, 30–2, 128, 149–50, 171
Aquinas, Saint Thomas, 21–32
Archimedes' Principle, 132–4, 162
assumptions, theistic, atheistic or neither, 127, 133–50, 161–8, 201
Augustine, Saint, 8–20, 23–4, 26, 32, 104–8
Ayer, Sir Alfred J., 171n

Barr, James, 228–30
Barth, Karl, 208–10, 223–8, 230
Baur, Ferdinand C., 80–1
belief, degrees of, 34, 101
belief evaluation, criteria for, 46–8, 49, 125–6, 169–207
beyond nature, 17, 104–8
Bradley, Francis H., 66–82, 227n
Bultmann, Rudolf K., 92–6, 162, 208, 228

Cato, Marcus Porcius Uticensis, 151
causality, 24, 74, 80–1
conceptions of miracle, 12–19, 21–4, 35–43, 42–8, 83–102, 103, 104–8, 112–18
Craig, Edward J., 143
cultural discontinuity, 5
Cupitt, Don, 230–53

Davies, Brian, 128n
demons, 25–30, 38, 41, 120

Descartes, Rene, 138
Diamond, Malcolm L., 201
Dummett, Michael, 91n, 253n

Edwards, Paul, 94
Enlightenment, the, 2–4, 74
epistemology, 4, 169–207
evaluative purpose, 5
explanation, 74, 172–201

faith, 2, 85, 95–102, 257
Flew, Antony G. N., 124n, 164–7, 193n
foundations for a religious system, 62, 124–5, 144–50, 156, 169–207
freedom, 85, 95–6
Fuller, Reginald H., 85

Grant, Robert M., 12n, 14n, 16n

Hacking, Ian, 115n
Hampshire, Stuart, 167
Hansen, James, 4n
Harvey, Anthony E., 89
Harvey, Van A., 256n
Hastings, James, 67n
Hawking, Stephen W., 238–9
Heidegger, Martin, 93–4
Helm, Paul, 85n, 91n
Herodotus, 74
Hick, John H., 2, 118n, 201, 230n
historical critical method, 66–82, 83–4, 208–30
Holtzer, Steven W., 190n
Houston, Joseph, 85n, 91n 190n
Humanism, 74
Hume, David, 1–4, 49–65, 83–120, 124–5, 131–68, 203–7, 209, 221, 231, 255–7
Hume's check, 128

262